I0643995

SPECTACULAR ACCUMULATION

SPECTACULAR ACCUMULATION

Material Culture, Tokugawa Ieyasu, and Samurai Sociability

Morgan Pitelka

University of Hawai'i Press
HONOLULU

© 2016 University of Hawai'i Press

All rights reserved

Paperback edition 2018

Printed in the United States of America

23 22 21 20 19 18   6 5 4 3 2 1

Library of Congress Cataloging-in-Publication Data

Pitelka, Morgan, author.
Spectacular accumulation : material culture, Tokugawa Ieyasu, and samurai sociability / Morgan Pitelka.
pages cm
Includes bibliographical references and index.
ISBN 978-0-8248-5157-6 (hardcover : alk. paper)
1. Japan—History—Azuchi-Momoyama period, 1568–1603. 2. Japan—History—Tokugawa period, 1600–1868. 3. Material culture—Political aspects—Japan. 4. Samurai—Social life and customs. 5. Tokugawa, Ieyasu, 1543–1616. I. Title.
DS868.P58 2016
952′.025—dc23

2015015814

ISBN 978-0-8248-7681-4 (pbk.)

Portions of chapter 2 previously appeared in the following essay, and are included here with permission from Wiley Global: Morgan Pitelka, "Art, Agency, and Networks in the Career of Tokugawa Ieyasu," in *A Companion to Asian Art and Architecture*, ed. Rebecca M. Brown and Deborah S. Hutton. New York: Wiley-Blackwell, 2011.

University of Hawai'i Press books are printed on acid-free paper and meet the guidelines for permanence and durability of the Council on Library Resources.

For Brenda, Ravi, and Luca

Contents

List of Illustrations
ix

Acknowledgments
xi

Prologue
1

CHAPTER ONE
Famous Objects:
Treasures, Trophies, and Warrior Power
17

CHAPTER TWO
Grand Spectacle:
Material Culture and Contingency
42

CHAPTER THREE
The Politics of Sociability:
Gift Giving and Ritual Performance
65

CHAPTER FOUR

Lordly Sport:

Raptors, Falconry, and the Control of Land

94

CHAPTER FIVE

Severed Heads and Salvaged Swords:

The Material Culture of War

118

CHAPTER SIX

Apotheosis:

Ieyasu's Early Modern and Modern Afterlives

143

Epilogue:

Museums and Japanese History

171

Notes 177

Bibliography 201

Index 217

Illustrations

Figure 1. Map of Japan xiv
Figure 2. Map of the Tōkaidō xv
Figure 3. Map of Western Japan xvi
Figure 4. Map of Kyoto xvii
Figure 5. Broadsheet of the fall of Osaka Castle, 1615 3
Figure 6. Tea caddy named Tsukumo Nasu 4
Figure 7. X-ray of tea caddy named Tsukumo Nasu 4
Figure 8. Portrait of Tokugawa Ieyasu at the Battle of Mikatagahara 12
Figure 9. *Tenmoku* tea bowl 21
Figure 10. Folding screen illustrating the Sumiyoshi festival, detail 29
Figure 11. Wood-block print triptych, the Battle of Okehazama in Bishû, Owari Province. Utagawa Toyonobu 37
Figure 12. Tea caddy named Hatsuhana 46
Figure 13. Ubaguchi-shaped tea kettle 48
Figure 14. Mishima-style tea bowl named Mishima-oke 49
Figure 15. Calligraphy, Xutang Zhiyu 58
Figure 16. Tea jar named Shōka 60
Figure 17. Letter from Toyotomi Hideyoshi to the Kutsuki house 71
Figure 18. Letter from Tokugawa Ieyasu to the Kutsuki house 72
Figure 19. Tea caddy named Yokota 73
Figure 20. Sword (*tachi*) named Torigai Kunitoshi 82

Figure 21. Dagger (*tantō*) named Fudō Masamune 90
Figure 22. Black kite (*Milvus migrans*) 95
Figure 23. Steller's sea eagle (*Haliaeetus pelagicus*) 96
Figure 24. A falcon trainer 97
Figure 25. Illustration of hunting in Hizen Province, detail. Kizaki Moritaka 104
Figure 26. Image from album of hawks and calligraphy. Kano Tsunenobu 115
Figure 27. Folding screen illustrating the Battle of Sekigahara, detail 123
Figure 28. Folding screen illustrating the Summer Siege of Osaka 134
Figure 29. Print of Tokugawa Ieyasu Examining a Head. Tsukioka Yoshitoshi 136
Figure 30. Dagger (*tantō*) named Ebina Kokaji 139
Figure 31. Nikkō Tōshōgū carving details 144
Figure 32. Nikkō Tōshōgū 150
Figure 33. Record of probate from Sunpu, Owari Tokugawa family 152
Figure 34. Painting of a returning sailboat. Yujian 154
Figure 35. Suit of armor (*gusoku*) with rising-sun design 155
Figure 36. Dream portrait of Tōshō Daigongen. Kano Tan'yū 159
Figure 37. Painted handscroll of the Nagoya Tōshōgū festival. Mori Takamasa 162
Figure 38. The Tomb of Iyeyasu Tokugawa. John La Farge 165
Figure 39. Tokugawa Art Museum 168

Acknowledgments

My interest in the material culture of sixteenth- and seventeenth-century elite warriors, particularly Tokugawa Ieyasu, was piqued during my participation in the Kyoto University Japanese history graduate research trip to Ise and Mikawa in the fall of 1998. Traveling with my friends and fellow graduate students to sites ranging from Tahara Castle to Ise Shrine to the Takisan Tōshōgū in the company of Professor Fujii Jōji was an edifying experience. Fujii's patience as I began to explore my interest in the warlords of the period—all while I was researching the Raku family—was generous. I also benefited then and on repeated trips to Nagoya from the generosity of the staff of the Tokugawa Art Museum, a remarkable institution to which I extend my gratitude. Tani Akira of the Nomura Art Museum in Kyoto has continued to be a generous friend who has answered countless questions. Kitagawa Hiroshi at the Osaka Castle Museum has also been munificent with his advice and time. I also extend my thanks to the Tokyo National Museum, Rinnōji, the Nikkō Tōshōgū, and many other museums, archives, and libraries in Japan. Thanks also to Satow Morihiro, Tanimura Reiko, Yagi Akira and Sakiyo, and others in Japan for their friendship.

I started work on this book during my first sabbatical, a semester of leave from teaching at Occidental College in the fall of 2004. Many thanks to the Richard C. Rudolph East Asian Library at the University of California–Los Angeles (UCLA), for their open lending policies and to the Interlibrary Loan librarians at Occidental for their miraculous work borrowing books from all over the world. Multiple research trips to Japan were funded by the Dean's Office of Occidental College, vital support that made work on this project not just feasible but enjoyable. In 2007–2008 I had a National Endowment for the Humanities Fellowship to spend a year working on the project, which allowed me to complete much of the research and write several chapters. I also benefited from the support and advice of many colleagues at Occidental, including Anthony Chase, Amy Lyford, Warren Montag, Alexandra Puerto, Martha Ronk, Lisa Sousa, Marla Stone, Kristi Upson-Saia, Dale Wright, and Louise Yuhas. After moving to the University of North Carolina–Chapel Hill (UNC) in 2010, I again benefited from the support of colleagues in the Asian Studies and History departments, including Jan Bardsley, Mark Driscoll, Miles Fletcher, Michelle King, Michael Tsin, Brett Whalen, and Nadia Yaqub. The larger Japanese studies community in the Triangle—including David Ambaras, Barbara Ambros, Inger Brodey, Harry Harootunian, Richard Jaffe, Chris Nelson, Simon Partner, Gen Weisenfeld, and graduate students such as Laurel Foote-Hudson, Magdalena Kolodziej, Daniele Lauro, and Matt Mitchell—has been stimulating and supportive. At the end of the project, a writing group with Pat Parker, Rachel Pollack, Michelle Robinson, and Nadia Yaqub inspired me to complete the manuscript. Along the way, the work of various research assistants at Occidental and UNC, including Tim Anderson, Emma La Fleur, Jeff Oakley, and Mishio Yamanaka was invaluable as well.

Opportunities to present facets of this research to scholarly audiences were enlightening, including presentations in 2007 at Princeton University and Columbia University and to the Japanese Art Society of America. Matthew Stavros' generous invitation to give a keynote lecture at the University of Sydney, which resulted in my article "The Empire of Things," was transformative, and I extend my thanks to him. Similarly, chances to present new research on Ieyasu's material culture at Beloit College, the Bowers Museum, UCLA's Fowler Museum, Harvard's Reischauer Institute of Japanese Studies, and the University of California–Irvine in 2009 proved to be instructive. Thanks to John Duncan, the Japan Foundation of Australia, Jennifer Jung-Kim, Matthew McKelway, Ian Miller, Mari Takamatsu, Allison Tolman, the UCLA Asia Institute, Anne Walthall, and Daniel Youd.

My close collaboration with David Eason, Suzanne Gay, Eric Rath, Peter Shapinsky, David Spafford, and others in a reevaluation of the shift from medieval to early modern in Japanese history informed this project throughout. Our "Japan's Long Sixteenth Century" research group held its first meeting at the University of Southern California in 2008, thanks to the support of Joan Piggott's Project for Premodern Japan. This event was followed by a symposium at Princeton University in 2009, a symposium at the University of California–Berkeley in 2010, and an international conference on the topic at the University of Michigan in 2011. Thanks to Kurushima Noriko and Umezawa Fumiko for their advice and suggestions that resulted from our interactions at that Michigan conference.

I was able to spend the 2011–2012 year as a fellow at the National Humanities Center, where the library staff provided remarkable support. Thanks to Karen Carroll for her copyediting and to all of the staff of the center for all that they do. I extend my gratitude also to Carol Shannon for her editing and to Scott Flodin for his work on the maps. Thanks as always to Pat Crosby at the University of Hawai'i Press for her support and general excellence, as well as to Stephanie Chun. Support from the UNC Department of History and the Triangle Center for Japanese Studies made the inclusion of color images possible. Lastly, to my parents Linda and Vince, I extend my love and thanks.

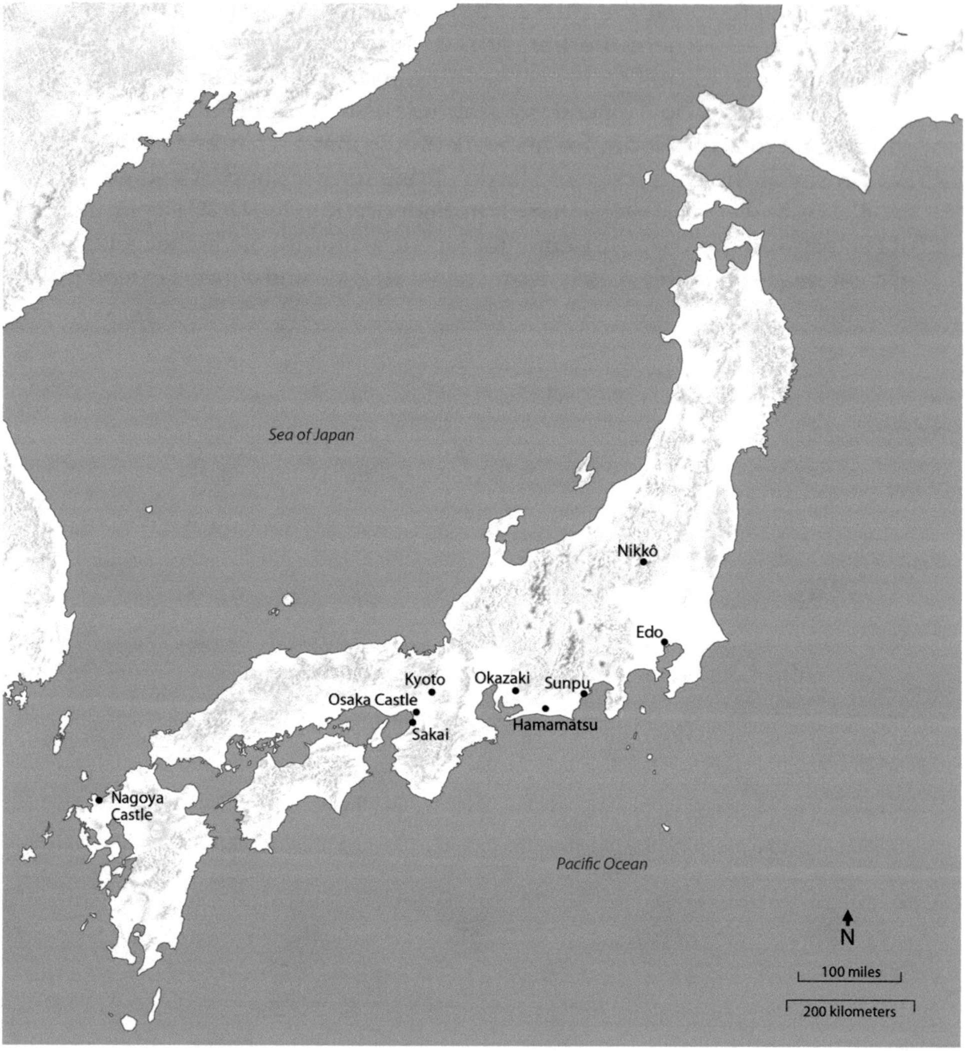

Figure 1. Map of Japan, by Scott Flodin

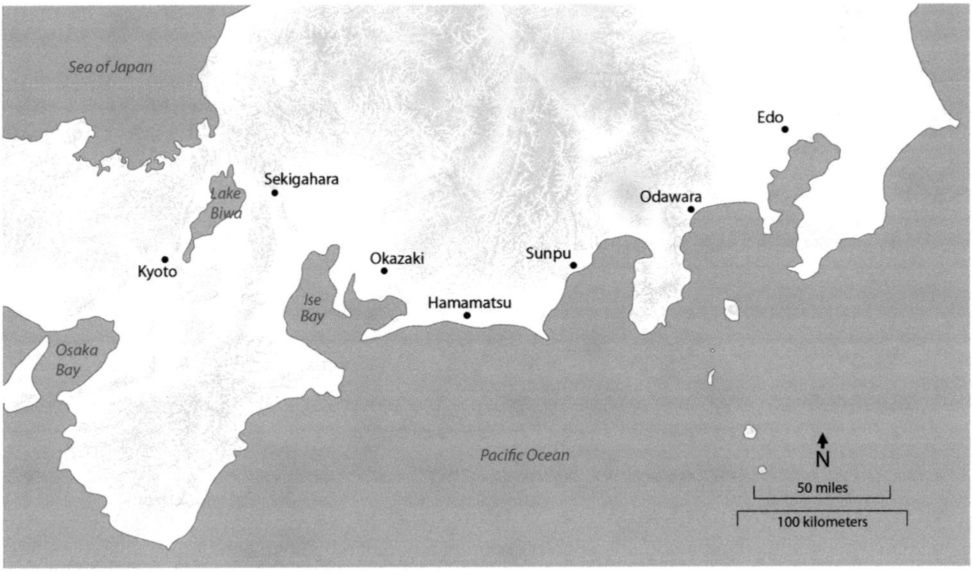

Figure 2. Map of the Tōkaidō, by Scott Flodin

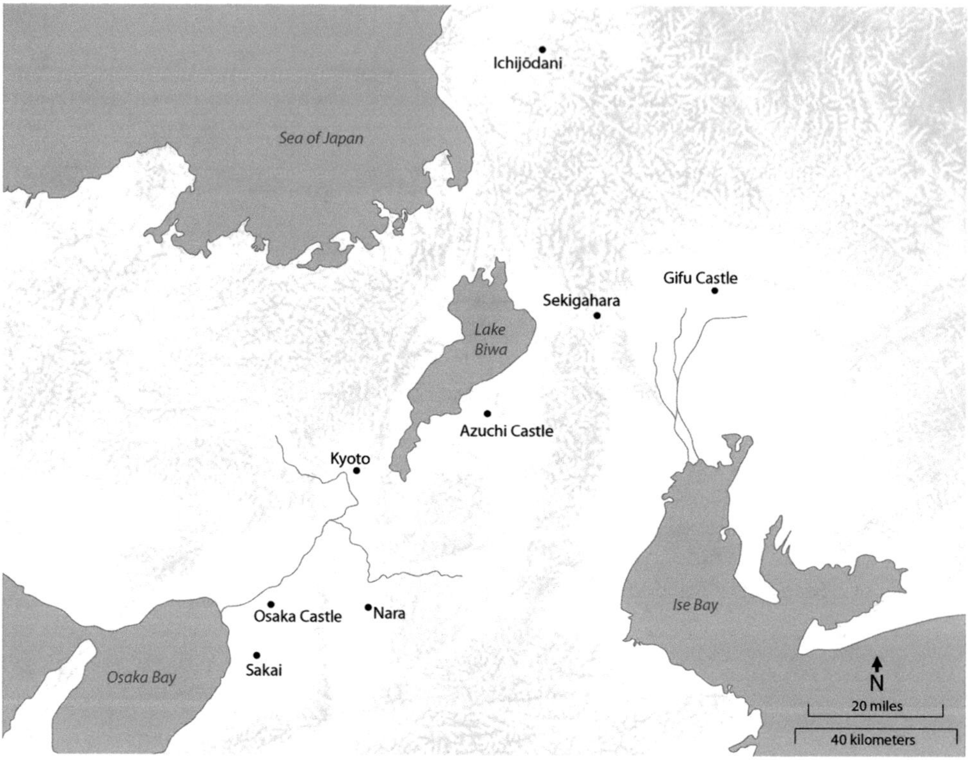

Figure 3. Map of Western Japan, by Scott Flodin

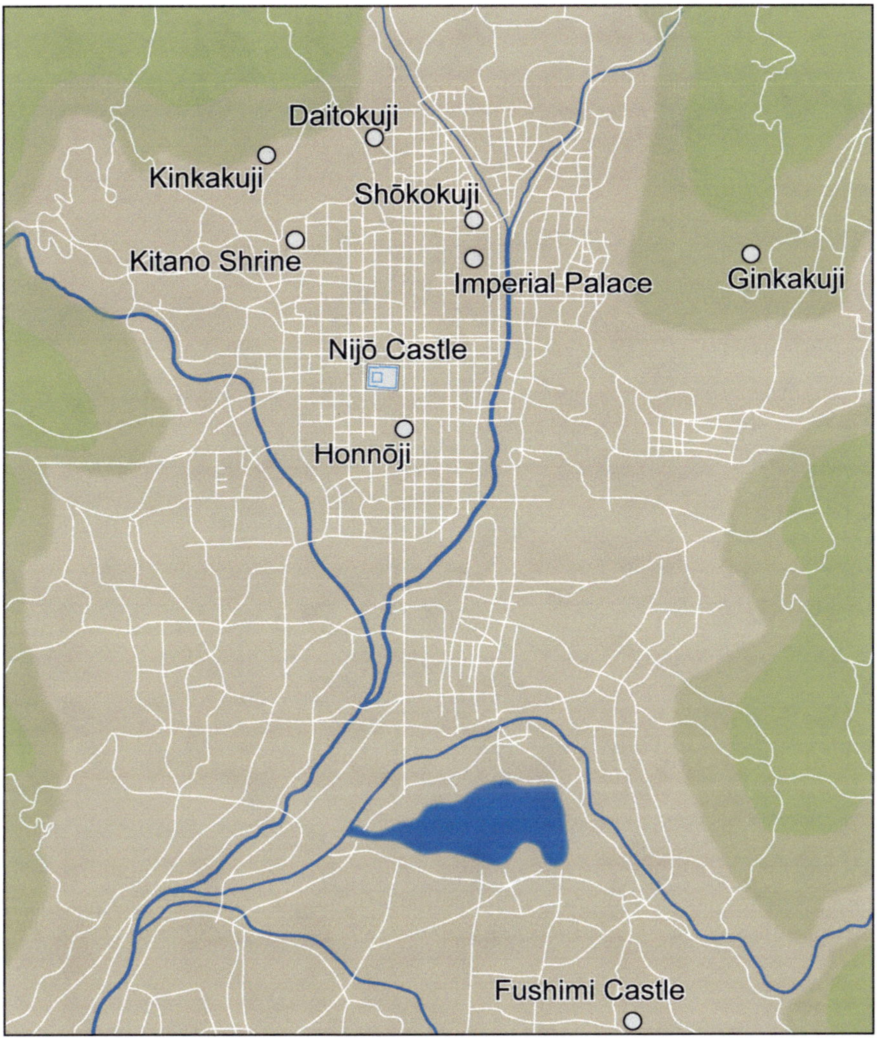

Figure 4. Map of Kyoto, by Matthew Stavros

Prologue

> History is culturally ordered, differently so in different societies, according to meaningful schemes of things.
>
> —Marshall Sahlins, *Islands of History*

In the fifth month of 1615, the retired shogun Tokugawa Ieyasu (1543–1616) launched a final assault on his rivals, the Toyotomi, who were ensconced in Osaka Castle. His primary target—and his former protectee—was Toyotomi Hideyori, the increasingly confident Toyotomi heir who was advised by a politically savvy mother and who knew that the Imperial Court in Kyoto preferred his graceful and youthful promise to the gruff old politicking of the seventy-two-year-old Tokugawa patriarch. Hideyori had inherited much of the wealth of his father, Toyotomi Hideyoshi, the second hegemon of the age, and had soared through the ranks of the Imperial Court to the point that his position was higher than that of Ieyasu or his son, the shogun Hidetada. Hideyori was beloved on the streets of Osaka and Kyoto, not to mention in the audience halls of many of the powerful warlords of Japan. The Tokugawa were determined to destroy him. The first assault had occurred in 1614 and resulted in a stalemate that allowed the Tokugawa to fill in the moats around the otherwise impenetrable Osaka Castle. Ieyasu had raised a huge army, and this time would face little serious resistance.[1]

Hideyori waited in the castle with his mother, his wife (the granddaughter of Ieyasu), his vassals, and a host of *rōnin,* samurai who had been uprooted and disenfranchised in the Tokugawa settlement of the past fifteen years. He was also accompanied by much of the material culture assembled by his father, Hideyoshi, one of the greatest collectors in premodern Japanese history, a man of humble origins who had devoted nearly as much energy to mastering the culture of tea, Noh theater, the arts of poetry and calligraphy, and diverse courtly rituals as to unifying the provinces of Japan and (unsuccessfully) conquering the Chinese continent. Displayed in the castle's reception halls and installed in its storage rooms was a plethora of swords, Chinese ceramics, paintings, Noh masks, and other treasures with distinguished pedigrees and significant symbolic and economic value. Some had once been owned by the Ashikaga shoguns of the late fourteenth and early fifteenth centuries; others had been given to the Toyotomi by merchant tea masters and powerful warlords after Hideyoshi came to power in 1582. Like the castle in which they resided, these famous objects represented the past accomplishments, the present power, and the future potential of the Toyotomi house.

It took just two days for the Tokugawa to cut down Hideyori's much smaller force and topple the outer defenses of the castle. Most of the Toyotomi took their own lives, and the castle itself was burnt to the ground, as seen in the block-printed broadsheet depicting the fall of the castle from 1615 (figure 5). However, Ieyasu was not finished dismantling the legacy of the Toyotomi. In the weeks that followed, he ordered several trusted vassals to organize search parties to comb the wreckage of the fortress in search of the broken pieces and scattered shards of the famous objects the Toyotomi had owned and displayed for so many years.[2] He then commanded smiths to reforge the heirloom swords that had been recovered and lacquerers to piece together and re-form tea caddies and other famous tea ceramics.[3] The brief references to this rather fantastical sounding endeavor in the documentary record are supported by recent scientific research conducted on extant ceramic pieces that had been owned previously by the Toyotomi and that then passed into the Tokugawa collection after the destruction of Osaka Castle. Notably, the Seikadō Art Museum x-rayed several tea caddies and discovered fracture lines that had been completely masked by the careful application of lacquer. The famous tea caddy named Tsukumo Nasu (also known as Matsumoto Nasu) (figure 6), for example, looks like a perfectly preserved specimen of a Chinese-produced, Song-dynasty container, originally used for medicine, but repurposed in Japan to hold and display powdered green tea during a tea gathering. Shaped like an eggplant (*nasu*) and covered with a luscious iron-brown glaze, the piece exhibits the slightly cloudy surface patterns that resulted from the random atmospheric conditions of the kiln, which were highly prized by tea practitioners in the sixteenth and early seventeenth centuries. X-rays (figure 7), however, reveal a shattered and carefully reconstructed tea caddy that is as much a result of Tokugawa-sponsored lacquer repair and reproduction as of the original Fujianese ceramic craftsmanship.[4]

A great deal of work was expended in the retrieval of fragments of swords and ceramics from the ashes of Osaka Castle, and even more in their meticulous, almost ritualized refurbishment. The investment paid hand-

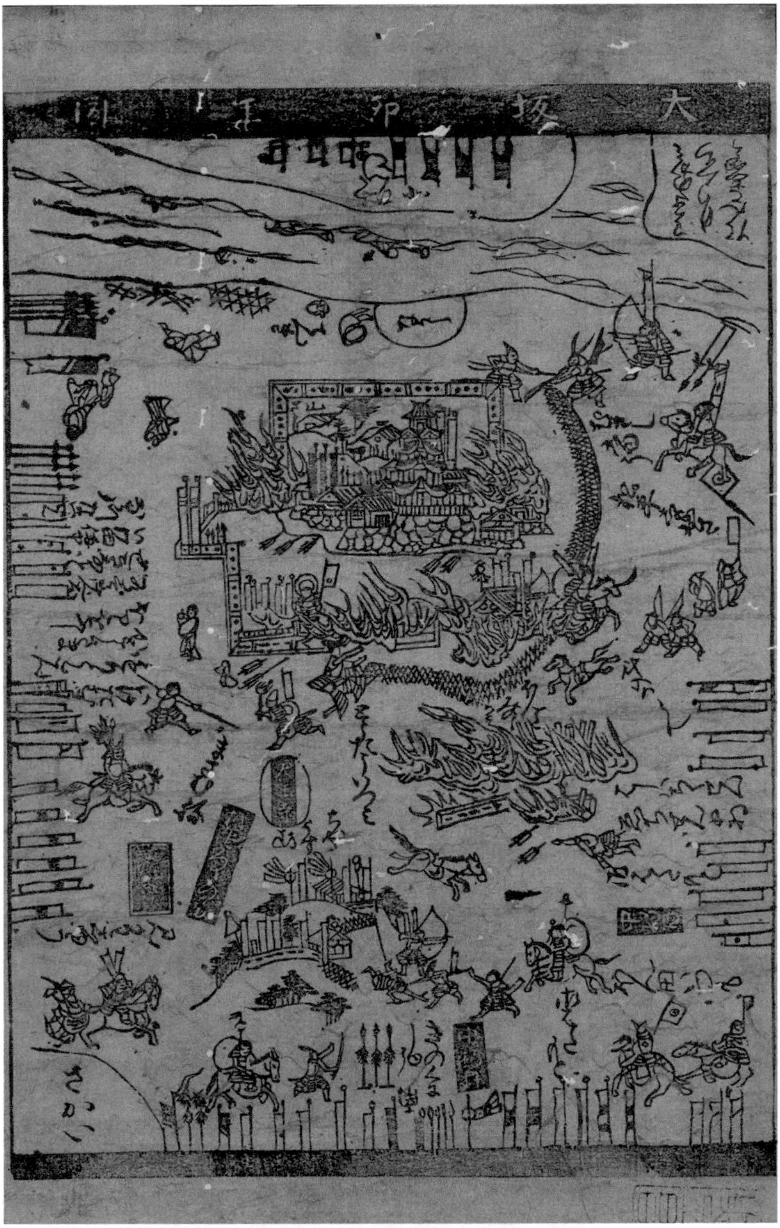

Figure 5. Broadsheet of the fall of Osaka Castle. 1615. 71 x 33 cm. National Archive of Japan

Figure 6. Tea caddy named Tsukumo Nasu. Chinese, Song dynasty, 12th–13th century. Height 6 cm. Seikadō Art Museum

Figure 7. X-ray of tea caddy named Tsukumo Nasu. Seikadō Art Museum

some dividends, however. The pieces that entered the Tokugawa collection as a result of this process were among the most sought-after, famous objects in the land. The example of the tea caddy Tsukumo Nasu reveals an astounding, though for this group of objects, typical, pedigree: it had been owned by Matsumoto Shūhō (15th c.), an early merchant and tea collector of Chinese ceramics; Takeno Jōō (1502–1555), one of the most famed merchant and tea collectors of the early sixteenth century; Oda Nobunaga, the first warlord to collect famous objects as an overtly political practice; and of course Toyotomi Hideyoshi, Ieyasu's former rival and liege. It is perhaps too much of an exaggeration to argue that possession of these objects extended to the Tokugawa a kind of symbolic authority over their previous owners;[5] nevertheless, the acquisition, exchange, and display of material culture such as swords and tea caddies was a profoundly political act and one of the key dynamics of this period of social and political change. Like the exchange of hostages, the collection of heads, and the command of massive armies numbering in some cases in excess of one hundred thousand men, art collecting was a form of what I call *spectacular accumulation* that represents the apogee of warrior power.

Although related to histories of collecting,[6] this book uses the notion of spectacular accumulation to contextualize the acquisition of "art" (an Enlightenment-era concept that doesn't appear in sixteenth-century Japanese texts) within a larger complex of practices aimed at establishing political authority, demonstrating military dominance, reifying hierarchy, and advertising wealth. I first encountered the phrase "spectacular accumulation" in Simon Schama's description of the Dutch city of Antwerp at the height of its imperial glory. His account of the "dialectical encounter of the sumptuous and the severe" in seventeenth-century Dutch paintings, informed by the huge range of goods flowing into Dutch ports as a result of imperial and colonial resource extraction and trade, resonated with the collecting patterns of late sixteenth-century tea practitioners in Japan, who were devoted to selecting and arranging (practices known in Japanese tea culture as *toriawase*) imported Chinese art alongside appropriated Japanese objects. I later studied Anna Tsing's conception of "spectacular accumulation" as the interaction between global capitalism, local franchise cronyism, and a kind of "wild west" frontier culture that characterized Indonesia before the 1997 Asian Financial Crisis. Both inform my reading of the late sixteenth-century relationship between elite warrior control over human bodies and famous objects, and the eventual deployment of both forms of accumulation in rituals of sociability, highly political spectacles that culminated in the apotheosis of Ieyasu and his enshrinement at the Tōshōgū.[7] Although the audiences changed in dynamic ways, acquiring, stockpiling, activating, and displaying valuable things was, this book argues, one of the defining characteristics of sixteenth-century power.

MATERIAL CULTURE

This book examines the elite material culture of Japan's late sixteenth and early seventeenth centuries, particularly the accumulation of a category of things that were so sought-after by those in power that they came to be known as "famous objects," or *meibutsu.* Used variously to describe antique masterpieces of Asian art coveted by tea practitioners, heirloom swords passed down in warrior lineages, and prized products of far-flung regions of Japan, the notion of the famous object is key to understanding the canonization of cultural practices and forms that occurred in the shift from medieval to early modern. Late medieval warrior collections of Chinese paintings and ceramics, for example, influenced the patronage and production of new Japanese art for centuries, while antique swords were exchanged as gifts and displayed as symbols of martial heritage and familial wealth and prestige before they became symbols of samurai identity in the early modern status system. The pages that follow introduce many examples of the famous objects of this period that are now considered among the most treasured pieces of the heritage of Japan, masterpieces celebrated as "national treasures" (*kokuhō*) and "important cultural properties" (*jūyō bunkazai*) in the modern system of cultural property protection and proudly displayed in public and private museums in Japan and abroad.

This study is not concerned, however, with the formal and aesthetic qualities of the famous objects of the late sixteenth and early seventeenth centuries. Instead, it attempts to contextualize the process by which certain types of material culture came to be instrumental in the politics of this turbulent moment, a period of civil war foreclosed by a development that has been dubbed "national unification."[8] The book avoids the artificial distinction between cultural history and political history, between narratives of beautiful things and narratives of military exploits, between a history of art and a history of politics. The famed cultural efflorescence of these years was not subsidiary to the landscape of political conflict, battlefield maneuvering, and massive acts of violence fomented by infamous hegemons such as Ieyasu, but constitutive of it. I thus consider the collection and deployment of nonhuman subjects such as falcons as a correlated practice, as well as the taking of heads and other body parts during and after battle. These are all examples of spectacular accumulation, the practice of hoarding symbolically significant things and aggressively displaying and deploying them for cultural and political gain.

My approach has been influenced by the larger academic field that is sometimes referred to as material culture studies, though this book is fundamentally a study of history. Though historians increasingly include things in the spectrum of evidence they examine, as can be seen in works on Japan by historians such as Susan Hanley (1997), Peter Kornicki (1998), and Jordan Sand (2005), they do so in profoundly different ways, indicative of the diversity of origins from which the field of material history—really more a heterogeneous assemblage of intellectual practices than an academic discipline—emerges.[9] My approach is thus influenced by other disciplines as well. Art history has of course always been concerned with the meaning and value of the object, first in formal, aesthetic terms and gradually in the last decades of the twentieth century, in larger contextual and cultural terms.[10] Archaeology and sociocultural anthropology were the next academic disciplines to turn to things as a serious form of evidence, and in Britain in particular the cultural turn in these fields was accompanied by a material turn.[11] Daniel Miller's work on the material culture of mass consumption has inspired increased interest in the role of everyday goods in the lives of people both in the past and the present, while Alfred Gell's work on the agency of art has suggested that objects could be understood not just as products of a society, but as constitutive actors within it.[12] Both of these approaches have influenced my interest in what D. Miller has referred to as "materiality and power" or the way in which a culture, in producing and placing value on things, also defines the value of human life itself. What Karl Marx called objectification and its resulting condition of alienation are key to understanding the profound *asymmetrical power* formations that emerged in the rise of the three hegemons of the late sixteenth century—sometimes called the Three Unifiers—who appear repeatedly throughout this book.

The implications of this study for our understanding of the relationship between late medieval warfare, social reorganization, and the establishment of the early modern system are considerable. The system of authority that resulted from the violent civil wars of the era—the Pax Tokugawa—was not a capitalist system, of course, but it rested on a cultural foundation in which the influence of certain kinds of art (activated through ritual, as I discuss later in this prologue) and the objectification of human bodies (seen particularly clearly in the status system and the system of alternate attendance) acted in complex but related ways to create stability through cultural and political domination. The hallmarks of Tokugawa society were a rigorous and hierarchical structure that maintained peace through inequity, the threat of violence, and the promise of the pleasures of the new arts of play and other increasingly accessible forms of consumer culture, which offered both the exploration of a reified form of identity and distraction from the conditions of the surrounding society.[13] This book explores the process through which these foundations were laid. This perspective is not meant to minimize the appeal of things or the beauty of art; it is not my intention to deny the varied and contingent values placed on the objects of material culture examined in this book, but rather to emphasize their social influence and their role within constructions of power.

TOKUGAWA IEYASU

The life story of the founder of the Tokugawa military government and the last of the Three Unifiers, Tokugawa Ieyasu, is useful as one anchor of this study because the trajectory of his rise to power—as a warlord, shogun, retired shogun, and ultimately as a deity—allows us to trace the concomitant shifts in the meaning and influence of material culture. Ieyasu was neither the most important collector nor the most significant participant in a social and cultural system that privileged the use, display, and exchange of famous objects, and in fact the opening chapters of this book devote considerable attention to other collectors—the Ashikaga shoguns, Oda Nobunaga, and Toyotomi Hideyoshi. However, the story of Ieyasu's career and afterlife illustrates the close relationship between people, things, and politics and offers us insights into the nature of the shift from medieval to early modern and indeed the role of material culture in the shaping of historical knowledge.

Ieyasu's legacy is the source of significant debate within Japanese historiography.[14] Many see him as an opportunist, who took advantage of Hideyoshi's death and the youth of the Toyotomi heir to pilfer the prize of hegemony for himself, in effect appropriating the revolutionary innovations of Nobunaga and Hideyoshi. Others, conversely, see his accomplishments as eclipsing the work of his predecessors. Ieyasu's first biography in English, for example, is a 1937 study titled *The Maker of Modern Japan* by the British-born, Oxford-trained A. L. Sadler. One of the founding fathers of Australia's robust Japanese studies tradition, Sadler saw Ieyasu as "unquestionably one of the greatest men the world has yet seen" and in the unfolding of Ieyasu's life and career read nothing less than the providential emergence of modern "Nippon."[15] Beginning with the Tokugawa founder's childhood tribulations as a hostage and extending through his battlefield victories, the establishment of Edo as the political capital, and various legislative innovations, Sadler considered Ieyasu the heroic figure who "made the system under which Japan as we know it was forged into shape." Sadler acknowledges that many in Japan have a preference for Nobunaga and Hideyoshi; yet in Sadler's eyes Ieyasu not only outshines the first two Unifiers, but was a more brilliant military leader and statesman than far-flung contemporaries such as "Henry VIII and Elizabeth, Francis I, Akbar, Ivan the Terrible, and Suleyman the Magnificent."[16] In truth, the Tokugawa military regime that Ieyasu established in 1603 and solidified in 1615 represented the end to Japan's civil wars. The successful perpetuation of the regime until 1868 by Ieyasu's descendants did indeed shape a set of social and cultural practices and institutions that have continued to influence national identity even as Japan's political institutions and international position have changed dramatically.

Another champion of Ieyasu's contribution is the prolific American historian of early modern Japan, Conrad Totman, who echoed Sadler's tone in his short 1983 biography *Tokugawa Ieyasu, Shogun*. Although less triumphalist than Sadler, Totman too sees Ieyasu's career as a heroic tale of one man's triumph over adversity. The author uses Ieyasu's victory at the titanic Battle of Sekigahara in 1600 as a framing device for the entire book, telling the Tokugawa lord's whole life story through flashbacks and other vignettes that punctuate the buildup to and aftermath of the conflict. Indeed, it is hard to argue with the significance of this battle, in which Ieyasu and his allies met the armies of an alliance opposed to Tokugawa rule, with the clash probably involving well over 150,000 men. The Imperial Court recognized Ieyasu's military superiority in 1603 by awarding him the post of shogun, which in turn allowed him to establish the warrior government in Edo that would rule Japan until 1868. Ieyasu rewarded his vassals with large domains that produced considerable income, or in some cases, with influential positions within his new administration. He carefully contained those who had opposed him by assigning them to domains that were large enough to prevent resentment but isolated enough to render them harmless. Totman argues that Ieyasu's entire life was in some sense a process of preparing him for this conflict and the opportunities it would afford him and that his win at the Battle of Sekigahara determined the shape and character of early modern Japan.

However, much of the literature on Ieyasu has been insufficiently attentive to the problematic connection between hagiography and historiography. The accounts of Sadler and Totman are typical in this regard: both are lively and entertaining, filled with anecdotes about Ieyasu's exploits as well as confident statements about his inner thoughts and feelings. Sadler tells us that Ieyasu responded delicately and respectfully to the sight of a defeated enemy's decapitated head (112); ordered huge stores of rice to be stockpiled ahead of a major battle, demonstrating his "usual foresight" (158); and was "delighted" to pardon a former opponent (219). "Ieyasu's Personal Habits and Views," a chapter in Sadler, reveals that the Shogun was skilled at swimming, prone to laughter, liked a blade to be well-polished, and became short-tempered as he aged. Totman's book, likewise, illuminates Ieyasu's innermost thoughts throughout the narrative. Ieyasu was not alarmed, for example, by the activities of Uesugi Kagekatsu in 1599 (12), "could only marvel at how the times had changed" as he traveled through Mikawa in 1600 (31), was not upset by Hideyoshi's rise (50), and was enraged by missionaries in 1612 (136). In a sense, both authors shape their narratives in this fashion to accomplish the goal of biographical writing: to allow the reader a glimpse of the inner life of the historical subject.

Something significant is lost, however, in these accounts. The sources for Sadler's quotes and anecdotes, it turns out, are hagiographic texts written or compiled well after Ieyasu's death. The Tokugawa lord underwent a process of apotheosis in 1616 and became a major cult deity in the mid-seventeenth century and beyond. Deification combined with Ieyasu's status as the founder of the ruling regime to create a highly mythologized and symbolically significant figure in the landscape of Tokugawa culture. Therefore, after his death, Ieyasu was not and could not be the object of an honest or empirical process of remembering. Among the reliable documents from the period of Ieyasu's life, none illuminate his inner life. The texture that enlivens Sadler's narrative—the innermost thoughts, loudly expressed feelings, and rich evocations of character—is best understood as a fictitious gloss that falsely brings a familiar character to life in our imagination, but does little to help us understand the powerful eddies and currents of the historical period of the sixteenth century.

Likewise, Totman takes his information, as he readily admits in his acknowledgments, "almost entirely from one source, *Ieyasuden*" (195) by the Japanese historian, Nakamura Kōya (1885–1970). Nakamura had a remarkable career, for example, publishing a biography of Admiral Tōgō Heihachirō in 1937 and researching and teaching Japanese history at Tokyo Imperial University throughout the war years. His work on Ieyasu extended across six decades, beginning with the publication of *Biography of the Light of the East (Tōshōkōden)* in 1915 and ending with *Ieyasu's Politics, Economics, and Vassals (Ieyasu no seiji keizai shinryō),* posthumously published in 1978. In books such as *Biography of Ieyasu* (the aforementioned *Ieyasu den*) and the four volumes of sources and commentary in *Research on the Documents of Tokugawa Ieyasu (Tokugawa Ieyasu monjo no kenkyū),* Nakamura organized and drew upon all known primary sources related to the Tokugawa founder, including some that are now seen as problematic or that date to significantly after Ieyasu's death. (I draw throughout this book on the primary source collections that Nakamkura edited.) But Nakamura also received significant support for his publications from the Tōshōgū (Shrine to the Light of the East) at Nikkō, the largest and most important shrine-temple complex dedicated to the worship of Ieyasu as a god. Totman's reliance solely on materials taken from this prolific Japanese historian to illuminate Ieyasu's thoughts and feelings can be seen either as evocative but fictional narrative devices—necessary to maintain his nonlinear structure built around the Battle of Sekigahara—or as an English translation of the mythologization that sometimes creeps into the work of the otherwise reliable Nakamura. Although the goal of these scholars was surely the articulation of something objectively true about these significant historical figures, the assumptions that undergird their biographical projects lead to an ideological reappropriation, a modern fantasy.

This book is not a biography of Tokugawa Ieyasu (figure 8) and does not strive to provide coverage of his life, his career, or indeed of the period in which he lived. Although the narrative is roughly chronological, it jumps forward and backward to pursue the argument in each chapter and to flesh out the themes and topics of each section. Ieyasu is, rather, one of the foci of this study because his role was unparalleled in the objectification of human bodies through warfare and the politics of détente and in his influence on the culture of collecting and display that would be institutionalized in Tokugawa-era practices of the display of power and wealth. Ieyasu's hagiography, in other words, or the fact of his elevation to the status of a god and the concomitant complications that result for the positivist historian are, in my methodology, welcome indicators of the symbolic valence of material culture in the construction of historical knowledge. The spectacular deployment of his huge art collection in the transference of his authority to his heirs is a rare and significant illustration of the politics of culture in Japanese history, the role that things have played in relocating authority over the generations and in shaping the historical consciousness of both historical actors in the past and historians in the present.

SAMURAI SOCIABILITY

Examining material culture, particularly those objects that were significant in the lives of the Three Unifiers of the late sixteenth century, allows me to foreground the politics of culture in this age of civil war. I pursue this goal in the chapters that follow by focusing on the role of sociability—which I understand as cultural practices such as the tea ceremony and social rituals such as gift exchange—in the interactions between warlords and other powerful agents. Cultural practices and social rituals are key to understanding the relationship between war and stability, between agency and power, because they serve to order social relations. I do not see practices such as

Figure 8. Portrait of Tokugawa Ieyasu at the Battle of Mikatagahara. Muromachi period, 1573. 37.8 x 21.8 cm. Tokugawa Art Museum Collection, by permission of the Tokugawa Art Museum/DNPartcom

tea, art display, gift giving, and falconry as "symbolic" acts that point in the direction of real politics; rather, I understand these forms of sociability as the political process by which the hierarchy of warrior society was made. Rulers such as the Three Unifiers placed limits on the cultural and social practices that other warriors could engage in and also empowered selected retainers through gifts and the extension of special cultural privileges. These acts created a kind of consensus regarding the distribution of power among those with different positions within the developing political structure. Bearing in mind that those institutions established by the Tokugawa endured and had widespread effects on Japanese society and culture, we should take seriously the role that cultural practices and social rituals played in the establishment and indeed the maintenance of early modernity in Japan.

The term "sociability" is often found in studies of late seventeenth- and eighteenth-century elite culture and politics in England, as well as in a prominent study of freemasonry in Germany in the nineteenth century, among many other works of social and cultural history.[17] In general, these analyses take up networks—such as writers' associations or craft guilds—and sites of social interaction—such as court salons or lodges—to argue that sociability is a form of work and a part of politics. Implicit in most of these analyses is the notion that these types of social interactions in early modern Europe participated in, or were related to the development of, civil society and the public sphere. My interpretation of social interactions in sixteenth- and seventeenth-century Japan is less focused on an ostensible shared moral code and idealistic goals of liberation; rather, I see cultural practices and social rituals such as tea, falconry, formal visits (*onari*), and gift giving as tools for the reification of hierarchy and the replication of social distinction. This approach helps to provide context for the usual narratives of institution building and political progress. Paying attention to the politics of sociability in this "age of unification" serves, among other things, to deemphasize the individual as the primary engine of historical change and cultural production and to situate historical actors in their communities of practice.

Central to my analysis is the contention that cultural and social practices were not merely politically significant, but were ritually articulated. This work builds on a new wave of scholarship in English and Japanese that helps to foreground ritual texts, practices, and meanings as a major theme in premodern Japanese history. We now know, for example, that ritual played a central role in Japan's medieval conflicts over sovereignty, temporal authority, and sacred sites. Thomas Conlan argues that "in the midst of the wrenching political and institutional changes of the fourteenth century, a new epistemology arose in the language of ritual and legitimacy."[18] Conlan sees ritual as a dynamic and reactive tool that allowed warrior leaders to offer solutions to social and political problems that emerged from the violent and irruptive outcomes of war. Mahayana Buddhist rites of the Shingon school proved particularly significant in warrior leaders' attempts to reproduce and reinvent the rituals of state pioneered by Kyoto aristocrats in the new context of the Ashikaga warrior government. Matthew Stavros' work on the ritual politics of location in the history of Kyoto as both the imperial capital and the home of the Ashikaga shogunate also highlights the reach of what we might think of as ritual grammar, which played a role not just in ceremonies of state or social interactions but in the most foundational decisions about where to construct the edifices and institutions of power.[19]

Perhaps the most productive scholar of ritual in premodern warrior society has been Futaki Ken'ichi, who has excavated the regular ritual practices of the Kamakura and Ashikaga military governments, calling attention to the fundamental relationship between ritual practices, social standing, and rank within military organizations. Ceremony, and by extension rank, is often thought of as some sort of façade or decorative performance, but as Futaki's work shows and as my discussion of the Battle of Sekigahara in this book argues, ritualistic regulations and the resulting standards of comportment could determine the outcome of major military encounters.[20] Futaki's work also demonstrates the way in which ritual serves as a kind of social and political connective tissue linking medieval warrior regimes with the new institutional structures of the late sixteenth-century unifiers. Futaki demonstrates that Toyotomi Hideyoshi, in particular, labored to reproduce the ritualistic practices and semi-public performances of rank that had been established under the Ashikaga shogunate, anchoring his rule in the structures of legitimacy that had, for a time at least, defined the previous, stable warrior government.[21] The Tokugawa administration likewise drew on the ritualistic codes and norms of prior warrior regimes, enacting requirements about dress, hairstyle, comportment, and indeed acts of cultural consumption as part of a longer genealogy of ritualistic, warrior social norms.[22] This book builds on these findings by arguing that the Tokugawa regime of proper behavior included the acquisition, use, and display of material culture and that this entire package of ritual was central both to the authority of the Tokugawa, as well as the attempts of feudal lords and their vassals to reproduce and to challenge it.

Acknowledging the continuity of medieval social structures based in previous warrior regimes and manifested and maintained through the use of cultural practices and social rituals raises significant issues in the history of Japan. The question of how a military organization maintained peaceful rule for so long without regularly resorting to battle has been addressed by many historians of early modern Japan, but recently two scholars have posed related answers. Luke Roberts argues that Tokugawa authority was performed on public and semipublic stages in early modern Japan, often through ritualistic practices, alongside equally compelling and broadly understood performances, on slightly smaller and more local stages, of the authority and relative independence of domainal lords.[23] This reliance on ritual relates to the argument of Watanabe Hiroshi that the Tokugawa ruled not so much by force as by the image of force, by the performance of power rather than its actuation on the battlefield (though we must not ignore the ongoing threat of violence throughout the early modern period). In the parades and processions that dotted the highways of Japan as a result of the system of alternate attendance (*sankin kōtai*)—a descendent of the systems of hostage exchange that I examine in this volume—as well as in the rituals of reception, gift exchange, and banqueting that could be found in Edo Castle, the Tokugawa shoguns demanded veneration, inspired awe, and projected their legitimate authority despite the many crises they faced.[24] This book explores the late sixteenth-century refinement of the warrior social rituals and cultural practices—including those related to warfare—that would form part of the bedrock of Tokugawa authority, and focuses on the institutionalization of these politics in the career and deification of Tokugawa Ieyasu.

GOALS AND STRUCTURE

One of the goals of this project is to challenge the prevalent historiography on late sixteenth-century Japan and its aftermath, which tends to privilege the unification of the country as a process of early modern institution building and progress toward the nation-state. This book aims instead to relink war and culture. By examining the social practices, rituals, and interactions between people and things in this period in terms of the notion of spectacular accumulation, I draw attention to the continuity of a set of distinctly medieval power formations into the seventeenth century. Another goal is to highlight the significance of Tokugawa Ieyasu, not only as the founder of the Tokugawa shogunate but as a ruler whose attention to acquisition and spectacle defined a pattern of materialism that would influence social and cultural formations for centuries. Lastly, I consistently highlight the social lives of things and the influence of the survival of most (but not all) of Ieyasu's collection in the storehouses of his descendants, in the shrines devoted to his worship, and eventually in modern museums devoted to particular forms of cultural representation. I hope to challenge the aestheticization of the samurai and the sanitization of their cultural legacy.

The structure of the book proceeds in roughly chronological order, beginning with the practices of collecting and display under the Ashikaga, next considering the cultural politics of Nobunaga and Hideyoshi, and then focusing on material culture in the career of Ieyasu and in his apotheosis. The first chapter, "Famous Objects: Treasures, Trophies, and Warrior Power," considers the resonance between the elite warrior acquisition of Chinese art in the sixteenth century and the increase in human objectification in the form of hostage exchanges; it also introduces the story of the rise of Tokugawa Ieyasu from a hostage to a warlord. The second chapter, "Grand Spectacle: Material Culture and Contingency," looks at the public and social deployment of material culture by elite warriors in the late sixteenth century and reflects on the problems of agency and contingency as historical forces. The third chapter, "The Politics of Sociability," surveys gift exchange among elite warriors and in particular in the career of Ieyasu and considers the role of such transactions in a society at war. The fourth chapter, "Lordly Sport: Raptors, Falconry, and the Control of Land," relates the practice of falconry and the accumulation of raptors to the previously examined issues of collecting, hostage exchange, and gift exchange, with particular attention to the hawking activities of Ieyasu. The fifth chapter, "Severed Heads and Salvaged Swords: The Material Culture of War," examines the two largest battles of Ieyasu's career—Sekigahara and the sieges of Osaka—in relation to rituals of head taking, as well as the practice of collecting swords, and argues that these practices helped to structure hierarchy and power relations within the warrior class. The sixth chapter, "Apotheosis," recounts the deification of Ieyasu after his death in 1616, focusing on the use of material culture associated with his life in mortuary rituals, pilgrimages, and other practices that acted to legitimize Tokugawa authority. This chapter also considers the modern apotheosis of Ieyasu and his material culture in the founding of the Tokugawa Art Museum in Nagoya in 1935 by one of his descendants, a philanthropist and colonial administrator. The epilogue, "Museums and Japanese History," considers the politics of museum display in postwar Japan and in particular the new social lives of pieces of Ieyasu's material culture in exhibitions that are imbricated in nationalistic discourses and monolithic representations of Japanese culture and history, a related but distinctly modern form of spectacular accumulation.

CHAPTER ONE

Famous Objects

Treasures, Trophies, and Warrior Power

On New Year's Day, 1574, Oda Nobunaga presided merrily over a daylong banquet and celebration in Gifu. The previous year had been good to him. One of the greatest potential threats to his rule, the warlord Takeda Shingen, had died suddenly of unknown causes. Nobunaga had attacked northern Kyoto to frighten the recalcitrant shogun, Ashikaga Yoshiaki; when Yoshiaki fled, Nobunaga's forces successfully captured and exiled him. Nobunaga had also comprehensively defeated two of his most determined opponents, the warlords Asakura Yoshikage of Echizen Province and Azai Nagamasa of Ōmi Province. Though he still faced considerable opposition from forces across the archipelago, at this moment he occupied a more powerful and secure position than any other ruler with hegemonic pretensions had attained in decades. "Everybody who was anybody in Kyoto and its neighboring provinces presented himself before Nobunaga in Gifu," according to *The Chronicle of Lord Nobunaga*.[1]

The public celebration was followed by a second, private banquet for Nobunaga's closest companions, a group of bodyguards and elite soldiers known as the Horse Guards (*umamawarishū*). Lacquered and gilt objects were displayed while sake was served. "The men made merry, reciting lines from plays and disporting themselves in general. Nobunaga was in unbounded, limitless high spirits. He was exhilarated."[2] This gathering was in one sense typical: occasions involving the ritualized serving and consumption of food and drink, as well as the presentation of important ritual art objects, had served as opportunities to cement social bonds, observe distinctions in rank, and celebrate seasonal and calendrical breaks for centuries among elite warriors. In another sense, however, this gathering was unique:

the displayed lacquered and gilt objects were not simple containers, but the skulls of three warlords dispatched the year before, the severed and preserved heads of Asakura Yoshikage, Azai Hisamasa, and his son Azai Nagamasa.

Nobunaga's gathering and purported sense of exhilaration must be placed in the context of a broader shift in the grammar of warrior power that occurred in the second half of the sixteenth century, in which warriors exchanged people and things and objectified both in ceremonies such as this banquet with great regularity. Some of the elements in play were not new: the taking of the heads of enemies was not a novel phenomenon, but rather one of the key rituals employed after battles and military campaigns to assess the productivity of those involved, a kind of quantification of killing that reduced historical subjects to inert objects. Lacquering the heads was innovative, but it can be compared to the display of lacquered treasures looted from the ruins of conquered enemies, another regular practice. What was different about this gathering, perhaps, was the spectacle of the accrual of power and control in the hands of one individual, Nobunaga, rather than in an institution such as the shogunate. Though our initial reaction to the description of this banquet might be disgust or the attribution of brutality or even insanity to Nobunaga, the gathering makes sense in the shifting politics of culture and the profoundly asymmetrical power dynamics of its moment.

This chapter examines these shifts by proposing that the late sixteenth-century transformation in warrior control of material culture, particularly in the intensive accumulation of artworks of the sort known as "famous objects" (*meibutsu*) in the world of tea, is related to shifts in elite warrior control of people, seen in an increase in hostage exchanges. In both cases, the most powerful members of warrior society, warlords (*daimyō*), exchanged entities over which they had some hegemony—a famous tea bowl in one instance, a vassal's son or daughter in another instance—as part of a political calculation. Such acts of exchange created value for both the exchanged objects and people and transferred some of this value to the actors conducting the exchange. Even when the value was not commoditized or monetized, as in the case of gift exchanges of tea utensils or hostage exchanges of family members, a system of social and cultural hierarchy was inscribed through the act of exchange and accumulation. Collecting famous objects and exchanging hostages represented significant forms of warrior power that informed the larger institutional shifts of the late sixteenth century, spectacular forms of accumulation that helped to define the grammar of politics.

TEA AND LORDLY THINGS

In the study of Japanese material culture, no cultural practice is as vital for understanding the play between the patronage and preservation of art as is tea culture. Not all forms of Japanese art played a role in tea culture; medieval Buddhist statuary or early modern woodblock prints, for example, almost never appeared in the tea room. But no attempt to map the social context for the creation, use, and survival of famous objects of the sort craved by Nobunaga and his peers would be complete without careful attention to the world of tea practitioners. The ritualized preparation and serving of tea became an opportunity for tea devotees to use and display a range of artworks and to enjoy the exquisitely planned spaces in which they hosted their guests. Tea practitioners commissioned new works, collected domestic and imported antiques, and even experimented with the production of their own artworks. Entire artistic industries were born and sustained—some into the twenty-first century—through the networks of patronage and exchange of the tea world.[3] Likewise, tea collectors meticulously preserved examples of genres of art that might have been lost to the ravages of time if not for the attention they paid to the storage and preservation of their beloved treasures.[4]

Though elites and later people of all statuses drank tea daily and in informal contexts after the late medieval period, the cultural practice that sustained art production and preservation and that appears throughout this book, known as *chanoyu* in Japanese, was more ritualized and choreographed. It was, and continues to be today, a practice centered on procedures for making tea (*temae*), which change according to the season, level of formality of the occasion, and types of utensils being used. The two main categories of tea ritual are thin tea (*usucha*) and thick tea (*koicha*), with those of the first category being less complex and formal than those of the latter category. Rules for making tea form the basis of any tea gathering (*chakai*), which involves a host and several guests (during the early modern period usually no more than five). While the order of a tea gathering changes according to time of day and season, the basic elements are that the host lays charcoal, serves a meal (*kaiseki*), and prepares a bowl of thick tea shared by all of the guests and a bowl of thin tea for each guest. The guests' movements and interactions with the host and other guests are also governed by rules and set patterns. Thus, both the host and guests must be knowledgeable about tea culture for a meeting to function smoothly. Tea gatherings are an occasion for displaying the knowledge, refinement, and accumulation of material wealth (through the display of utensils) of both the host and the guests. They are also occasions at which social and political ties can be fostered and cemented.[5]

The origins of tea drinking in East Asia are not well documented, but scholars assume that the spread of the consumption of the beverage emerged from its basic medicinal characteristics: tea stimulates the mind and body while improving health.[6] An added benefit is that the daily ritual of making, drinking, and sharing tea is a reassuring habit that promotes sociability. These may have been the motivations of early tea drinkers in China, where the broad-leafed evergreen bushes (*Camellia sinensis*) from which tea buds were picked grew naturally. Early authors such as Lu Yu (ca. 733–803) of the Tang dynasty demonstrated a dedication to every aspect of the production and preparation of the beverage to get the most effective and pleasurable effects.[7] Tea was seen both as a medicinal brew that promoted alertness and as a soothing, agreeable way of entertaining guests. This dual character would define tea culture as the practice of tea expanded geographically and changed over the centuries.

Around the time that Lu Yu was writing about tea in China, Japanese Buddhist monks brought tea, books, and utensils home from their studies on the continent. Some Sinophiles in the Kyoto court enjoyed the beverage, but tea drinking did not spread widely until the Zen monk Eisai (1141–1215), who also studied in China and brought back to Japan canonical Zen scriptures as well as tea seeds or seedlings, wrote a treatise devoted to the health benefits of the practice and introduced tea-drinking rituals into monastic life.[8] By the late fourteenth century, aristocrats and elite warriors were not just drinking tea, but holding contests known as tea battles (*tōcha*) to discern different varieties.[9] Commoners also drank tea more frequently, as sellers proliferated around Buddhist temple complexes and in urban marketplaces.

In the early fifteenth century, members of the warrior elite began to construct special rooms, lavishly decorated with domestic and imported art objects, for social gatherings. The Ashikaga shoguns—notably the third shogun, Yoshimitsu (1358–1408); the sixth shogun, Yoshinori (1394–1441); and the eighth shogun, Yoshimasa (1436–1490)—employed cultural advisers (*dōbōshū*) to collect and catalog art, design gardens, and stage theatrical performances.[10] The shoguns and their advisers valued Chinese things (*karamono*) in particular and regularly used calligraphy and paintings by Chinese Chan monks (such as the now canonical works by Mu Qi and Zhang Sigong), as well as *tenmoku* tea bowls (made in Fujian, China) in the course of their elaborate tea gatherings. Several distinctive architectural and decorative features emerged from this period of innovation and soon became standard elements in high-quality architecture. First, tea battles gradually

Figure 9. Tenmoku tea bowl. Chinese, Song dynasty, 12th–13th century. Height 6 cm. Tokugawa Art Museum Collection, by permission of the Tokugawa Art Museum/DNPartcom

evolved into similarly rule-bound but less competitive tea gatherings, so Ashikaga shoguns constructed gathering rooms (*kaisho*) for tea, linked-verse poetry, banquets, and other forms of cultural exchange. Second, warrior elites wanted to display their newly acquired treasures from China, so residential tea gathering rooms increasingly included special features such as a built-in desk (*oshiita*) for scholarly writing implements, a decorative alcove (*tokonoma*) for hanging scrolls and flower arrangements, and staggered shelves (*chigaidana*) for incense burners, tea containers, or other small vessels.[11] Objects that became core to the culture of tea, such as the Chinese-manufactured tea bowls referred to as *tenmoku* (figure 9) in Japanese, were well suited both to the rituals of banqueting and of display in these palaces. By the late fifteenth century, therefore, the basic characteristics of Japanese tea culture had been established, with warrior elites collecting, using, and displaying art from China; hiring commoners as technical specialists and assistants; and constructing carefully planned spaces—what Takemoto Chizu calls banqueting sites—for social gatherings in which tea and related practices could be pursued.[12]

A tremendously significant but largely overlooked product of this fifteenth-century culture of shogunal sociability and art display was a new genre of documentation that might be anachronistically labeled the "art catalog," but which at the time encompassed a heterogeneous assortment of writings on display procedures, registers of paintings and ceramics, and somewhat haphazard lists of famous objects. The first known example, attributed to the shogunal cultural adviser Nōami (1397–1471) but perhaps recorded by his grandson Sōami (d. 1525), was the 1460s-era document entitled *Catalog of Lordly Paintings (Gomotsu on'e mokuroku).*[13] A Tokugawa-period transcription, now in the collection of the Tokyo National Museum, enumerates the names and painters of Chinese works from the Song and Yuan dynasties that were owned by the Ashikaga. Organized by size, the paintings do not share any common theme or style, but rather point to the Sinophilic gaze of the Ashikaga shoguns, the intense intention to acquire, possess, and display art associated with Chinese civilization. The spectacle of this collection was key to its function; the Ashikaga shoguns regularly invited elite warriors, shrine and temple priests, and members of the imperial court to visit their palaces. The visits of emperors, such as the well-documented call of Emperor Go-Hanazono on Shogun Ashikaga Yoshinori in the Muromachi Palace in 1437 (Eikyō 9/9/26), functioned as opportunities for elaborate displays of paintings, ceramics, and other works of Chinese art that were artfully thematized and displayed in purpose-built structures.[14] The objects in this collection were collectively designated *gomotsu* (also readable as *gyomotsu* or *gyobutsu*), a term that is often translated as "imperial treasures," in reference to the materials in the Shōsōin storehouse in Nara, associated with sovereigns of the 730s and 740s; in the context of the Ashikaga collection, however, a better translation might be "lordly things," as the method of acquisition was a hierarchical ritual culture of exchange that was central to the medieval conception of political authority.

Medieval calendrical anniversaries and other ritually observed temporal markers provided opportunities for gift giving that supplied the Ashikaga shoguns with some of their impressive collection. For example, Manzai (1378–1435), the abbot of the Kyoto temple Daigōji, recorded a range of gifts presented to the shoguns Ashikaga Yoshimochi and Yoshinori to mark celebrations such as Eighth Month (*hassaku*), which was observed the first day of the eighth lunar month.[15] Objects presented included painted screens, fans, ceramics (including tea bowls, water jars, and incense containers), and gold and silver vessels. In return, the shoguns sometimes offered swords, ceramics, or other precious objects.[16] The collection thus advertised not only the wealth and, in theory, political power of the Ashikaga shoguns, but the network of vassals, allies, and relations through which these objects had traveled to reach their palaces in Kyoto. Of course, many treasures of the Ashikaga were acquired through purchase from merchants or via relations with institutions, such as Zen Buddhist temples with connections to China. But the Eighth Month and other calendrical exchanges serve as a reminder that elite material culture was peripatetic in medieval Japan because of its instrumentality in social rituals, even when a sustained collecting effort such as that of the Ashikaga shoguns created a kind of centripetal force on valuable Chinese things.[17]

Perhaps the most influential record of the Muromachi Palace culture of sociability and display, a document that would be reproduced in various formats for the next several hundred years, was the *Manual of the Attendant of the Shogunal Collection (Kundaikan sōchōki)*.[18] Attributed to Sōami, one of the cultural advisers to Ashikaga Yoshimasa, this decorative and connoisseurial guide in fact represented an already fading snapshot of the glory of the Ashikaga shogunal world of lordly things, seen from the vantage point of its dissolution and destruction. Shogun Yoshimasa famously presided over the collapse of Ashikaga authority, as the Ōnin War raged through Kyoto and spread into the provinces, while the shogun and his peers pursued their cultural interests in the Silver Pavilion and other luxurious palaces around the capital city, some of which were soon after destroyed.[19] After Yoshimasa's death in 1490 and the installment of a child shogun, the Ashikaga collection began to scatter, sold to raise funds, given away in desperate attempts to shore up shogunal authority, and generally dispersed to warlords and wealthy urban commoners. Now those who had previously witnessed the sophisticated displays and social graces of the Ashikaga could purchase the very Chinese treasures that bore the seals and pedigrees of Ashikaga ownership. The dispersal of this collection created an opportunity for Sōami, who was perhaps reflexively aware of his position as the last cultural adviser to the Ashikaga shoguns. He may have written the *Manual* as a way to profit from the desire of the new owners of Ashikaga treasures to identify, store, and display their acquisitions properly. Drawing on his memories and perhaps on notes left by Nōami, he drafted and probably sold copies of the *Manual*. The first documentary reference to the *Manual* appeared in 1511; then, as Sōami or others produced more manuscript copies, the text was mentioned in letters and diaries with increasing frequency, until the rise of the new generation of commoner tea masters and warrior collectors in the second half of the sixteenth century.[20]

The spread of both the Ashikaga collection of famous objects and copies of the *Manual* in the early sixteenth century had the curious effect of popularizing an elite practice that was socially significant as a means of creating distinction precisely because of the previous limits on access. This disrupted the power dynamic in the field of collecting within tea culture, opening up the possibility of the ownership of lordly things, at least initially, to wealthy commoners such as merchants from the city of Sakai, who became innovative leaders in the development of new tea practices, assemblages of objects, and performance sites that adopted Ashikaga elements in smaller, more contained formats. The story of the origins of this "rustic tea" (*wabicha*) style, with precise emphasis on the figures of Murata Jukō and Takeno Jōō, has been well explored in both Japanese and English.[21] Linking the collapse of the Ashikaga collection to the rise of commoner tea, however, was the *Manual,* which delineated a lexicon of classification and methods of display that allowed individuals of various backgrounds and economic means to acquire, or at least aspire to acquire, lordly things.

HUNTING FOR FAMOUS OBJECTS

Collecting of tea objects by elite warriors did not come to a halt with the dispersal of the Ashikaga collection and the rise of commoner tea but continued with a widened scope. The Asakura house of warlords, for example, who had commandeered the rule of Echizen Province from the Shiba in the wake of the Ōnin War, were patrons of many forms of culture popular in Kyoto in the late fifteenth century. In fact the Asakura are explicitly mentioned in the prologue of one extant version of the *Manual of the Attendant of the Shogunal Collection* as having sponsored the writing of that copy, at least, by Sōami.[22] They amassed a significant collection of Chinese art in the late fifteenth and early sixteenth centuries, as noted in contemporaneous records, such as the Yamashina family diaries and the Chinese poetry anthology *Collection of Literature of the Five Phoenixes (Kanrin gohōshū).*[23] These archival references are supported by massive archaeological excavations of the Asakura's castle town of Ichijōdani, which unearthed significant quantities of high-quality Chinese ceramics.[24]

The Asakura were not alone in their activities. Similar accumulative practices are apparent in records of famous objects (*meibutsuki*) and tea diaries (*chakaiki*), two genres of record keeping that emerged in the early sixteenth century in response to the spread of the *Manual,* the dispersal of the Ashikaga collection, and the growth of rustic tea among a class of highly literate urban commoners. Lists of lordly things, which were increasingly referred to as *meibutsu,* or "famous objects," began to circulate in this period, both in the capital and in the provinces.[25] The early text, *Record of Praiseworthy Famous Objects (Seigan meibutsuki),* for example, lists 414 objects by category and also notes previous and current owners by location, up to the end of the Tenbun period (1532–1555), when such details were known. The majority of objects are listed as being located in Kyoto and Sakai, the centers of the new rustic tea practice, but significant quantities are also described as in the collections of provincial warriors, including the Hosokawa, Asakura, Takeda, Miyoshi, and many other warrior families.[26]

Similarly, the earliest tea diaries, such as the *Gathering Records of Tennōjiya (Tennōjiya kaiki)* of the Tsuda family of Sakai, which begins in 1533, and *Gathering Records of Matsuya (Matsuya kaiki)* of the Matsuya family of Nara, which begins in 1548, record warlord participants in tea gatherings and note numerous famous objects that these warlords acquired, owned, and used in the vibrant urban context of tea culture. The previously mentioned Asakura, for example, possessed at least thirty-two famous objects, according to the documentary records of this period.[27] One of these pieces, a Chinese-produced tea caddy (used to hold powdered green tea during the actual ritual of preparing and serving tea) known as Eggplant Tsukumo (Tsukumo Nasu), was mentioned in the prologue and had previously been in the Ashikaga collection. Even more impressive was the warlord Matsunaga Hisahide (1510–1577), who was centrally involved in the betrayals, wars, and capital politics of the 1560s. As an ardent tea practitioner and collector, he reportedly owned at least fifty-nine famous objects, eight of which had previously been part of the Ashikaga collection.[28]

If provincial leaders such as the Asakura and upstart politicians such as Matsunaga Hisahide represent the commitment of individual, regional warlords to the symbolic value of famous objects, it was the ambitious young warrior from Owari Province, Oda Nobunaga, who brought tea and the acquisition of Chinese things back onto the political center stage. Nobunaga was first exposed to such objects by his father, Oda Nobuhide (1510–1552), who collected Chinese things. *The Record of Praiseworthy Famous Objects* lists a water pitcher (*mizutsugi*) that was probably a Chinese ceramic; a yellow *tenmoku* bowl, made in Fujian, China; and a hanging scroll painting, *Mountain Village After a Storm (Sanshi seiran)* by the thirteenth-century Chinese painter Mu Qi, as being owned by the Oda.[29] Nobunaga probably inherited Nobuhide's collection of Chinese things when his father died, but did not begin his own acquisition of famous objects until well after he had consolidated his hold on the Oda house in 1558 and eliminated the threat of his neighbor Imagawa Yoshimoto in 1560. It was in fact in 1568, when Nobunaga marched toward the capital city of Kyoto with the intent of installing the scheming Ashikaga Yoshiaki as shogun, that this brash leader began to accumulate what would become a truly spectacular collection.

Not long after Nobunaga's victory in a series of battles as he escorted Ashikaga Yoshiaki from Ōmi to Kyoto early in the tenth month of 1568, the Oda lord began to receive gifts and accolades acknowledging his pacification of the Five Home Provinces (Yamashiro, Yamato, Kawachi, Izumi, and Settsu). Matsunaga Hisahide, one of those who had opposed Nobunaga (and been involved in the murder of the previous shogun), saluted him with a kingly gift: the Chinese tea caddy Eggplant Tsukumo, previously in the collection of the Asakura and before that part of the Ashikaga collection.[30] Likewise, the Sakai merchant and entrepreneurial tea master Imai Sōkyū—who was well connected among the politically and economically powerful merchants of the region's key port city, and who also was at the center of the burgeoning rustic tea movement—gave Nobunaga two impressive pieces. The first, a Chinese-made ceramic tea jar (*chatsubo*) called Matsushima, had previously been in the Ashikaga collection before being acquired by the warlord Miyoshi Masanaga, who owned an impressive array of famous objects before his death in 1549. Later it was owned by Takeno Jōō, one of the most influential tea masters of the age and Sōkyū's father-in-law. The second was an unnamed eggplant-shaped tea caddy (*nasu*), a common description for the small, Chinese ceramic containers with larger, bulbous bottoms and slightly smaller tops; this particular example is believed to have been another famous object known as Jōō Eggplant, previously in the collection of the Ashikaga, that Sōkyū inherited from Jōō along with Matsushima.[31] Lastly, an unnamed party presented a unique piece of armor to Nobunaga, a suit that the twelfth-century hero, Minamoto no Yoshitsune, wore as he "stormed down Tekkai Cliff at the Battle of Ichinotani." In short, in this moment the close linkage between political authority and the ownership of famous objects can be seen, a linkage that helps to clarify why accumulation was a strategically important practice for ambitious warlords in this era. Nobunaga's most significant accomplishment to date—the elimination of the barriers to the installment of Ashikaga Yoshiaki as shogun in Kyoto—marked the beginning of his career as a hegemon with aspirations of widespread dominance, as well as the beginning of his education as a devoted collector of tea utensils, or what *The Chronicle of Lord Nobunaga* calls his acquisition of "the greatest of rarities from our country and from foreign lands."[32] The trajectories of these two pursuits—the accumulation of political power and the accumulation of treasures—were inextricably linked by acts of violence and sociability.

Nobunaga's appetite was apparently whetted by the receipt of these gifts, and he soon embarked upon a campaign known as the Hunt for Famous Objects (*meibutsu gari*). Between 1569 and 1570, Nobunaga acquired at least ten of the most prized tea utensils in Japan, using his authority as the rising political and military leader to persuade, and when necessary force, owners to part with their treasures. According to book 2 of the *Chronicle:*

> Whereas Nobunaga had no shortage of gold, silver, rice, or cash, he decided that he should furthermore acquire Chinese things as well as the most famous pieces of this realm for his collection. First, from Upper Kyoto,
>
> | | |
> |---|---|
> | Item: [the tea caddy] Hatsuhana | owned by Daimonjiya [Sōkan] |
> | Item: [the tea caddy] Fujinasubi | from Yūjōbō |
> | Item: bamboo tea ladle | from Hōkōbō |
> | Item [the flower vase] Kaburanashi | belonging to Ikegami Jokei |
> | Item: painting of wild geese | Sano |
> | Item: [the flower container] Mokusoko | Emura |
>
> Yūkan and Niwa Gorōzaemon acted as the emissaries in making payment in gold and silver or rice on Nobunaga's behalf.[33]

Politically and economically, northern or "upper" Kyoto represented the heart of the capital city, home to the imperial court and its aristocratic families, as well as the artisanal and merchant families that served them. Not surprisingly, this population had acquired a number of objects from the Ashikaga collection and was also at the forefront of the growing rustic tea movement among wealthy urban commoners. Nobunaga sent two of his most trusted vassals—Matsui Yūkan (active late 16th c.) and Niwa Gorōzaemon (1535–1585; Nagahide)—to act as collection agents. The first famous object they acquired for Nobunaga according to this account was a tea caddy previously owned by Ashikaga Yoshimasa, and ostensibly named after a line in the *Kokinshū* poetry anthology: Hatsuhana, or "First Flower."[34] After its dispersal from the Ashikaga collection, it was owned by the influential tea master Murata Jukō (1423–1502) before being acquired by Daimonjiya Sōkan, a merchant and noted tea practitioner, who appears numerous times in the tea diaries of the day.[35] By obtaining it, Nobunaga now possessed a tea caddy that a later tea practitioner would refer to as one of the three most important famous objects in Japan.[36] The other pieces listed above (with the exception of the bamboo tea ladle) had similar pedigrees: originating in China, passing through the Ashikaga collection, and then scattering into various merchant collections before being reunited in Nobunaga's tea utensil hunt.

According to book 3 of the *Chronicle*, Nobunaga turned his acquisitive gaze toward Sakai in the following year:

> At that time, the most famous objects of art in the realm were the following tea ceremony articles, which were to be found in Sakai:
>
> | | |
> |---|---|
> | Item: painting of sweets[37] | Tennōjiya Sōgyū |
> | Item: [the tea leaf jar] Komatsushima | Yakushiin |
> | Item: [the flower container] Kōjiguchi | Aburaya Jōyū |
> | Item: painting of a bell | Matsunaga Danjō [Hisahide] |

> Each of them was truly a famous object. Using Yūkan and Niwa Gorōzaemon as his emissaries, Nobunaga let it be known that he wanted them for his own collection. The owners, who could not possibly disobey Nobunaga's orders, presented the articles without demur. Nobunaga ordered that they be given gold and silver in exchange.[38]

It was no accident that these works of art were "to be found" in the entrepot of Sakai, one of the most vibrant commercial cities of the period. In the fifteenth and sixteenth centuries, the port was home to international and national shipping organizations, wholesalers who dealt with the transshipment of estate rents, a range of merchants, and powerful temple complexes.[39] The city was by all accounts teeming with activity. Genre screens from the period, such as the painting of the Sumiyoshi festival (Sumiyoshi sairei-zu byōbu), show shops selling goods to festival participants and bystanders on a network of densely crowded streets (figure 10).[40] Sakai was home to a class of wealthy merchants who were quite independent and managed to shield their city from much of the violence that visited other parts of Japan in a period of political instability. One Jesuit visitor to the city in the 1560s remarked,

> Unlike Sakai, Japan in general is not a tranquil country. In the provinces, there are disturbances everywhere. These are unknown in Sakai. Vanquished and victors can come here to live in peace. Here, they talk, instead of fighting. There is no disorder in the city's districts. . . . In each district are lookout towers ready to intervene in case of brawls. . . . The city has a secure position, surrounded by the sea and by moats filled with water.[41]

In fact, the leading council of the city's merchant elders maintained a certain degree of independence and safety by negotiating with surrounding warlords and using their broad influence to ensure their collective safety.

From 1469 to 1510, Sakai had served as the gateway for official missions to Ming China, which included significant mercantile activity.[42] This trade contributed much to the long-standing importation of Chinese ceramics, paintings, and other objects that were treasured by Buddhist, urban commoner, and warrior elites. Even after the official Ming expeditions came to a halt, Sakai continued to function as a center for the exchange of various types of art objects, including Chinese and Japanese ceramics. Excavations of late sixteenth-century archaeological sites in the city have yielded significant objects, including carved Mishima bowls from Korea, Lonqquan celadons from China, Chinese blue and white porcelains from a variety of kilns, and even wares from Southeast Asia.[43] Many of the prominent Japanese ceramic styles that became increasingly popular among tea practitioners in

Figure 10. Folding screen illustrating the Sumiyoshi festival, detail. Edo period, 17th century. 107.6 x 263 cm. Sakai City Museum

the second half of the sixteenth century are also found in these sites, making it clear that Sakai was a major center for the trade in famous things. These details were not incidental to the political successes of leading merchants and tea practitioners or to the interest in the city for warlords, such as Nobunaga.

The first famous object in this entry from the *Chronicle* noted previously, for example, was taken from a prominent figure in the Sakai tea world, Tsuda Sōgyū (d. 1591), the son of a particularly successful merchant and tea practitioner who had been one of the first to record his tea experiences in a tea diary (*chakaiki*). Like his father, Sōgyū was extremely active in tea circles, as well as an avid chronicler of his activities, and aided by the wealth that his family had acquired through their Tennōjiya business, he was able to put together a notable collection of utensils. Along with Imai Sōkyū and the up-and-coming tea master Sen no Rikyū (also Sen Sōeki; 1522–1591), Sōgyū was one of the most influential members of Sakai's tea community. The painting of sweets (*kashi*) is attributed to the Chinese painter Zhao Chang, active during the Northern Song dynasty (960–1127). The second famous object, a tea leaf jar of Chinese manufacture named Komatsushima, belonged to a prominent Sakai doctor. The third object, a metal Chinese flower container named Kōjiguchi, was owned by a Sakai merchant, while the fourth object, an ink painting attributed to the popular Chinese artist Mu Qi, came from the collection of Matsunaga Hisahide. Eguchi Kōzō notes that while these objects were widely considered to be valuable treasures, there was a political purpose beyond, or perhaps intertwined with, these acquisitions in Sakai. The merchant families from which Nobunaga requisitioned these famous objects were not the old leaders of the city that had dominated the ruling council (*egōshū*) and navigated the tumultuous political tides of the 1540s and 1550s; instead, there is a new commercial and cultural elite emerging from these interactions with Nobunaga.[44] Although these Hunts for Famous Objects can be read as straightforward deployments of power by a young hegemon, they are better understood as instances of exchange, in which Nobunaga reciprocally extends some form of political protection to the rising merchants of Sakai.

Armed now with a small but extraordinary collection of famous objects, as well as with substantiated connections to some of the tea luminaries of Sakai, Nobunaga entered the world of tea as a practitioner in 1571 by hosting a small gathering at Gifu Castle.[45] From this point onward, Nobunaga actively enlarged his collection of famous objects. Reliable historical sources record at least 109 objects owned by Nobunaga based on the firsthand observations of the authors. Other sources record an additional 73 objects in his collection based on thirdhand knowledge, though the actual total may have been much higher.[46] *Tenmoku* tea bowls originally made in Fujian, China; ink paintings brushed during the Song dynasty; and imported ceramic tea caddies "with shoulders" (*katatsuki*) all appeared in the pages of the diaries of tea practitioners such as Imai Sōkyū and Tsuda Sōgyū as objects that Nobunaga used at gatherings in the decade after 1571. These events were often planned to showcase Nobunaga's growing collection to a large audience of practitioners; the tea gathering became an opportunity for Nobunaga to not only perform his growing devotion to the choreographed movements of tea ritual, but also to sponsor a spectacle that would "caress the exterior senses,"[47] while concretizing the power of the hegemon. In the tenth month of 1575, for example, he invited seventeen tea practitioners from the capital and Sakai to a tea gathering at Myōkakuji, a temple in northern Kyoto. The event is well known in tea historiography because it represents one of the first appearances of Sen Sōeki, who would later change his name to Rikyū, on the main stage of political pageantry. Although by 1575, Nobunaga already regularly relied on Imai Sōkyū and Tsuda Sōgyū as tea masters and consultants, his choice of Sōeki as the host for this performance seems significant considering the meteoric rise of both men in the decade that followed.[48] In the alcove of the tea room, Sōeki hung the prized Chinese ink painting *Evening Bell* (probably the same piece referred to earlier as *Painting of a Bell*, acquired from Matsunaga Hisahide in 1570), which had previously been part of the Ashikaga collection.[49] He also placed the tea jar Mikazuki, which Nobunaga's vassal Miyoshi Yasunaga (also Shōgan; dates unknown) had given the Oda lord just a week earlier, underneath the hanging scroll. On the staggered shelves (*chigaidana*), Sōeki displayed the white *tenmoku* tea bowl that Nobunaga had earlier received from the prince-abbot (*monzeki*) of the Honganji of Osaka.[50] This treasure was itself seated on a stand, while the tea caddy Tsukumo—that first famous object that Matsunaga Hisahide had given to Nobunaga in 1569—sat on a tray decorated with a red lacquer interior. On the tatami mat, Sōeki had arranged an iron teakettle named Otogoze and the tea jar Matsushima, a previous gift from Imai Sōkyū. In later centuries, *otogoze* became a designation for a specific kettle shape, with a bulbous form, a flat top, and a concave mouth; the description of this gathering in the *Chronicle,* however, is the first known use of the name in tea. According to the text, the gathering was "an occasion that all would remember gratefully for the rest of their lives."[51]

With the exception of the kettle and probably the stand and tray, all of the objects that Nobunaga displayed at this gathering were Chinese in origin, part of the outpouring of famous objects that circulated among warlords and wealthy urban commoners in the wake of the dispersion of the Ashikaga collection. Although the appearance of Sōeki at this event is heralded as a key moment in the history of rustic tea and the Sen tea tradition, what is most striking in this instance is the intensity with which Nobunaga replicated (with the goal of surpassing) the Ashikaga assemblage of Chinese famous objects. Though Nobunaga had driven out Yoshiaki, the last Ashikaga shogun, from Kyoto two years before this gathering, the visual and material grammar of power established by Ashikaga Yoshimitsu, Yoshinori, and Yoshimasa was still appealing to the Oda lord as a means of what Theodore Ludwig called "establishing his claims of hegemony and ritualizing his position."[52]

WAR AND HOSTAGE EXCHANGE

Nobunaga's instrumentalization of material culture to demonstrate his power and authority was complemented by his activities on the battlefield; both practices highlight the increasingly asymmetrical forms of power of late sixteenth-century Japan. Nobunaga embraced violence as a means of effecting change even more determinedly than he did collecting Chinese things and sponsoring tea gatherings. Perhaps the most spectacular example was his 1571 assault on the influential temple complex of Enryakuji, located in the Higashiyama hills outside of Kyoto and well established as one of the cultural and economic buttresses of the capital region's medieval system.

In 1570, Enryakuji's Tendai monks had sided with the Azai and the Asakura in their resistance to Nobunaga, despite the Oda lord's strong warnings to the temple to either support his cause or stay out of the conflict. As punishment, and to make a statement to other religious institutions, Nobunaga ordered his men to burn down the temples and shrines of Enryakuji, giving off what one diarist recorded as "clouds of black smoke."[53] But more than buildings suffered the "wrath of Nobunaga":[54] according to the *Chronicle,* advancing Oda soldiers "cut off the heads of priests and laymen, children, wise men, and holy men alike," and presented the trophies for examination. Even the large numbers of "beautiful women and boys" found in the temple complex—evidence, perhaps of the ostensible "lewdness" of the Enryakuji priests—were executed despite their desperate requests for clemency. "One by one, they had their heads chopped off, a scene horrible to behold. Thousands of corpses lay scattered about like so many little sticks, a pitiful end."[55]

Nobunaga's destruction of the temple complex on Mount Hiei stands out as a singular act of violence in the late sixteenth century, but in fact the broader trajectory of war in this period was toward larger conflicts. Battles between armies numbering in the tens of thousands occurred with some regularity.[56] The taking of heads, sometimes in the thousands, as a means of quantifying the labor of war, likewise appears with such frequency in records of this period that it becomes ubiquitous, making it almost easy to ignore. But Nobunaga's rise to power was lifted by a tide of decapitation. For example, in the months before his army's attack on Mt. Hiei, his forces took 670 heads in an attack on Shimura Castle, and in the seventh month of 1572, one of Nobunaga's generals led forces in a successful attack against light infantry: "His men cut them to ribbons and took more than fifty heads."[57] The heads of high-ranking enemies were particularly valuable and were often recorded in lists, but decapitation in general was a means of receiving acknowledgment and even financial rewards. In Nobunaga's campaign against the Azai, his forces explicitly used the accumulation of enemy trophies for this purpose, "bringing back captured banners, flags, and armaments; not a day went by without their presenting two or three heads to him. Nobunaga rewarded his men in proportion to their exploits, so their determination was extraordinary."[58] The ritual of head collection and head counting thereby reduced the singular human body to an exchangeable object, which was literally traded for economic remuneration or its equivalent in social capital. (This topic is discussed in more detail in chapter 5.)[59]

Another common practice in sixteenth-century warrior society, linked by the theme of *accumulation* to hunting for famous objects as well as hunting for heads, was the exchange of hostages (*hitojichi*).[60] Hostage taking is now closely associated with late twentieth- and early twenty-first-century instances of kidnapping and terrorism, but as Adam Kosto has shown in the context of medieval Europe, the hostage was by no means a monolithic category. Rulers gave hostages to secure rights or guarantee agreements; generals took hostages in warfare; warlords exchanged people as hostages, as prisoners, and as slaves; and individuals sold themselves into servitude to pay off debts.[61] While recognizing that the commoditization of people, and the resulting trafficking of individuals against their will, "was and is a tragedy," as Joseph Miller wrote in *The Problem of Slavery as History,* hostage exchange in Japan's late sixteenth century can be understood as another manifestation of the increasingly asymmetrical formations of warrior power.[62]

Records from this period are littered with references to hostage exchange.[63] In the *Chronicle,* for example, we see references to warriors taking hostages (*hitojichi o tori*) to buttress military positions as early as 1552 and to combatants presenting hostages (*hitojichi idashi*) as guarantees of loyalty in 1553.[64] In 1567, a group of warrior leaders from Mino defected to the side of Oda Nobunaga and "asked him to accept hostages from them" (*hotojichi o ouke tori*) as proof of their sincere intentions, one of many similar examples.[65] Hostages were also central to what was perhaps Nobunaga's most significant moment of political ascension: his victory over Ashikaga Yoshiaki, the shogun whom he had helped to install in Kyoto and the last representative of the previous warrior regime's authority. In 1573, after Yoshiaki had openly turned against Nobunaga, the Oda lord entered Kyoto with a large army and surrounded the shogun's castle at Nijō. "Amazed at the size of his army, the shogun's men offered apologies and hostages to Nobunaga; all of them joined his camp."[66] When Nobunaga caught Yoshiaki soon after, he exiled the shogun rather than killing him and, significantly, "kept Yoshiaki's infant son as a hostage," ostensibly a sign of his generosity.[67] These were not token gestures; Nobunaga and his peers were ruthless in their assessment of the outcomes of these hostage exchanges, even when the trafficked bodies were those of children, wives, or other family members. In 1579, for example, Nobunaga ordered the execution of more than six hundred hostages taken from the warlord Araki Yoshishige, including the public spectacle of parading about thirty of his family members through the streets of Kyoto on carts before beheading them.[68] The message to the residents of Kyoto, and indeed to all who contemplated resisting Nobunaga, was clear. In the words of the author of the *Chronicle,* "Anyone who tried to oppose Nobunaga was overcome. The measure of his power and his glory was utterly incalculable."[69]

TOKUGAWA IEYASU: FROM HOSTAGE TO WARLORD

The hostages who were exchanged in the political maneuverings and battlefield divisions of spoils of the sixteenth century were often unnamed and therefore remain unknown to us today. A notable exception was Tokugawa Ieyasu, the third of the Three Unifiers and the founder of the Tokugawa shogunate. The story of his youth, constrained by the relative weakness of his family, and his notable rise illustrate the profound differentials in power that marked this period. Ieyasu was born in Okazaki Castle (present-day Okazaki city, Aichi Prefecture) in the province of Mikawa on 1543/12/26.[70] He was the first son of the sixteen-year-old lord of Okazaki, Matsudaira Hirotada (1526–1549) and his fourteen-year-old wife Odai no Kata (1528–1602). In 1547 Ieyasu was sent as a hostage to the Imagawa clan. Along the way, he was captured by another warlord, Oda Nobuhide (the father of Nobunaga). In early 1549, two years into his life as a hostage of the Oda clan, Ieyasu's father died. Later that year, Ieyasu was sent along with one of the Oda sons as a hostage to the warlord Imagawa Yoshimoto, the ruler of the provinces of Suruga and Tōtōmi, who had his headquarters in Sunpu Castle, where Ieyasu would live until he was a young man.[71]

Later hagiographies and collections of sayings attributed to Ieyasu record various stories from this period that imply that his life under the Imagawa was trying. *The Tale of Mikawa (Mikawa monogatari),* for example, claims that "these were fearful times for Ieyasu, more than can be expressed in words."[72] Other stories, probably apocryphal, record instances of the young man acting in a brazen or proud fashion, implying that he was destined for greatness.[73] We must remember, however, that while a hostage of the Imagawa, Ieyasu still received a full education, trained in the cultural and military practices typical for a young man of his status, and participated—at his lord's command—in military engagements, a marriage, and other actions.[74] Rather than seeing Ieyasu's objectification as a hostage as a kind of test of his mettle or a step on the inevitable and providential road to greatness, perhaps we should identify this moment of precarity as all too typical an experience. Vassalage itself represented an inherently unequal relationship, and such inequalities defined the structure of warrior society. In an age of war many lacked agency, above all those of lower status and wealth, but even those elites with less say over the movement of their own bodies, such as samurai women and children, could find themselves in constrained and highly objectified positions.[75]

The status of Ieyasu as a captive hostage was reified in various ways. Yoshimoto arranged in 1555 for Ieyasu to undergo the ceremony of manhood at the age of thirteen, when he received a new name, (Matsudaira Jirosaburō) Motonobu, in exchange for his childhood name of Takechiyo.[76] The ceremony was a privilege, in a sense, but in this instance too we see a sign of Ieyasu's objectified position in a naming ritual that can be found throughout the pages of warrior documents from the long sixteenth century. His new name, *Moto*nobu, begins with a character taken from his master's given name, Yoshi*moto*. Although a common trend among families and vassal bands, in this context it may not have been welcome, though that may be an anachronistic reading of what was then a common practice.

The following year brought Ieyasu the chance to travel to Okazaki and visit the graves of his ancestors and finally to conduct a proper Buddhist memorial service for his father.[77] Ieyasu wrote an early letter (the first extant) during this visit to Okazaki, a missive that commended control over his ancestral temple of Daisenji to the temple itself and also lays out several prohibitions:

> As to the matter of Daisenji in Okazaki, extending from Sawatari in the east, to Kaido in the south, to where the valleys meet, to the edge of the fields of Konawate, and also to the edge of the fields in the north, I commend this in perpetuity. While previous letters of donation have been misplaced, it is important that if at any time someone were to come forward with a previous letter of donation, he should be considered a thief:
>
> Item: Taking of life is prohibited
> Item: Cutting bamboo in front of or inside the temple grounds is prohibited
> Item: Debts held by the temple are relieved
> Item: The temple is exempt from the building tax, gate tax, and labor services
> If anyone violates these articles, he will be strictly punished.
> 1556/6/24 Matsudaira Jirosaburō, Motonobu [seal][78]

Ieyasu seems to have been claiming the mantle of adulthood by reestablishing his connection with his ancestors and particularly his deceased father, as well as exercising one of the key rights of a wealthy warrior, the commendation of land.

Another manifestation of the asymmetrical power relations that served as the foundation of warrior society as arranged, forced marriages among vassals, a kind of trafficking in which young women's bodies were used to cement feudal ties, reward efficacious actions, or guarantee loyalty. In 1557, Imagawa Yoshimoto arranged for Ieyasu to marry the daughter of Sekiguchi Yoshihiro, an Imagawa vassal and relative by marriage, in a ceremony at the Imagawa hall in Sunpu.[79] Ieyasu would turn fifteen that year, and although his wife's exact age is unknown, some sources claim she was several years older.[80]

Ieyasu began to assume more responsibility as an active warrior during this period. In 1558, he traveled with Yoshimoto and his forces in an assault on a castle on the outskirts of a neighboring domain, controlled by the Oda. After burning the castle, they attacked other defenses in the region before returning to Sunpu.[81] Several former vassals of Ieyasu's father, now in the service of Yoshimoto, saw this as an opportune moment to argue for the development and maturity of Ieyasu as a potential leader; they petitioned Yoshimoto to request that Ieyasu be permitted to return to Okazaki Castle to take up his position as head of the family. Yoshimoto, however, was unwilling to release his hostage. He instead gifted a sword to Ieyasu as a reward for his contribution to the raid.[82] Under these circumstances, the gift of a sword may have symbolized more than just his martial accomplishment; perhaps the object served to remind the young man of his submission to the Imagawa and thus his inability to be an independent ruler at that moment.

In the third month of 1559, Ieyasu's wife gave birth to their first child, a boy whom they named Takechiyo like his father (and who would later take the name Nobuyasu). Ieyasu in this year began to use the name Motoyasu, reflecting his accomplishments but also his continued position as a hostage of Yoshimoto, who seemed determined to keep the young warrior in check. For example, he ordered Ieyasu to send a set of firm instructions to his vassals in Okazaki to prevent a recurrence of their previous petition. The document stipulates that Ieyasu's vassals should not speak of the matter of when he would be allowed to return to Okazaki to govern. Furthermore, they should obey Ieyasu's orders (meaning, in effect, Yoshimoto's) even while he was in Sunpu. Those who failed to fulfill their duties would be punished.[83]

The year 1560 was transformative for Ieyasu, who shifted from his precarious position as a hostage to the relative agency of a young warlord. In the fifth month, Yoshimoto set out from Sunpu with an army of approximately twenty-five thousand men and made his way toward Owari in a campaign with unclear goals. Ieyasu led the advance guard. After a week of marching, Yoshimoto on the nineteenth day sent Ieyasu and his forces to lay siege to one of the Oda fortifications, Marune Castle, but he soon reversed himself and dispatched Ieyasu to protect Ōdaka Castle, a key location in the supply of provisions.[84] This diversion may have saved Ieyasu's life. The same day, the young, neighboring warlord Oda Nobunaga left his headquarters at Kiyosu Castle and led a small force (estimated by some to be no more than eighteen hundred men) toward Yoshimoto's main army (perhaps five thousand men), which was encamped in the narrow Dengaku Hazama basin in the direction of Okehazama. Supposedly under cover of a fierce storm, the

Figure 11. Wood-block print triptych, the Battle of Okehazama in Bishû, Owari Province. Utagawa Toyonobu (active 1880s). Meiji period, 1883. 35.3 x 71.7 cm. Harvard Art Museums/Arthur M. Sackler Museum

attackers descended upon Yoshimoto's army, which could not form ranks and scattered amid a tide of slaughter. The *Chronicle* records the battle as follows (excerpts):

> Nobunaga ordered his troops to press on to the hillside. At that very moment there was a cloudburst. Hailstones pelted the enemy in the face, while ours felt the storm in their back. . . . Seeing that the skies were clearing, Nobunaga seized a spear and shouted at the top of his voice, "Now! Attack, attack!" Yoshimoto's men only saw a black cloud of dust storming towards them, and their line instantly collapsed as if washed away by water. Their bows, spears, harquebuses, banners, and flags lay scattered like so many little sticks all over the battle field. . . . Mōri Shinsuke struck down Yoshimoto and cut off his head.[85]

Though some of the details of the account may be apocryphal, the significance of the conflict, known as the Battle of Okehazama (figure 11), is clear. Ieyasu's captor was dead, and Ieyasu, who had escaped the battle by following Yoshimoto's own instructions, was now free to reclaim his position as lord of Okazaki. Yoshimoto's life—not to mention his most prized sword, Samonji—were taken from him by Nobunaga, while Ieyasu gained the opportunity to reclaim his birthright.[86]

In the spring of 1561, almost a year after Yoshimoto's death and Ieyasu's subsequent return to Okazaki Castle, Ieyasu made peace with the young but rising Oda Nobunaga.[87] This new alliance represented a substantial shift, away from the Imagawa—still the most powerful warrior clan in the region—to the impressive but still relatively small domain of Oda. This fortuitous association benefited both men and had a great impact on Japanese history. Ieyasu also began the process in this period of consolidating and then gradually extending his rule, as can be seen in a stream of missives sent to vassals, village leaders, and temples that confirmed or confiscated holdings, conciliated disputes, and rewarded meritorious service.[88] It was not, of course, the act of writing itself that empowered Ieyasu in this or later periods; his letters were buttressed by his position as head of his clan and ultimately by the threat of force from the ranks of samurai who pledged their service to him. But the relationship between his and his vassals' actions—invading a castle or exchanging hostages, for example—and the letters he inevitably sent soon after is clear: documenting the uses and consequences of force clarified the aftermath and lessened the need for further conflict.

Strategic alliances among warlords were often sealed through the exchange of family members as hostages or, in a similar use of familial bodies as a form of political capital, in the betrothal of children. In a sense, then, Ieyasu's rise from hostage to warlord is best illustrated by his participation in the asymmetrical power relations of warrior society as a subject who trafficked in bodies rather than as the object of such trafficking. The year 1563 marked Ieyasu's first foray into this arena when he sanctioned the betrothal of his first son, Takechiyo (later known as Nobuyasu), to Oda Nobunaga's daughter Tokuhime. Since both children were four years old at this time, the vow was initially symbolic of the beneficial truce between Nobunaga and Ieyasu.[89] Eventually, however, as Ieyasu acquired more land and vassals, and as Nobunaga grew in strength and standing, the marriage was consummated and became a cornerstone of the relationship between these two warlords.

This relationship was tested, and the balance between familial ties and feudal ties was measured, in a crisis that occurred much later, in 1579, when Nobunaga and Ieyasu had been collaborating for almost two decades. Unfortunately, the details of the crisis are unclear, as no extant letters from or to Ieyasu mention the incident and references in later sources are vague. Based on limited traces, historians hypothesize that the source of the problem was the marriage of Nobuyasu while still a boy to Nobunaga's daughter Tokuhime. For unknown reasons, the marriage deteriorated and Nobuyasu and his mother grew increasingly dissatisfied with Tokuhime and, in a much broader sense, the entire Tokugawa-Oda alliance. In the 1570s Nobuyasu began participating in the military activities of his father and must have felt more empowered to act as a warrior. In 1579 he was twenty years old, the same age that Ieyasu had been when he first forged an alliance with

Nobunaga. Proud of his Tokugawa heritage and Ieyasu's accomplishments, it may have exasperated Nobuyasu to think that his wife's father was in a superior position to his own. Whatever the source of friction, Tokuhime apparently wrote to Nobunaga in 1579 to report that her husband and mother-in-law were engaged in serious scheming against the Oda cause and perhaps were in league with Takeda Katsuyori. Nobunaga took the threat seriously. When some of Ieyasu's vassals arrived at Azuchi Castle in the seventh month with a gift of a fine horse for Nobunaga, perhaps in anticipation of the tension to come, the Oda lord demanded that Ieyasu order his son to "cut his belly."[90] One contemporaneous account of Ieyasu's actions at this time, *The Diary of Ietada,* though not particularly illuminating regarding Ieyasu's response to this grim news, paints a dark picture of the climate around the Tokugawa lord in this period, as though the natural world were promoting what Ieyasu could not. Entry after entry records heavy rain, until the last entry for the eighth month seems to encompass the whole affair: "An earthquake struck this afternoon."[91] Ieyasu met with Nobuyasu around this time to deliver his verdict, and on 9/15 Nobuyasu committed ritual suicide. To completely obliterate any possibility of further offending Nobunaga, Ieyasu also sent several of his vassals to find and kill his wife, Tsukiyama, who was traveling by boat to Hamamatsu.[92] Ieyasu did have other children, all born to the concubines whom he had installed near his quarters in Hamamatsu Castle: his two daughters were named Kamehime and Tokuhime (written with a different character than Nobunaga's daughter), and his two surviving sons were Hideyasu and Hidetada, the latter of which had just been born five months before Nobuyasu's death and would go on to succeed his father as head of the Tokugawa clan.

Ieyasu, of course, would marry again and have many more children, which illustrates the point that the authority of these men was based on a surplus that was not simply political or economic in nature but was in fact corporeal. The Tokugawa lord's cold calculus of feudal versus familial loyalty, influenced, perhaps, by the harsh decisions his own father had had to make about his fate as a child, is a reminder of the pressures and stakes of a nation at war with itself and the objectification and violence against children and women that resulted. Warlords were constrained by the power of their peers, or as in this case, Ieyasu was limited by his alliance with a military superior like Nobunaga, but such men also possessed a surplus of power over their own family and vassals, a surplus that allowed the sacrifice of a child or a spouse.[93] The logic of this objectification served as the platform for warrior rule, defining the right to wage war and expend human bodies in the name of accruing power, in increasingly large numbers and in progressively more destructive acts of violence throughout the long sixteenth century, all of which blurred the lines between the personal and the political. Mary Elizabeth Berry perhaps put it best when she noted that warrior relations in this period were defined in "relentlessly physical terms. Personal relations were not an ornamental or recreational dimension of an otherwise bureaucratized system of rule; they were, rather, the system of rule itself."[94]

CONCLUSION

In 1582, Nobunaga and Ieyasu defeated one of the most significant warlord families to resist the Oda lord: the Takeda, based in Kai Province (present-day Yamanashi Prefecture), with whom Nobunaga and Ieyasu had been fighting for more than a decade. Nobunaga next turned to a review of his newly acquired territory and the division of the spoils. He rewarded Ieyasu with the entire province of Suruga, further extending Tokugawa lands to the east and giving him control over the entire coast from the edge of Owari to Suruga Bay. Ieyasu had the opportunity to thank Nobunaga on 4/12, when the latter completed his military tour of Kai and met the young Tokugawa lord in Suruga. Ieyasu threw a banquet and gave Nobunaga a series of gifts, including a long sword, a short sword, and three good horses.[95] The importance of this victory to both men cannot be overstated; like the destruction of the Imagawa twenty-two years earlier that had launched both Nobunaga and Ieyasu on their individual paths to independent authority, the elimination of the Takeda cleared the way for Nobunaga to continue his expansion and for his ally Ieyasu to continue his growth in the central and most strategic region of the archipelago.

It is fitting that Ieyasu marked the end of this conflict with an offering of swords to his senior partner.[96] Nobunaga, as a leader who intended to conquer Japan, ruled overwhelmingly by the sword, both symbolically (for his use of military dominance) and literally, in the use of indiscriminate violence as means to this end. Ieyasu, likewise, had received a sword from his master Imagawa Yoshimoto in what seems to have been an objectifying rather than empowering gift, reinforcing the young Ieyasu's servility in the guise of emboldening him with a weapon. As Ieyasu claimed his hereditary position as leader of the Matsudaira, however, he increasingly possessed the authority to give swords of his own, as a means of cementing alliances, sending thanks, or making requests. Likewise, the sword also symbolized Ieyasu's ability to objectify the bodies of those with less power than him—his warriors sent into battle, his children trafficked in the name of marriage politics, or his own heir and wife, killed in the name of feudal duty—which marked his rise into the upper stratum of the warrior elite.

Ieyasu's reversal from the position of child hostage, separated from his home and his family, to that of a wealthy and independent warlord is startling. But we must note that this transformation in his position and relative power emerged not from a rejection of the elite warrior social and political system that had relegated him to a childhood spent with the Imagawa in Sunpu, but rather from his success and luck in navigating it. Ieyasu, like many of his peers, seems to have accepted the objectification of human subjects alongside the force granted to valuable things as part of the cultural logic of his age. To return to the anecdote that opened this chapter, the image of Nobunaga celebrating his victory over his enemies by displaying the lacquered and gilded heads of his victims seems, perhaps, less gratuitously brutal and more representative of the grammar of warrior power over both people and things in this age of war.

CHAPTER TWO

Grand Spectacle

Material Culture and Contingency

In the summer of 1587, the warlord Toyotomi Hideyoshi announced a grand spectacle: a massive tea gathering to be held that autumn on the grounds of the Kitano Shrine complex in northern Kyoto, a site of natural beauty and symbolic significance. The written and publically posted invitation articulated a plan that was innovative in scope, aiming to bring together "all earnest practitioners of chanoyu, also warriors' attendants, townspeople, or farmers, and even those of lower station," not to mention "people on the continent." Although the name of the event, the Kitano Grand Tea Gathering (Kitano ōchanoyu no kai) implied a performance similar to the personal and intimate gatherings that dominated the field of tea practice, the intention seems to have been closer to a public exposition: "Lord Hideyoshi will assemble his entire collection of famous objects, omitting not a single one, in order to show them to serious followers of *suki* [tea]." Indeed, Hideyoshi's overwhelming concern that his collection be witnessed by as many people as possible may explain the threatening tenor of one passage in the invitation: "Lord Hideyoshi's attendance is motivated by his feeling of compassion for *wabi* [rustic or insufficient] tea men. Any among such people who fail to attend will be prohibited hereafter from preparing even *kogashi* [a cheap tea substitute], and anyone paying a visit to such a person will suffer the same punishment." In short, viewing the spectacle of Hideyoshi's collection of famous objects was mandatory for all participants in the burgeoning world of tea culture.[1]

The previous chapter examined the resonance between the collection of famous objects and the exchange of hostages in the second half of the sixteenth century, arguing that both were manifestations of the asymmetrical power relations of a society at war. This chapter explores the issue of warrior power and the destabilization of society from a different angle, that of the spectacle of the display and circulation of prized pieces of material culture. Did the increasing attention paid to a small group of objects grant them an unusual level of influence in warrior and elite commoner society? Could famous art objects like the named Chinese ceramics that elite warriors craved effect the relations and events around them? Alternatively, might the trajectories of these objects through the lives of warlords and generals have acted to expose men such as Hideyoshi to contingent historical forces? In other words, what were the social and cultural effects and implications of the instrumentalization of "famous objects" in elite warrior society?

A difficulty confronting historians of the sixteenth century is the problem of individual agency. In particular, our conception of the significance of this period has been hindered by the set of assumptions underlying the theory of the Three Unifiers.[2] This hermeneutic presupposes that these men were inherently extraordinary, somehow uniquely qualified to prepare for and win the battles that would allow them to establish the early modern political system. It also assumes a kind of providential intentionality in their goals and actions; they were not only capable of leading, but were driven and determined to rule the entire country. Indeed, such a theory takes as a given the causal and linear connection between the life and career of the unifiers and the eventual entry of Japan into the modern world. These are reasonable assumptions if we accept Nobunaga, Hideyoshi, and Ieyasu as archetypal historical actors in the heroic mode.[3] But this conception is itself a historical product, the result of a process by which the unifiers' names have become synonymous with late medieval and early modern Japan: in Japanese the latter half of the sixteenth century is often referred to as the "Oda and Toyotomi period" (Shokuhōki), and of course the entire age from Ieyasu's victory at Sekigahara in 1600 to the fall of the shogunate in 1868 is conventionally called the Tokugawa period (Tokugawa jidai). The inscription of these men's individual biographies into Japan's national chronology is typical of the top-down approach to history in which astonishing individuals transform the foreign past into the domesticated present. Rather than focusing on the personalities and quirks of these three men, whereby their imagined individual virtues or immoralities lead readers to engage in a kind of historicist celebrity worship, this chapter focuses on material culture and the circulation of objects through the elite circles of warlords and their commoner advisers to raise the possibility that works of art had a kind of agency in this society at war. This approach is not meant to imply, of course, that famous objects were conscious or made choices. Rather, the increasing instrumentalization of certain categories and examples of material culture imbued them with singular value such that they seem to have affected the human subjects with which they came into contact. Ascribing agency to a famous Chinese tea ceramic is an interpretive and narrative device of the historian, an attempt to decenter the individualist hagiographies of the Three Unifiers and to understand the period in terms of broader social and cultural changes.[4]

Another method that I employ in this chapter in my attempt to make sense of the role of material culture in late sixteenth-century Japan is to call attention to the role of contingency in the process of unification. This, too, helps us to consider historical transformations without relying on causal explanations of progress toward modernity or the heroic greatness of the unifiers. By contingency, I do not mean discourses about chance or the culture of the accidental in sixteenth-century Japan, a topic fruitfully explored by Michael Witmore for England in this same period.[5] Instead, I follow the Renaissance historian Gene Brucker in considering contingency as "fortuitous and unpredictable" developments in a period of rapid and complex historical change.[6] Contingency is thus not equivalent to mathematical randomness, but represents a "conjuncture of preceding states."[7] As I explain in the following sections, the influence of elite material culture—the great value that warlords and tea practitioners placed on "famous objects" and the resulting effect they had on the actions of human subjects—heightened the significance of contingency as a historical force by bringing another system of value and meaning into play in social and political relations. The results were indeed often unpredictable, particularly from the point of view of the participants at the time.

THE PRIVILEGE OF ACCESS

Acquiring and Using Tea Utensils under Nobunaga

By 1571, as discussed in the previous chapter, Nobunaga had acquired a substantial collection of tea utensils, as well as firm relations with a number of tea practitioners in Kyoto and Sakai that would enable him to engage in further activity in the world of tea. Over the course of the following decade, his actions demonstrate that he saw his collection of famous Chinese ceramics, paintings, and other objects not as a static investment to be hoarded or protected from the ravages of time, but as an instrument in the politics and social maneuverings of unification. As Nobunaga continued the process of conquering recalcitrant warlords and their domains, enticing new allies to join him, and motivating his generals to manage this work on the ground, rewards of not only tea utensils but also special licenses to practice tea proved to be useful. Previous accounts of the history of tea culture in Japan tended to criticize the collection and instrumentalization of tea utensils by Nobunaga and his peers as "blatant cupidity" and "misuses as emblems of political prestige and power."[8] Such assertions create excessive delineation between an idealized "spiritual world" of tea and the politics of a society at war, presuming that the tea practice of commoners like Imai Sōkyū and Sen no Rikyū, who were less directly involved in the wars of unification, somehow trumped the tea practice of Nobunaga, Hideyoshi, and others.

The ostensibly distinct realms of culture and war were not so easily separated.[9] Sakai merchants such as Sōkyū and Rikyū, who are best known to us today as tea masters, also worked as merchants of various goods, including weapons and ammunition.[10] Nobunaga, conversely, began to use tea culture as an instrument of rule. Tentatively in the early years of his ownership of famous objects, and with drastically increasing frequency as his military expansion was successful, the Oda lord dispersed important tea utensils among his vassals and allies with great vigor. For example, in 1574 Rikyū and Tsuda Sōgyū both received unusual gifts from Nobunaga: pieces of the famous resin wood log, known as Ranjatai, used in incense ceremonies. This object, which is believed to have originated in Southeast Asia, was (and is today) part of the imperial collection in the Shōsōin storehouse at the Buddhist temple complex Tōdaiji in Nara and required court permission to handle and remove pieces. Ashikaga Yoshimasa had famously received permission to cut off a piece in 1465,[11] and Nobunaga followed suit in 1574. The ritual of examining the piece in the Room for Shogunal Visits in front of his valued Horse Guards was "a reflection of Nobunaga's glory," as the *Chronicle* puts it, as well as another instance of his reiteration of the political culture of the Ashikaga shogunate.[12]

The following month, Nobunaga sponsored a tea gathering at Shōkokuji, one of the five Gozan Zen temples of Kyoto. Tsuda Sōgyū recorded the event in his tea diary, and he is particularly eloquent in his discussion of the tea caddy named Hatsuhana, a piece that would later enter the collection of Ieyasu and play a role in the politics of his relationship with Hideyoshi (figure 12):

> Fourth month, third day, daytime, his lordship's improvised tea at Shōkokuji
> In the alcove: *Landscape of Ten Thousand Miles* [Banri Kōzan] by Yujian [J: Gyokukan, active mid-13th c. in China], owned by his lordship.[13]
> The tea caddy "First Flower" and the Yasui tea bowl were placed on a long tray.
> The brazier, on a lacquered board (*koita*); a flat kettle on a tripod; the brazier itself was helmet-shaped (*hōate-buro*).
> Shutoku bamboo tea scoop, Baisetsu made tea.

This was my first time seeing First Flower, [the tea caddy] with shoulders. It had three dripping striations [in the glaze], and the lips of the mouth are slightly flat. The glaze was applied to look like light persimmon under dark persimmon. The clay had a purplish color, and the base was like the bottom of a *go*-stone bowl. The color of the glaze seemed to contain something of the purple color of the clay, making it look still more graceful. The back of the jar was truly beautiful in appearance. The glaze was neither too light nor did it throb with brush marks. It goes without saying that the balance was excellent. Glaze drips (*nadare*) could be seen on just one side, which made its features somewhat more noticeable. It was a noble and harmonious object. Even if we can say it was a bit tall, that suited it. Similarly, we can say that the mouth was a bit low, but it fit the proportions.

In the course of the gathering, Sōeki [Sen no Rikyū] and Sōgyū [the author] received from his lordship Ranjatai fragments presented on open fans, which were also gifts. As Sōeki and Sōgyū both own incense burners, each obtained 2 *to* [approximately 2.6 liters] of the [aromatic] material bestowed by Tōdaiji. Other Sakai townspeople received nothing. The fans received from his lordship were decorated with cut gold foil.[14]

Sōgyū's documentation of this gathering and his and Rikyū's ritual receipt of gifts from Nobunaga conveys something of the significance of these encounters between powerful men of different status and the objects they mutually craved. Sōgyū's thick description of the tea caddy First Flower drips with appreciation, to the point that his praise hints at a barely hidden acquisitive lust. He describes the object not in terms of its distinguished ped-

Figure 12. Tea caddy named Hatsuhana. Chinese, Song dynasty, 13th century. Height 8.8 cm. Tokugawa Memorial Foundation

igree but rather its formal qualities, yet the social biography of the piece and the power and munificence of its present owner surely influenced his assessment. The privilege of being granted access to these famous objects and of receiving gifts from Nobunaga—"Other Sakai townspeople received nothing"—is key to the meaning of the encounter. On different occasions Nobunaga similarly gave tea utensils to other elite commoners, such as the doctor Manase Dōsan, the tea practitioner Yamanoe Sōji, and the Kyoto merchant Hariya Sōwa, in exchange for confiscated famous objects or as recompense for services.[15]

Nobunaga likewise awarded tea utensils to his military commanders with some frequency. Niwa Nagahide (1535–1585), for example, had served Nobunaga since the time of their youth and had played a major role in his rise, both as a commander on the battlefield and as a trusted lieutenant involved in the Hunt for Famous Objects. In 1576, to mark his appreciation for Nagahide's work on the initial phase of the construction of Azuchi Castle, Nobunaga awarded him a Chinese celadon tea bowl formerly owned by the Sakai tea master Murata Jukō. Nagahide was, according to the *Chronicle*, "most thankful."[16] Later that year, after working on further construction at Azuchi Castle, Nagahide again received a famous object as a reward from Nobunaga: the painting *The Marketplace* by the Chinese artist Yujian (J: Gyokukan, active mid-13th c. in China), while Hideyoshi, also involved in the construction, received a hanging scroll. According to the *Chronicle*, "The two counted their blessings. Their ability to acquire such precious items was, they knew, a reflection of their lord's power and his glory."[17]

Numerous generals received famous objects from Nobunaga to mark their notable accomplishments or cooperation, including Akechi Mitsuhide—the vassal who would ultimately betray Nobunaga—and the father and son pair of Sakuma Nobumori and Nobuhide. Among the rewarded vassals, two in particular stand out. Hideyoshi, who as noted earlier also participated in the construction of Azuchi Castle and received his first famous object from Nobunaga in 1576, was the most highly compensated of all of the Oda lord's generals. In late 1577 and early 1578, Hideyoshi sought to distinguish himself as a commander after being criticized by Nobunaga and took it upon himself to pacify various hostile forces in Tajima and Harima Provinces (current-day Hyōgo Prefecture). He surrounded and lay siege to Kōzuki Castle, for example, and his force was sufficiently intimidating that the soldiers in the castle killed their own commander and brought his head to Hideyoshi to plead clemency. Hideyoshi responded by sending the head to Nobunaga for inspection and then crucifying all of the remaining enemy soldiers, a statement of intent aimed at his superior but articulated through violence on the bodies of his enemies. He turned next to the neighboring

Figure 13. Ubaguchi-shaped tea kettle. Muromachi period, 15th century. Height 17 cm. Tokugawa Art Museum Collection, by permission of the Tokugawa Art Museum / DNPartcom

castle of Fukuokano, which he toppled, taking 250 heads in the process. Nobunaga's response to these extreme acts was to reward Hideyoshi with a famous object, a tea kettle (figure 13), a curious but meaningful representation of the value of human life versus the value of artworks in the politics of the day.[18] Hideyoshi's largest reward came in 1581, after he successfully pacified much of western Honshū. At the end of the year, upon returning from his endeavors, Hideyoshi "presented two hundred lined silk garments to Nobunaga by way of felicitations at year's end. In addition, he gave presents to each of the ladies. Such stupendous munificence, unwitnessed in past or present, left everyone, high and low, completely amazed."[19] Nobunaga responded by presenting Hideyoshi with twelve famous objects, all of them tea utensils, from his own massive collection, including a Korean tea bowl, a tea caddy "with shoulders" (*katatsuki*) formerly owned by the Asakura clan, and other well-known pieces.[20] This act of exchange of objects such as Korean tea bowls, which were becoming increasingly popular among tea practitioners (figure 14), served to emphasize Nobunaga's great appreciation for Hideyoshi and the premium value he placed on the young

Figure 14. Mishima-style tea bowl named Mishima-oke. Korean, Yi dynasty, 16th century. Height 8.9 cm. Tokugawa Art Museum Collection, by permission of the Tokugawa Art Museum / DNPartcom

lord's leadership and entrepreneurship, at least as understood in the particular context of the late sixteenth century.

Another recipient of pieces from Nobunaga's collection, though in a different type of relationship, was Oda Nobutada (1557–1582), Nobunaga's eldest son and heir. Nobutada had been increasingly involved in his father's campaigns since 1573, when he took part in the war in Echizen Province against the Asakura. In 1575, Nobunaga passed the headship of the Oda house to his son, along with the rule of Mino and Owari Provinces, the castle at Gifu, "the great sword Hishikiri . . . and the rest of the priceless implements that he had collected." The *Chronicle* notes that Nobunaga kept "only his tea ceremony implements for himself."[21] Two years later, in late 1577, Nobunaga presented Nobutada with at least eleven of these very treasured famous objects, including the aforementioned Chinese ceramic tea caddy named "First Flower" (Hatsuhana).[22] These gifts represented a form of probate, by which some of the material wealth and symbolic authority that Nobunaga had accrued would be transferred to Nobutada; they also represented a reward for meritorious service, particularly Nobutada's effective destruction of Matsunaga Hisahide, who had suddenly turned against Nobunaga earlier that year.[23] It may be that the delay represented a trial period in which Nobunaga assessed Nobutada's suitability as a ruler before granting him these most important of gifts.[24]

Perhaps the clearest example of Nobunaga's deployment of tea in the realm of politics came in 1581, not long after his gift to Hideyoshi of various famous objects. Now Nobunaga extended Hideyoshi's privileges in the field of tea to the three core, most significant practices: Hideyoshi was allowed to (1) host tea gatherings using the famous objects received from Nobunaga; (2) employ tea masters from Sakai; and (3) gift tea utensils to his own vassals.[25] Hideyoshi quickly made use of these privileges, holding an impromptu tea gathering that was attended by Tsuda Sōgyū.[26] Nobunaga thus appropriated the symbolic authority of the previous, legitimate warrior government of the Ashikaga and reified the warrior hierarchy in his own organization through the targeted dispersal of privileges. He did so carefully, monopolizing these privileges and only bestowing them when useful to prevent any diminishment in their effect. The famous objects from his own collection played a similar role, serving as symbols of his authority and stand-ins for his own personage—a process that the anthropologist Richard Werbner calls "dividuation," or a sharing of self and risks through ritual exchanges—which allowed the Oda lord to fortify the hierarchical bonds of his warrior collective.[27] Gifting famous objects and bestowing privileges such as the right to employ tea masters, in other words, represented moments in which warrior society itself was constituted.

SAVED BY TEA

The fifth month of 1582 marked the beginning of a new stage in Oda Nobunaga's seemingly unstoppable drive to unify Japan. The elimination of the Takeda and the increased control this gave Nobunaga over central Japan only increased his growing roster of vassals and their armies, which of course included Ieyasu but was by no means limited to him. This allowed Nobunaga to begin planning major assaults on more peripheral regions of the country that required significant mobilization and preparation. He aimed his sights first on the island of Shikoku, but was distracted by news from his lieutenant Hideyoshi, who was in the middle of a struggle against the mighty clan of Mōri in southern Honshū. Hideyoshi reported that the Mōri were emerging in force and that he would need reinforcements. From Nobunaga's perspective, this was a golden opportunity to crush a resilient opponent. He therefore ordered six of his generals to reinforce Hideyoshi, and he began preparations to travel to the south himself. Plans for the invasion of Shikoku also continued, meaning that he would mount two major offensives simultaneously, a clear sign of his strength and confidence. He left for Kyoto in the company of a small group of retainers, as well as much of his collection of Chinese art, secure in his control of the central region of the country and looking forward to the chance to show off his precious things to the aristocrats and elite commoners of the capital.[28]

Ieyasu had just left the capital as part of a leisurely tour of Kyoto, Nara, and Osaka that he took on his way to Sakai to prepare his troops for the invasion of Shikoku.[29] He arrived in Sakai on the same day that Nobunaga entered Kyoto. This was Ieyasu's first visit to the city after spending most of his life in Mikawa and neighboring provinces. Two days later he took advantage of the opportunity to meet with two of the most important sources of information and providers of tea utensils in Japan: Sōkyū and Sōgyū.[30] That afternoon he joined another tea gathering, and in the late afternoon he attended a dance performance. He topped off this rather long day with a banquet in the evening. Nobunaga, at precisely the same moment, was enjoying a celebration in Kyoto put on by members of the court and other local elites, who clearly recognized that the Oda lord was the undisputed master of the temporal realm (*tenka*).

Unbeknownst to Nobunaga and Ieyasu, however, one of the Oda vassals assigned to support Hideyoshi, the warlord Akechi Mitsuhide, had decided to seize this chance to overthrow Nobunaga and his family and take the Oda territory and vassals by force. As the *Chronicle* put it, "But then events took an unexpected turn."[31] In an attack that has become one of the most famous acts of treason in Japanese history, Mitsuhide and his army of thirteen thousand diverged suddenly from their route to the south and entered Kyoto in the early hours of 1562/6/2, surrounding Honnōji where Nobunaga was staying in quiet luxury. Again, the *Chronicle*'s dramatic account is useful, if flowery:

> In no time at all, the enemy surrounded the Honnōji, the temple where Lord Nobunaga was staying and came busting in tumultuously from all four sides. At first Nobunaga and his pages thought that a passing quarrel had broken out among the lower orders, but nothing could have been further from the truth. The enemy raised the battle cry and blasted Nobunaga's residential quarters with their guns. "This is treason!" Nobunaga stated. "Whose plot is it?" "They look like Akechi's men," Mori Ran replied. Nobunaga's response was, "What's done is done."[32]

Amid rising flames, with gunfire echoing around him, and suffering from a wound from his own attempts to fight off the treasonous attackers, Nobunaga reportedly killed himself rather than fall into the hands of his enemy.[33]

Mitsuhide next turned to attack Nobunaga's eldest son Nobutada, who was staying in the capital, and he too was soon dead by his own hand. In a single night the rule of Nobunaga had descended from well-appointed confidence to complete disarray, as his vassals and surviving family members scrambled to make sense of these events and ensure that they and their domains were not also under attack. Many citizens of Kyoto, afraid of further violence, retreated to the Imperial Court in search of sanctuary.[34] Ieyasu, hearing of the Honnōji event later in the morning, immediately left Sakai and hurried warily home.[35] He arrived at Okazaki Castle, after a difficult trek, on the fourth day of the month and took some time to recuperate, acquire information, and get organized.[36]

Akechi Mitsuhide, meanwhile, had attacked Azuchi Castle and sent a messenger to the Mōri clan to arrange a truce, hoping to join forces and crush Hideyoshi between them. Unfortunately for Mitsuhide, Hideyoshi's men captured the messenger and thereby learned of both the treasonous attack on Nobunaga and Mitsuhide's plan against them. Hideyoshi quickly decided on a course of action that would immediately avenge Nobunaga and also put him in a leadership position. First, he cleverly negotiated a quick truce with the Mōri, who still did not know about Nobunaga's death. Then, two days later, he began marching his forces north to directly confront Mitsuhide and anyone who had decided to support him.[37] It took him only a few days to reach Osaka, where his army was reinforced by the soldiers of Nobunaga's vassal Niwa Nagahide and Nobunaga's second son Oda Nobukatsu. Hideyoshi led this army into Yamashiro Province and set up camp close to Mitsuhide's forces in Yamazaki. On 6/13, Hideyoshi attacked. His forces proved to be both in better condition and more numerous, and the Akechi forces were quickly defeated. According to one account, the Katsura River nearby was filled with dead bodies.[38] Mitsuhide himself fled to the north on horseback with about twenty of his men, but was set upon by villagers and killed.[39] Hideyoshi soon after viewed the head to verify the death of Nobunaga's killer and then set his sights on forming a new coalition to continue the work of unification begun by his liege.

Ieyasu's presence in Sakai at the time of Nobunaga's assassination was, of course, a contingency. It is easy to imagine that Ieyasu might have stayed in Kyoto with Nobunaga and been trapped in the flames of Honnōji or, equally likely, stayed a bit longer in his home castle, which would have put him in an ideal position to seek rapid vengeance against Mitsuhide. The chance to share tea, examine famous objects, and consort with knowledgeable merchants in Sakai, however, drew him down a different path. Objects such as the Chinese art desired by tea practitioners played a major role in shaping the range of possibilities in the historical past. Thus, the significance of these small moments of cultural practice are striking in the larger picture of national politics; gatherings such as this one counter the notion that culture lies outside of the realm of national politics. Historians often comment on the fact that, unlike Nobunaga and Hideyoshi, who were such devoted students of tea ritual, Ieyasu was only a grudging participant. At the time of the Honnōji attack, however, it is not too much of an exaggeration to say that the ritual significance of the culture of tea and the influence and authority of the tea master merchants who practiced it saved Ieyasu's life by drawing him away from the capital and into Sakai.

Ieyasu characteristically left no record of his thoughts or emotions at this most critical juncture in his career. How he may have felt personally about Nobunaga's death is impossible to know. Certainly Nobunaga had been his closest and most powerful ally for decades. Though Ieyasu had clearly been in the inferior position both in terms of age and resources, the two men seem to have viewed each other as peers. Ieyasu did appear to have considered going after Mitsuhide himself and on 6/11 launched his forces out of Okazaki toward the west. However, upon hearing of Hideyoshi's victory over Mitsuhide at the Battle of Yamazaki on 6/13, he returned to Hamamatsu.[40] At the very least, Ieyasu probably took Nobunaga's death as a reminder, if he needed one, of the capricious changes in fate that awaited any warlord who let his guard down.

According to the logic of the sixteenth century, Ieyasu also must have understood the tragedy, at least in part, as an opportunity to take advantage of, not unlike the chance afforded by Nobunaga's killing of Imagawa Yoshimoto so many years before, which had propelled him onto the path of leadership. Most immediately, the lands of the recently defeated Takeda to the north, no longer under strong Oda control, needed to be dealt with before any competitor could acquire them. This would provide security and would furthermore strengthen his position vis-à-vis any potential future enemies, such as his peers Hideyoshi and Shibata Katsuie. Ieyasu first cautiously assigned a vassal to construct a fortress inside of Kai Province.[41] He then began much more ambitious plans to administer both Kai and Shinano and officially receive oaths of fealty from former Takeda vassals, which would massively increase his territory and the forces at his disposal.[42] This was no easy task because the leaders of the Hōjō clan, his allies and rivals to the east, were also looking at the former Takeda lands with an eye toward expansion and security. The job was accomplished by largely avoiding open military engagement with Hōjō forces, and instead waging a war on the field of diplomacy and letter writing. Ieyasu left Hamamatsu for Kai and Shinano in the seventh month, and stayed until the end of the year. During this time, and continuing to the end of 1583, Ieyasu wrote hundreds of commendation letters to warriors and temples in Kai and Shinano.[43] Despite many skirmishes with the Hōjō, he was determined to avoid all-out war. The gradual appointment of magistrates to the region illustrates his growing control despite Hōjō concerns; his offer of his daughter, Tokuhime, as wife to the Hōjō heir Ujinao as part of larger peace negotiations in 10/1582, demonstrates his skillful victory in one of the most important conflicts of his career, again using human bodies—in this case those of his own family—as tools in the expansion and stabilization of his territory.[44]

FIRST FLOWER AS AMBASSADOR

On the Power of Objects

While Ieyasu was busy cementing his hold on the six provinces to the east of his ancestral home of Mikawa, Hideyoshi was creating a powerful alliance from the former vassals of Nobunaga. In 1583, Hideyoshi defeated the armies of Shibata Katsuie, a major rival, and the next day Ieyasu sent him a congratulatory letter:

> When Shibata advanced to the southern border of Echizen, you rode north to Nagahara. Your situation worried me so I sent a messenger. It is now clear the enemy strategy was unsound. Shibata advanced to seize Kyutaro's fortress and fighting erupted. I am delighted to hear that his forces were crushed and larger numbers slain by your incomparable performance. I am very gratified to hear the details of these developments. Here I have thoroughly quieted Shinano and when I have a respite shall unsaddle my horses, so please feel at ease.[45]

This letter was clearly designed to show Hideyoshi how much Ieyasu knew and also to remind him that the Tokugawa, too, were expanding their territories. It was followed by a present delivered in person by one of Ieyasu's most trusted vassals, Ishikawa Kazumasa. The gift was a famous object that has already appeared in this story, the Chinese ceramic tea caddy (*chaire*) named First Flower (Hatsuhana) (Figure 12) that had previously been in Nobunaga's collection and which he then gave to Nobutada.[46] This small ceramic container was made in China during the Southern Song dynasty. It was thrown on a wheel and decorated with an iron-brown glaze that dripped down over the unglazed bottom half of the piece. Its shape is of a type described at the time as "having shoulders" (*katatsuki*) because of the relatively acute angle at which the exterior wall turns in to meet the neck of the vessel, which is accentuated by an impressed line. As was true for most ceramic tea caddies from this period, tea practitioners added an ivory lid and stored the piece in an attractive textile bag when using it to hold powdered green tea at a tea gathering. First Flower was widely thought to be one of the three most important tea caddies in Japan. It had previously been owned by a series of warlords including Oda Nobunaga and his son Nobutada; it survived the attack that killed its owner. After Nobutada's death it was recovered and given to Ieyasu, so passing it on to Hideyoshi was fraught with complicated references.[47] (Hideyoshi used the tea caddy dozens of times and seems to have considered it one of his most cherished possessions.)

Despite these sparring but still friendly exchanges, Ieyasu and Hideyoshi gradually drifted towards a military conflict that seemed likely, considering the long chain of victories Hideyoshi was amassing, to result in the defeat of Ieyasu. Instead, in the Battles of Komaki and Nagakute in 1584, Hideyoshi proved unable, even in advantageous circumstances, to pin down Ieyasu and his forces. Ever the pragmatist, Hideyoshi decided to wage a war of diplomacy.[48] He made sure that Ieyasu received word as more and more warlords threw their lot in with Hideyoshi, and he continued to badger Ieyasu with messages and requests. As more and more men joined Hideyoshi, the problem grew serious enough that Ieyasu held a council with his chief vassals to discuss the matter. Though the details are not known, Ieyasu was not swayed by those who counseled capitulation to Hideyoshi's demands.[49] These events provoked a crisis for which Ieyasu was entirely unprepared. One of the Tokugawa's most significant and experienced vassals, Ishikawa Kazumasa—the man who had delivered "First Flower" to Hideyoshi in person after his victory over Shibata Katsuie—decided to defect to what he saw as the stronger side. Kazumasa, who was the keeper of Okazaki Castle and had been one of Ieyasu's companions since childhood, left Okazaki surreptitiously with his wife and children and traveled to Osaka to pledge himself to Hideyoshi. He brought with him as a hostage a child of a former vassal of Nobunaga's who had nominally supported Ieyasu but now also chose to throw his lot in with Hideyoshi.[50]

Kazumasa's defection was a stunning development from Ieyasu's point of view. The move illustrated that dissatisfaction with Ieyasu's ongoing resistance to Hideyoshi ran deeper than he had dared to imagine. Of even greater concern than Ieyasu's loss of a lifelong companion was the inevitable exposure of his defenses, tactics, and military secrets to his most powerful adversary. Ieyasu therefore traveled immediately to Okazaki and reconfigured and refortified his interior and exterior defenses. But Hideyoshi continued to apply diplomatic pressure. In early 1586, he rather publicly rewarded Ishikawa Kazumasa for his defection from the Tokugawa with the rule of Izumi Province. This surely sent the message to Ieyasu, as well as to any other potential turncoats in the Tokugawa ranks of generals, that service to Hideyoshi was rewarding.[51] After a few more rounds of negotiation, Ieyasu seemed finally on the verge of giving in. Some final token was needed. Hideyoshi's solution to this vexing problem was yet another example of human objectification in the form of offering a hostage as guarantee. He sent to Okazaki emissaries who promised that Hideyoshi would use his own mother to guarantee Ieyasu's safety. In response to this unusual offer, Ieyasu conceded.

In late 1586, Hideyoshi's mother arrived in Okazaki, and Ieyasu, who had been staying at a different castle, came to verify the situation[52] and then set out for western Japan. A week later he arrived in Osaka, where he stayed in a residence provided by Hideyoshi. The following evening Hideyoshi visited Ieyasu, who invited him to sit inside "to his heart's content." The two men reportedly talked little but drank sake together, with Hideyoshi pouring and generously offering cup after cup to Ieyasu and the Tokugawa lord reciprocating.[53] Ieyasu soon visited Hideyoshi in the castle and formally declared his allegiance in front of the assembled warlords who already served Hideyoshi.[54] His duty done, Ieyasu returned to Okazaki and sent Hideyoshi's mother back to Osaka the following day. It is vital to remember that in this delicate political equation the primary catalyst was not Ieyasu but his vassal Ishikawa Kazumasa. Likewise, it is important to emphasize that Kazumasa himself was introduced to Hideyoshi, in effect, by the tea caddy First Flower. It is possible that had Ieyasu not submitted to Hideyoshi at this precise moment, the latter would not have felt secure enough to launch his invasion of Kyushu, probably opting instead for an invasion of Mikawa and the other Tokugawa domains. The history of Japan, suffice it to say, would likely have looked quite different.

SPECTACULAR DISPLAYS

Instead, Hideyoshi found himself in an even more secure position than Nobunaga had in 1582, demonstrating what Mary Elizabeth Berry called "that assurance in power which can inspire submission."[55] Coincident with this assurance were conspicuous displays of famous objects and other forms of symbolic capital that also projected Hideyoshi's power. These activities both appealed to precedent, particularly the might of previous warrior leaders such as Minamoto Yoritomo and the Ashikaga shoguns, and responded to the trends of the day and the evolving personal tastes of Hideyoshi as hegemon. In the tea gatherings that Hideyoshi hosted and participated in after Nobunaga's death, he deliberately and consistently attempted to use objects that he had received from Nobunaga, that had previously been in Nobunaga's collection or that Nobunaga had given to others and which Hideyoshi had subsequently acquired.[56] He also turned to increasingly public and symbolically fraught displays of his treasures. In 1584, for example, Hideyoshi invited a large group of leaders from the tea community to a gathering at Osaka Castle that lasted from morning until evening. This gathering was unprecedented for its inclusion of every major tea master and their potential heirs, as well as major warrior tea participants, all of whom gathered in Hideyoshi's presence and presumably used many of his tea utensils. The event illustrates Hideyoshi's interest in displaying his acquisitions to a large and diverse population of warrior and tea elites.[57] The group represented the inner core of Hideyoshi's tea regime, the core constituency of designers, aesthetes, collectors, and experts in the trade in famous objects.

More spectacularly, on 1585/3/8 Hideyoshi organized an unprecedented tea gathering at Daitokuji, a major Zen Buddhist temple complex in northern Kyoto and a significant center for cultural practices such as tea. The exact guest list is not known to us today, but the broad outline conveys the scope of Hideyoshi's ambition for the increasingly spectacular display of his acquisitions. Attendees included Hideyoshi's personal guard, various warlords, fifty residents of Kyoto, twenty-four residents of Sakai invited by Rikyū and Sōgyū, and at least one hundred fifty tea practitioners. The guests brought their prized tea utensils, set up small enclosed spaces using folding screens, and practiced tea. Hideyoshi displayed his utensils, many of them famous objects previously in Nobunaga's collection. These included Hideyoshi's beloved painting *Green Maples* by the Chinese artist Yujian, calligraphy (figure 15) by the Chinese Chan Buddhist priest Xutang Zhiyu (J: Kidō Chigu; 1185–1269), *Evening Bell from a Mist-Shrouded Temple*[58] by Yujian, the tea caddy Nasubi (an alternative name for the piece Eggplant Tsukumo mentioned previously), a lacquered tray with a red interior (Uchiaka no bon), a tea scoop attributed to Takeno Jōō, a Chinese white *tenmoku* tea bowl, and other works. Rikyū and Sōgyū, using other famous objects from Hideyoshi's collection, served tea throughout the day.[59] Absent from the accounts of this event is the image of tea practitioners as abstemious celebrators of the humble and rustic. Instead, Hideyoshi and the elite commoner tea masters who served him engaged in publicly ostentatious celebrations of the objects accumulated in the course of the previous three years of war and détente.

In late 1585, Hideyoshi organized a tea gathering at the Imperial Court, perhaps his most spectacular display of cultural power, though in a less public venue than the later Grand Kitano Tea Gathering. This event followed a series of recent promotions in his court rank that Hideyoshi had aggressively pursued through gift giving and financial support of the ailing imperial institution.[60] Hideyoshi was the first warrior to attain the rank of imperial chancellor (*kanpaku*), and he seems to have wanted to imprint his distinctive brand of cultural politics on this role. After days of preparation,

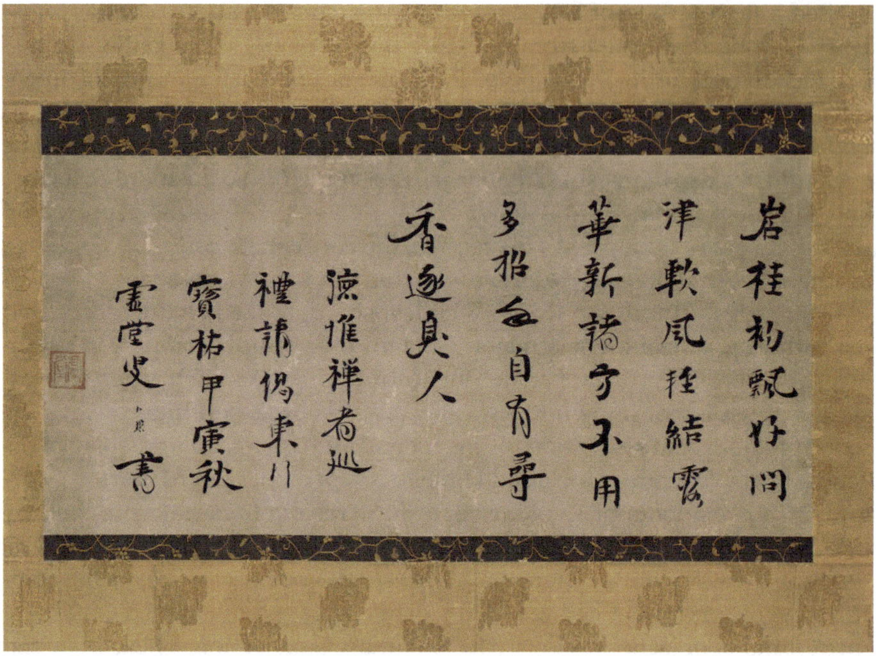

Figure 15. Calligraphy by Xutang Zhiyu (1185–1269). Chinese, Southern Song dynasty, 1254. 30.6 x 62.7 cm. Important Work of Art. Tokugawa Art Museum Collection, by permission of the Tokugawa Art Museum / DNPartcom

Hideyoshi arrived at the court in the morning on 10/7 and ritually greeted Emperor Ōgimachi in a residential building (*tsune no gosho*). Next, Hideyoshi's half-brother Hidenaga similarly exchanged ritual greetings in the Hall for State Ceremonies (Shishiden). Then Hideyoshi and his entourage moved to a banqueting room in which he performed the entire ritual of tea preparation and serving for the emperor and five nobles, with the guidance of Rikyū. Then Rikyū moved to another room and served the assembled nobles and imperial shrine and temple heads in groups of seven. The whole event represented an unprecedented opportunity for Hideyoshi to flaunt his most treasured famous objects to the members of the court; apparently his utensils were set up in two halls of the palace to maximize the quantity on show. We might even include Rikyū, who actually received his unique title (he had previously been known as "Sōeki") for this event, in the roster of Hideyoshi's coveted possessions.[61] The tea performance, along with a series of Noh plays presented to the court and other regular interactions meant to convey through patronage the munificence of Hideyoshi, was entirely successful, "the high point in the tea careers of both Hideyoshi and Rikyū" according to one historian.[62]

Having acquired a noteworthy collection of famous objects by the mid-1580s and flaunted them to the most symbolically significant cultural arbiter in the land, Hideyoshi next turned to the creation of a new addition to his collection: a small but flashy, portable tearoom, covered inside and out in gold leaf or plating. Though the details of the construction are not known, Hideyoshi appears to have first used this golden tearoom in early 1586, recorded by a courtier after it was brought to the Imperial Palace for display to the emperor and his court.[63] This event seems to have successfully impressed the intended audience, as Hideyoshi soon organized another gathering with the golden tearoom as the primary venue, this time at Osaka Castle. One attendee, the warlord Ōtomo Sōrin, noted that the room was "truly remarkable" (*makoto ni migoto*), with gold covering all of the major architectural elements. Almost all of the utensils were gold as well. "Even the wastewater container and incense container were gold."[64] Though historians have tended to see the golden tearoom as a characteristically vulgar expression of Hideyoshi's power and desire for recognition, precedents were plentiful: Ashikaga Yoshimitsu's luxurious Kinkaku (Golden Pavilion) is notable as a major architectural site that used gold in the interior and, in later refurbishment, on the exterior. Likewise, we find numerous examples of gold foil, dust, and lacquer in paintings, vessels, and architectural sites of the late sixteenth century.[65] What was new, perhaps, was Hideyoshi's deployment of these architectural and ornamental characteristics in a flexible and instrumental form. The golden tearoom stands out as a landmark in the politics of culture in this period: a portable and modular structure that could be transported, to create an exhibition of power, at nearly any location. Small and intimate on the one hand and sumptuously luxurious on the other, the golden tearoom's mobility points to the peripatetic quality of Hideyoshi's rule, which was not rooted in a single territory or tied to a discrete location, but which roamed with a kind of frenetic energy.

The spectacle of the Grand Kitano Tea Gathering of 1587 is significant as the logical culmination of trends outlined earlier, rather than as an entirely unique performance. Like the 1585 gathering at Daitokuji, which had included large numbers of elite guests from various status groups, and the 1585 performance and exhibition at the Imperial Court, the Kitano event was an explicit expression of Hideyoshi's power and ambition that demanded not only an audience but also a form of shared participation. It was through interaction with his public that Hideyoshi reified his own authority, and his displayed collection functioned perhaps in metonymic fashion, substituting

Figure 16. Tea jar named Shōka. Chinese, Southern Song or Yuan dynasty, 13th–14th century. Height 39.7 cm. Important Cultural Property. Tokugawa Art Museum Collection, by permission of the Tokugawa Art Museum / DNPartcom

for the supremacy of previous power-holders, ranging from the Ashikaga to Nobunaga. The tea jar named Shōka or "pine blossom" (figure 16), for example, was as distinguished a work as existed in the hegemon's tea collection, a Chinese-manufactured piece that had circulated through commoner and warrior collections since the early sixteenth century, and which had previously been owned by Nobunaga among many others. Tall with broad shoulders that are accentuated by the bold curtain of yellow-brown glaze that covers the upper two-thirds of the body, this object—widely praised in contemporaneous tea records—was precisely the kind of treasure that Hideyoshi sought to display to the world at Kitano.

However as Louise Cort has commented in her systematic study of the gathering, the performance did not follow Hideyoshi's script. "Although he summoned utensil-less *wabi* [rustic or insufficient] tea men, he had planned an unprecedented display of his own outstanding collection of tea utensils. Unexpectedly, the eccentrics seem to have captured the attention of the crowd and cast a shadow on Hideyoshi's utensils."[66] As a result the ten-day event was truncated, abandoned after one day, and perhaps with a lesson learned by the hegemon. Hideyoshi would not again attempt a major public display of his collection of tea utensils, but would instead limit himself to small, more easily curated gatherings attended by his elite warrior peers and a select few tea masters and urban commoner connoisseurs.

CONCLUSION

Rarely an active participant in Hideyoshi's spectacular displays, Ieyasu spent most of 1587 overseeing Matsudaira Ietada (the author of *Diary of Ietada*) as he managed the reconstruction of Sunpu Castle, also venturing into the countryside for the occasional hawking expedition, a growing passion that would come to occupy more of his time as the years went by. He traveled to Kyoto in the fall to see the Toyotomi lord and the imperial court, and spend some leisure time in the nearby Higashiyama Hills. Back in his home provinces, he continued in this leisurely fashion, going on hawking trips and sending out the occasional commendation letter.[67]

The next year required considerably more effort from Ieyasu as a vassal of Hideyoshi, though nothing like the dangerous military activities that had characterized his partnership with Nobunaga. In fact, it seemed that Ieyasu's own position of authority within the ranks of warlords made him an ideal mediator for Hideyoshi, the kind of diplomat who could help smooth out tensions and disagreements within the new Toyotomi realm. In the third month of 1588, for example, Ieyasu wrote several missives to Mogami Yoshiaki, lord of Yamagata Province in the north, to explain that Hideyoshi wished the warlord to make peace with the young but impressive warlord Date Masamune.[68] Ieyasu then traveled to Kyoto, where he met with Hideyoshi. On 3/29, the two went hawking in the suburbs of the capital, and Hideyoshi marked the occasion by giving Ieyasu a falcon.[69] Ieyasu continued writing to the Mogami from the capital in the next month and received gifts from Hideyoshi in exchange. These included a Hakata tea stand, an *imogashira* (potato-head-shaped) water jar, a tea caddy previously owned by the warlord Kanemori Arishige, a *tenmoku* tea bowl previously owned by Rikyū, and a large quantity of rice.[70] The particular *tenmoku* tea bowl from this interaction is no longer extant, but the well-known black *yōhen tenmoku* piece (figure 9) that still exists in the collection of the Tokugawa Art Museum, which Ieyasu owned and passed on to the Owari branch of the Tokugawa family at his death, indicates the kind of pieces beloved by tea practitioners in this period. Ieyasu played his role by attending the visit of Emperor Go-Yōzei to Hideyoshi's palace at Jurakutei, the newest location for Hideyoshi's pageantry in the capital city. This five-day imperial visit involved the assembled warlords of Japan as well as the key cultural leaders of the capital city, and the event included massive performances and displays of parades of arrival and reception, poetry and banqueting, gift giving, music and dance, and other ritualized social and cultural practices that were key to Hideyoshi's establishment of legitimacy.[71]

Ieyasu's contact with the Mogami was perhaps a dress rehearsal for the more important task of mediating between Hideyoshi and the Hōjō, the powerful warrior clan to Ieyasu's east who continued to resist Toyotomi rule. Hideyoshi had previously asked the Hōjō to attend him in Osaka and then in Kyoto for the imperial progression to Jurakutei Palace, but to no avail. Ieyasu, therefore, wrote a letter to the Hōjō explaining that Hideyoshi required the presence of Ujimasa, the retired warlord, and Ujinao, his son and the ostensible ruler, in Kyoto that month.[72] In mid-1588, Ieyasu traveled again to Kyoto, and wrote to one of his vassals to ask him to put pressure on the Hōjō to give into Hideyoshi's demands.[73] Hōjō Ujinao finally sent his uncle Ujinori to Kyoto in the eighth month, who conveyed a message from the senior Hōjō, Ujimasa: before he would come to Kyoto, Ujimasa wanted a decision on the Hōjō's ongoing conflict with Hideyoshi's vassal, Sanada Masayuki. This was not a satisfactory answer from Hideyoshi's point of view, but he let the problem lie for the time being.

A year passed before Hideyoshi rather suddenly and for unknown reasons decided that the Hōjō resistance had carried on long enough. In late 1589, Hideyoshi sent a public letter to the Hōjō informing them that all Toyotomi vassals were being instructed to raise troops and prepare for an assault on Odawara Castle, the main Hōjō stronghold. He sent copies of the letter to Ieyasu via a courier and ordered the Tokugawa lord to make sure that the Hōjō received a copy and also that all of the major Toyotomi vassals were aware of the need to prepare their troops. Ieyasu left for Kyoto soon after and, along with other major Toyotomi vassals like Uesugi Kagekatsu and Maeda Toshiie, worked with Hideyoshi to plan the assault on the Hōjō.[74] The year ended with all sides preparing for war. This conflict is particularly significant because it illustrates the connection between the politics of war and Hideyoshi's spectacular displays of tea culture.

In early 1590, Ieyasu sent a preliminary force to the east to begin setting up camp, and then he and Oda Nobukatsu arrived and began construction in earnest at Nagakubo (near present-day Mishima and Numazu). The attack on the Hōjō was an important military engagement for Hideyoshi, perhaps his final major domestic campaign against a warlord family known for its rapid expansion and impressive control of the Kantō region over the previous seventy years. He marshaled a massive army, with as many 150,000 men, to attack the Hōjō, who had fortified themselves in Odawara Castle. But the siege needed to maintain order and hierarchy to be successful. Spectacular gatherings that would allow Hideyoshi to project and perform his rule in front of his men, and that would provide both entertainment and similar opportunities to his generals, were a necessity. Therefore, the camp that Ieyasu and Nobukatsu constructed included a tea pavilion for the entertainment of Hideyoshi and the other warlords who would be in attendance.[75] Ieyasu emerges from the documentary record of these preparations as a kind of project manager, an expert in organizing large ventures who also had the authority and connections to contract out each piece of the groundwork to a different party.

The assault on Hōjō territory began at the end of the third month of 1589. One by one Hōjō forts and castles fell to the Toyotomi onslaught (including the fortress of Edo on 4/22).[76] Assaults on the wide swath of Hōjō territory, but concentrated in particular on the main Hōjō fortress of Odawara, raged on for more than two months. Finally, on 1590/7/5, Hōjō Ujinao submitted to Hideyoshi and reportedly asked that he take his own life in exchange for the freedom of his father. Hideyoshi, however, decided to spare the young man's life and instead send him and his companions into exile on Mount Kōya in Kii Prefecture. He commanded Hōjō Ujimasa and his brother Ujiteru, however, to take their own lives; these enemies were too old, experienced, and wily, from Hideyoshi's perspective, to be allowed to live. He entered Odawara in ceremonial fashion on the tenth day, and Ujimasa and Ujiteru left the castle, retired to the house of a local doctor, and "cut their bellies" (*hara o okirase sōrō*) the next day as ordered.[77] Their heads were later publically displayed in Kyoto, a brutal performance of victory that resonated with earlier displays by Nobunaga and his contemporaries.

The outcome of the siege of Odawara was never truly in doubt considering the size of the army that Hideyoshi could command at will. However, the process of dividing the spoils completely transformed Ieyasu's life and career. On 7/13, in a formal declaration in Odawara Castle, Hideyoshi announced that he was granting to Ieyasu the former Hōjō provinces of Izu, Sagami, Musashi, Kōzuke, Shimōsa, and Kazusa to the east, plus parts of Ōmi and Ise in central Japan.[78] This change removed Ieyasu completely from his hereditary lands in Mikawa Province, but it also pushed him further to the east, while massively increasing the size of his holdings. Ieyasu's total domain was now valued at approximately 2.4 million *koku* of rice, making him the wealthiest warlord in all of Japan.[79] It is unlikely that Ieyasu was consulted in more than a cursory regard; documents record that the shift was something that "must" happen, and ample evidence existed that defying Hideyoshi's decisions in these matters was unwise. Oda Nobukatsu, for example, responded to Hideyoshi's offer of Ieyasu's old territory with a desperate request to retain the former Oda lands of Owari and Ise. The Toyotomi lord, enraged, demoted Nobukatsu and stripped him of his holdings.[80] Suffice it to say that there is no indication that Ieyasu resisted the transfer.

Whether as a reward for effective project management or as a means of isolating a potential threat, Ieyasu's transfer to the Kantō had an impermeable impact on Japan's subsequent history. The town of Edo itself grew into one of the largest cities in the world. More broadly, Ieyasu's assimilation into the population of elite Toyotomi vassals through his inclusion in spectacles such as the imperial progression to Jurakutei in 1588 would have a similarly significant effect. As we will see in subsequent chapters, the practice of spectacular accumulation was adopted by Ieyasu and later by his descendants, the Tokugawa shoguns, as one of the foundational structures of the shogun's right to rule.

CHAPTER THREE

The Politics of Sociability

Gift Giving and Ritual Performance

A curious conflict occurred in early 1611 between Tokugawa Ieyasu and Toyotomi Hideyori, the son of Hideyoshi. Ieyasu, now nominally retired from the position of shogun, was staying at Nijō Castle in Kyoto after attending the abdication of Emperor Go-Yōzei and the inauguration of Go-Yōzei's son under the name Go-Mizunoo. The day after the court ceremony, Hideyori arrived at Nijō Castle and met with Ieyasu in person. According to one contemporaneous account, Ieyasu waited on the garden veranda as Hideyori approached, maintaining a higher (and thus symbolically superior) position. Hideyori expressed his gratitude to Ieyasu, who then moved into the center of the reception room while Hideyori made his way onto the veranda, a delicate dance of space and hierarchy played amid palpable political tension. Later that day, Hideyori visited the magnificent Toyokuni Shrine that housed the deified spirit of his father Hideyoshi, ostensibly to see the ongoing work on the reconstruction of the huge Great Buddha statue at Hōkōji next door.[1] He then returned home to Osaka Castle, marginalized from the rituals of abdication and enthronement, though crowds of commoners reportedly came out to see the arrival and departure of this young man who was popular with both urban residents and members of the court.[2]

Not long after, Ieyasu sent some of his sons to Osaka Castle with gifts for Hideyori, including a long sword, a black horse, three hundred gold pieces, and other precious objects. Though the intention of the gifts was not recorded, their grandiosity implies the generosity of a patriarch, a recognition on the part of a superior of the effort of an inferior. Hideyori, however, reciprocated somewhat forcefully, with a gift of a long sword by Mitsutada (one of the most famous names in the history of Japanese swords), one hundred gold pieces, as well as additional presents for members of Ieyasu's family. This then precipitated another round of gift giving, with Ieyasu sending a long sword, a short sword, three falcons, ten horses, and so on. Hideyori felt compelled to respond, sending a messenger bearing his thanks but also bringing one thousand silver pieces, a long sword, and a horse for Ieyasu, plus additional gifts for members of Ieyasu's family. This continued, with swords, horses, money, fine clothing, and other precious things hurled back and forth between Nijō and Osaka like missiles flung from rival catapults, though in the end no palpable damage resulted.[3] Ieyasu seemed to want the last word, while Hideyori, we can surmise, wanted to demonstrate to Ieyasu that he was no peripheral inferior, content to receive the munificence of the Tokugawa lord, but rather a wealthy and central power, inheritor of the Toyotomi tradition.

Examples of the politics of sociability in the age of unification like this one tell us much about the methods that elite warriors used to create stability and indeed "good government." Although premodern Japanese society was in many senses riven by hierarchies and social groupings that kept people relatively separate according to wealth, occupation, and other markers of identity, within social units and certainly among elites, a marked art of association defined membership in the class, including, but not limited to, gift exchange. These forms of sociability reinforced the relative positions of different elite populations—warlords, courtiers, the shogun, and so on—while reinscribing the high status held by each group. The Kyoto cultural gatherings and regularized offerings to and from Nobunaga, Hideyoshi, and Ieyasu served to reassure all those involved in celebrating the rise of these warlords that they still possessed power; ritualization through the politics of sociability, in other words, perpetuated the misrecognition that the authority monopolized by the hegemons was shared.[4]

This interpretation diverges somewhat from the notion of a connection between sociability and the emergence of Japanese national identity in the nineteenth century. Eiko Ikegami has argued that Japan's hierarchical system of manners and appreciation for "beauty" is a useful counterpart to civil society in the West. She argues that in Japan's case manners and aesthetic appreciation led to strong group identity, which in turn facilitated the emergence of the modern nation-state. This chapter complicates that argument by focusing on the connection between civility and violence, between networks and coercion, and between appreciation for beauty and the objectification of human subjects. The prominence of these themes in the late sixteenth century, and indeed in the foundations of the Tokugawa system, implies that sociability was a tool for dominance and aggression as much as it was for civility.[5]

This chapter examines ritualized acts of sociability such as gift giving in the late sixteenth and early seventeenth centuries among the three hegemons.[6] (The practice of falconry, the exchange of falcons, and banqueting organized around consumption of animals hunted via falconry is dealt with in the next chapter.) In particular, it highlights the role of these practices in Tokugawa Ieyasu's politics in the years after the Battle of Sekigahara as tools in the construction and maintenance of hierarchy through the creation of asymmetrical but mutual obligation. In the wake of that brief but violent and profoundly significant battle, Ieyasu's practices of sociability, particularly gift exchange, had, as Marcel Mauss put it, "the further aim of buying peace."[7] However, this chapter does not provide a schematic or comprehensive overview of gift giving in the sixteenth century. The meaning of gifts and the rules of gift exchange are frequently unclear in the lists of objects sent or received by Ieyasu and his contemporaries, and the relationship of these practices to the rich (but still tangled) threads of gift giving in modern Japan is likewise uncertain. As Katharine Rupp has noted,

> Models founded on static or essentialist notions of the Japanese sense of self, or models that presume a priori that the gift is a part or extension of the giver, or models of whole societies as gift societies or commodity societies are not very helpful because they say little about the complex details and variations across many different forms of giving. . . . There is not one kind of giving in Japan; there have been tremendous changes over time, and ways of giving and attitudes toward giving are extremely diverse.[8]

Rupp demonstrates that the meaning of gifts in Japan is determined by the social context and in particular by the relationships within which the exchange occurs. Thus, this chapter posits that for sixteenth-century warrior elites, gift giving and other forms of sociability were among the complicated techniques for acquiring, preserving, and displaying power, methods of collecting important examples of material culture and displaying them to the world in what was often a highly performative form of spectacle.

The prominence of gift giving among elite warriors was hardly new in the late sixteenth century; medieval society functioned in part through rituals of munificent exchange and obligation. Documentary evidence records the exchange of gifts between the Imperial Court and various elites, between the shogun and his retainers, between autonomous warriors, and between villages and landholders. The types and value of gifts exchanged differed depending on the place, time, and constituencies involved, but the valence of exchange itself stayed fairly constant. During the Kamakura period, for example, gifts of horses served the double purpose of increasing the military preparedness of the recipient, particularly the shogunate, while ritually affirming relationships of dominance. During the Muromachi period, luxury foodstuffs, including melons, became significant in gift-giving exchanges among elite warriors, connecting the rulership of agricultural land to the rituals of banqueting that characterized the urban sociability of Kyoto.[9] These exchanges were manifestations of the personal and reciprocal ties of warrior corporate units, a gift-exchange economy that overlapped with a growing, though still constrained, money economy.[10] Gift giving was a component in warrior leaders' campaigns to use "magnanimity and largesse" to win the support of other autonomous and independent warriors.[11] Such exchanges did not necessarily create loyalty, but they did create obligation that was closely tied to self-interest. These practices may seem simple or quotidian, but they are versions of a deliberate strategy that elites used to solidify authority, what Leora Auslander called "a rational investment in political power."[12]

An example from the career of Oda Nobunaga illustrates the ritualization and political intent that inhered in many gift exchanges among elite warriors. On 1580/3/10, the warlord Hōjō Ujimasa sent three envoys to Nobunaga, who was staying in Honnōji, the temple in Kyoto that he had appropriated as an occasional residence. The Hōjō envoys met with Nobunaga's representatives while Nobunaga observed. First, Nobunaga's chief delegate "ceremonially announced their presentation of a sword and cash to Nobunaga," a combination that indicated great respect. The visiting envoys then orally presented their request to Nobunaga's representatives; the Hōjō asked Nobunaga to consider a marriage alliance with the promise that this union would increase his sway over the six eastern provinces. This was followed by their presentation of gifts. In addition to the sword, these included twenty swans (to be used as prey in falconry), one box of dried abalone, three hundred abalone (either fresh or differently preserved), one box of dried sea cucumber, and two barrels of Egawa sake. Next, the envoys announced their "polite greetings" on behalf of the Hōjō, with separate declarations offered by each visitor. Lastly, Nobunaga declared his satisfaction with the proceedings and sent the envoys on a tour of the capital city, led by one of his vassals.[13] Nobunaga's approval of this alliance bore fruit: the Hōjō sided with Nobunaga in 1582 in the final conflict with the Takeda (though the planned marriage did not occur before Nobunaga's death later that same year). This interaction shows that gift giving occurred not only at set times in the annual calendar but was part of political negotiations and accompanied direct requests. Gift giving usually acknowledged the status of the recipient by offering a particular combination of gifts—in this case the sword and cash—which indicated respect. In addition, a range of pleasurable famous products of the region of the giver were included, and all of these were presented in what appears to have been a formal and ritualized procedure that both conveyed a positive feeling of cooperation and reinforced the hierarchy within the respective warrior bands and between the givers and their recipients. Such interactions played a significant role in both constructing and maintaining warrior society.

GIFT GIVING AND RECIPROCITY

Gift giving was certainly a core component of the practices of sociability seen throughout the premodern period.[14] However, the relative social and political chaos of the first half of the sixteenth century may have limited opportunities for grand gift-giving gestures or at the very least the survival of records of such exchanges. João Rodrigues, writing in the early seventeenth century, noted the following:

> Up to the time of Nobunaga and Taikō [Hideyoshi], while Japan suffered from extreme poverty and wretchedness on account of wars and uprisings, all this giving of gifts was done merely as a compliment with things of little value and sometimes even dissemblingly. . . . But since the time of Nobunaga the kingdom has enjoyed peace, the lords and city dwellers have become wealthy, and commerce has increased. It is impossible to describe the lengths to which this practice of giving costly presents has gone among the nobles. They give each other gold, silver, rich lengths of silk of various kinds, weapons, and silk robes.[15]

Though his account of the period preceding the unification was undoubtedly colored by late sixteenth-century hyperbolic notions of the "age of warring states," the suggestion that gift giving had, over the course of the reign of the Three Unifiers, increased correlates well with the indications in primary sources that such practices of sociability were in fact vital tools of their hegemony.

In the records of the rise of Oda Nobunaga, gifts appear with greater frequency once he begins, self-consciously, his campaign to win "eternal fame" (*matsudai no kōmyō*).[16] Immediately after his victory over Imagawa Yoshimoto in 1560 at the Battle of Okehazama, Nobunaga returned to his home base and began the inspection of the approximately three thousand heads that had been collected by his soldiers. He was aided in this process by "a special prisoner of war," a servant of Yoshimoto, who was able to assist Nobunaga in the identification of many of these inert and objectified body parts. As a reward, Nobunaga gave the attendant a sword and a dagger, both of which were accompanied by "gold-encrusted sheaths."[17] The monetary worth of these gifts points to the value of the service performed, from the point of view of Nobunaga, in the aftermath of such a significant victory. But the principle is still a self-interested form of reciprocity. In other examples from the early period of his career, he rewards allies (Shibata Katsuie) with land grants and potential allies (the Satō in Kii Province) with gold coins.[18] More prominently, once Nobunaga began his campaign in 1568 to woo Ashikaga Yoshiaki, the younger brother of the murdered shogun Ashikaga Yoshiteru (1536–1565), gift giving played an important role in his political advances. He sent envoys to meet Yoshiaki, presenting him with one thousand copper coins, a sword, a suit of armor, other military paraphernalia, a horse, and various other gifts.[19] When he successfully penetrated Kyoto and installed Yoshiaki as shogun, more gift giving ensued, with Nobunaga accepting gifts from Kyoto elites, giving gifts to the new shogun, and then receiving a range of gifts from the shogun. The purpose of these exchanges at this moment of confusion amidst hope for increased stability seems clear: various parties wanted to impress this ambitious warlord with their intention to cooperate, and Nobunaga, though cagey about his own role in the new polity, was still reliant on Yoshiaki for some legitimacy. As Irma Thoen noted in her study of gift exchange in seventeenth-century Holland, "People are bound together by the expectation of reciprocity."[20]

Examples of gift giving from Nobunaga's career after this point are numerous, but one particular case will illustrate the increasing emphasis on his own magnanimity, reinforcing the point that "largesse was an essential component of hegemonic leadership."[21] In 1576 Nobunaga was in the midst of fighting on numerous fronts. His forces continued to battle Takeda Katsuyori, the son of the deceased warlord Takeda Shingen. Likewise, his retainers continued to assault the Honganji in Osaka, with mixed levels of success, while dealing with the hostile Mōri to the south and the inland sea lords in their employ. Characteristically, Nobunaga was simultaneously engaged in one of the largest building projects of the age, the construction of a massive castle and town at Azuchi. This palatial structure was largely financed and erected through the particular exchange system known as corvée, which in earlier times had meant that all imperial subjects owed a certain amount of labor to the court. In the late sixteenth century, earthworks and construction projects, not unlike military operations, were completed with the obligatory "assistance" of warriors under the command of a hegemon such as Nobunaga. After beginning a new phase in the construction process in the seventh month of 1576, he rewarded those warriors who had participated in the project: "All exerted themselves to their utmost and were rewarded with an untold number of gifts. Some received garments, others gold and silver or Chinese objects of art," according to *The Chronicle of Lord Nobunaga*.[22] Although these objects were, undoubtedly,

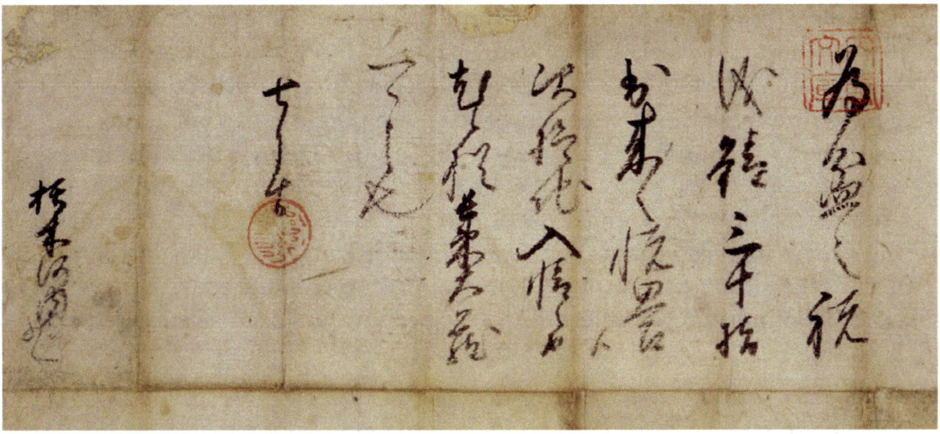

Figure 17. Letter from Toyotomi Hideyoshi to the Kutsuki house. 1590. National Archives of Japan

extremely valuable, it seems unlikely that they represented equivalent compensation for the labor and materials supplied in the work on Azuchi Castle. Instead, the obligation of these warriors under Nobunaga's command to supply corvée was noted, and the gifts from the hegemon marked the personal relationship that provided the logic of the asymmetrical exchange.

Hideyoshi, often the beneficiary of gifts from Nobunaga, was similarly enmeshed in this system of exchange as he consolidated and then expanded his authority as hegemon, seen in the voluminous records of gifts given and received among his letters (figure 17) and in the provenances of heirloom objects. The previous chapter recounted the story of Hideyoshi's and Ieyasu's rapprochement in 1586, with the vital use of Hideyoshi's own mother as a hostage to guarantee to Ieyasu his good intentions. What followed that successful ritual of obeisance was an intense bout of gift giving. Not long after Ieyasu returned from Osaka to his home domain, Hideyoshi sent him a tea jar, a short sword, a long sword, a falcon, and a formal coat (*haori*). Ieyasu in turn sent Hideyoshi ten horses, one hundred gold pieces, and a long sword. At the risk of stretching the meaning of this exchange a bit too far, we can see these gifts as a useful tally of the price of loyalty at this time.[23]

Hideyoshi also employed gift giving in his aggressive attempt to gain rank and prestige in the court. As discussed in the previous chapter, Hideyoshi made the Imperial Court the stage for his performances of authenticity and legitimacy on numerous occasions, but he did so in the context of reciprocal exchanges in which he funded the refurbishment of the significantly run-down palaces; provided cash and land to the emperor and his family; organized cultural events at the palace that emphasized the symbolic centrality of the imperial line; and gave a range of gifts, including commissioned art objects, to members of the court.[24] Hideyoshi's munificence and attention to the primacy of court ritual were reciprocated with ample and increasingly prestigious ranks. He became the first warrior to attain the rank of imperial chancellor (*kanpaku*) in 1585, and the rank of great minister of state (*daijō daijin*) in 1586. His relationship with the court, a powerful example of mutual self-interest and reciprocity, was seen as successful on both sides.

IEYASU'S GIFT GIVING AND SOCIABILITY UNDER HIDEYOSHI

Tokugawa Ieyasu's gift giving is better recorded than the practices of his peers for obvious reasons; the objects he exchanged, as well as the actual letters (figure 18) and other documents noting such practices, became valuable after Ieyasu's establishment of the shogunate in 1603 and even more so after his deification in 1616. These records reveal shifts in gift-giving practices according to Ieyasu's position and relative authority. Under Nobunaga, for example, Ieyasu was primarily limited to exchanges with neighboring warlords, such as a round of reciprocal gifts given and received with Uesugi Kenshin in 1571 (Ieyasu gave a helmet and received a horse) and 1573

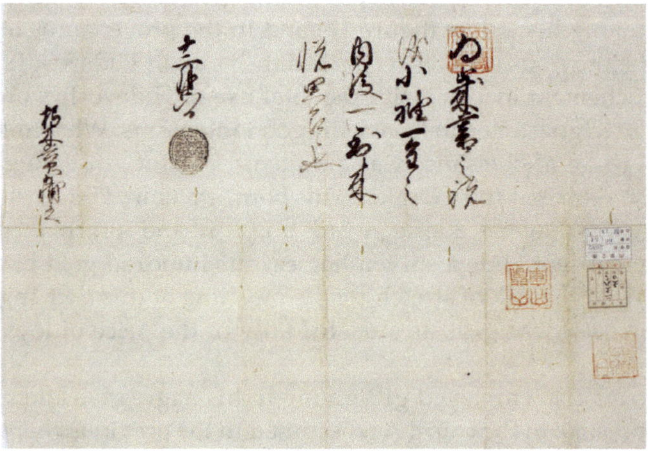

Figure 18. Letter from Tokugawa Ieyasu to the Kutsuki house (n.d.). National Archives of Japan

(Ieyasu gave a sword and received an unspecified present in return).[25] These exchanges occurred in the context of Ieyasu's and Kenshin's mutual conflict with Takeda Shingen. Another significant example comes from early 1582, after Nobunaga's defeat of Shingen's son Katsuyori. Nobunaga rewarded Ieyasu with the entire province of Suruga, further extending Tokugawa lands to the east and giving him control over the entire coast from the edge of Owari to Suruga Bay. Ieyasu had the opportunity to thank Nobunaga on 4/12, when the latter completed his military tour of Kai. Nobunaga came to Suruga and met the young Tokugawa lord. Ieyasu threw a banquet and gave Nobunaga a series of gifts, including a large sword (Ichimonji), a Yoshimitsu short sword, and several good horses.[26] Within a few months, the swords would be destroyed, along with many of Nobunaga's prized possessions, in the attacks that destroyed him and his legacy.

One oft-gifted artwork that avoided the destruction of so many objects in the betrayal of Nobunaga was the tea caddy named Yokota (figure 19), a

Figure 19. Tea caddy named Yokota. Seto ware. Muromachi period, 15th century. Height 13.9 cm. Tokugawa Art Museum Collection, by permission of the Tokugawa Art Museum / DNPartcom

cylindrical container made in the old Seto kilns and covered with a modest iron-brown glaze. According to a later box inscription, Ashikaga Yoshimasa acquired the piece and passed it down within his family until it came into the ownership of the last Ashikaga shogun, Yoshiaki. If true, the work is an unusual example of a lordly thing that avoided the centrifugal force that led to the scattering of the Ashikaga collection. As a domestic ceramic, it perhaps did not yet have the value in the late fifteenth century to merit selling or gifting it in the aftermath of the Ōnin War. Regardless, Yoshiaki reportedly gave the piece to Nobunaga, who later gave it to Hideyoshi, implying that the tea caddy had an impressive career accompanying those at the political center. Hideyoshi, in the period when he was attempting to convince Ieyasu to join him as an ally, in turn gifted the tea caddy to the Tokugawa lord. The receipt of such gifts thus marked Ieyasu as a major player on the stage of politics, an influential figure whose position on the hierarchy of warrior power was not only signified by but actually constructed in part by his participation in gift exchanges. The Tokugawa lord kept the now famous piece, Yokota, until his death, when it was bequeathed to the Owari Tokugawa house.[27]

Once Hideyoshi took center stage, Ieyasu's participation in gift exchanges increased almost tenfold, primarily in terms of items received rather than those given. It may be that the increase in the territory under his rule in 1582 and the increase in his responsibilities as one of Hideyoshi's allies (both as a general and as a kind of ambassador) after 1586 created more moments in which those below him in the social hierarchy sought to gain favor through gifts. Ieyasu received tea utensils, fish, swords, horses, clothing, and other objects in these years from his own retainers, from allies of Hideyoshi, and from temple and shrine complexes, particularly those in the provinces under his authority.[28] His own giving was more restrained and often practiced in the context of his service to Hideyoshi. In 1588, for example, Ieyasu sent the warlord Date Masamune a letter and gift of a short coat (*haori*) and some tea after Masamune peacefully resolved a dispute that Hideyoshi had hoped would come to an end.[29] In early 1592, Ieyasu sent a gift of culinary delicacies—mikan fruit and cured sea cucumber entrails (*konowata*)—to the warlord Gamō Ujisato, a general who faithfully served Hideyoshi and alongside whom Ieyasu had recently fought in northern Japan.[30]

The New Year of 1592 opened with a command from Hideyoshi that would shape the history of East Asia in complex and enduring ways and which is worth exploring in some detail. On the fifth day of the first month, Hideyoshi began to lay the groundwork for an unprecedented invasion of the Korean peninsula, with the ostensible goal of conquering Ming-dynasty China. There is some evidence that Oda Nobunaga first claimed his intention to conquer China in 1582, the year of his death. Following this, Hideyoshi had also spoken of his ambition to invade the continent, always with reference to divine imperative and the will of Heaven.[31] The year 1592, however, represented the beginning of the actual mobilization of troops, construction of a base of operations in southern Japan, and initiation of the conflict that we now know as the Imjin War, Japan's sole attack on another polity to that point in its history.

This momentous event also called for gift exchanges: on 1/11, Ieyasu wrote to Asano Nagayoshi, another of his recent collaborators in Hideyoshi's wars in the north, to thank him for his year-end gift of a kosode robe and to inform him that he would soon depart for Kyoto.[32]After arriving in Kyoto, Ieyasu visited with various important personages in the capital. On 2/25, for example, he saw the noble Yamashina Tokitsune, from whom he received a copy of the fourteenth-century encyclopedia, *Collection of Found Rubbish (Shūkaishō).*[33] This encounter was the first in a series that Ieyasu would have in this period with teachers and texts that would have a profound influence on his ideas about cultured governance, as will be seen later in this chapter. On 3/13 he visited the Imperial Court and the residence of the retired emperor, bringing gifts of swords and swans. On 3/15 he and Gamō Ujisato, an avid tea practitioner, visited the Kyoto tea house of Kamiya Sōtan for a tea gathering.[34] These practices of sociability were as important to the work of being a warrior as the act of preparing for battle; or, to put it a different way, the reification of relationships that resulted from these practices was, intrinsically, part of how warriors prepared for battle, a social, as much as a material, process.

Ieyasu departed for the island of Kyushu in southern Japan on 3/17 in the company of Date Masamune, Uesugi Kagekatsu, Satake Yoshinobu, and Nanbu Nobunao.[35] This voyage was a major one for Ieyasu, who was less well traveled than many of his contemporaries; it in fact represented his first and only trip south of Sakai and off of the main island of Honshū. On 3/25 the group arrived in Hizen Province, where Hideyoshi had ordered the construction of a castle the year before. This fortress was named Nagoya Castle (名護屋城), causing easy homophonic confusion with the later capital of Owari, also Nagoya Castle (名古屋城), though the two are usually written with a different second Chinese character. The former was located on the coast near the town of Hizen, facing Tsushima Island and the Korean peninsula to the north. It would serve as the base for Japan's assault on Korea until 1598 and as Ieyasu's home for a year and half. Ieyasu and his peers from eastern and northern Japan stationed their troops around Nagoya Castle and coordinated the movement of soldiers, laborers, and supplies to the islands of Iki and Tsushima and to Pusan in southern Korea. This was a monumental undertaking. Hideyoshi had requisitioned 158,000 men in nine divisions, primarily from the warlords of Kyushu and southern Japan, and also mobilized massive numbers of troops to protect Kyoto. As one historian has noted, "the mobilization for Hideyoshi's Korean venture encompassed the entire country of Japan, whether or not the troops were directly involved in operations on the continent."[36] The actual invasion began on 4/12 and enjoyed rapid success for several months: "The initial Japanese force under Konishi Yukinaga and Sō Yoshitoshi landed at Pusan in some 700 ships on May 23, 1592. In the vivid hyperbole of a popular Korean folktale about the war: 'the sun's rays dimmed, the air filled with death, waves touched the sky, black clouds covered the water as they approached. Countless thousands of Japanese ships covered the ocean, their three-tiered masts wrapped with blue awnings, the beat of drums and battle cries shaking the waves as they came.' "[37]

In truth, however, the Japanese soon were bogged down amid active guerilla and popular resistance. In 1593, the Korean admiral Yi Sun-sin enjoyed considerable success in cutting supply lines and defeating Japanese naval vessels, many of which were cobbled together from fishing or pirate boats. Yi reportedly described his strategy as follows:

> Previously, foreseeing the Japanese invasion, I had had a Turtle Ship specially built with a dragon's head, from whose mouth we could fire our cannons, and with iron spikes on its back to pierce the enemy's feet when they tried to board. Because it is in the shape of a turtle, our men can look out from inside, but the enemy cannot look in from outside. It moves so swiftly that it can plunge into the midst of even many hundreds of enemy vessels in any weather to attack them with cannon balls and fire-throwers.[38]

This bold naval action prevented the Japanese forces from attacking the Korean peninsula from both sides as originally intended and protected the land route from China to the west. As a result, Chinese troops began to arrive and provided formidable resistance, forcing the northernmost Japanese forces south with overwhelmingly superior numbers. In the fifth month, Hideyoshi commanded Ieyasu and Toshiie to prepare a reception for an ambassador from the Ming court who was traveling to Nagoya Castle with Ishida Mitsunari and other warlords who had been fighting in Korea. Hideyoshi met and feasted with the ambassador on 5/23 and a week later held a banquet and tea gathering for him in camp. A truce of sorts was reached on 6/28; a few select warlords began to return from Korea, and Hideyoshi headed home to Osaka.[39] Japanese forces continued to occupy southern Korea, but the agreement with the Ming held for the time being.

Ieyasu departed Nagoya in the eighth month and headed north to join Hideyoshi in Osaka. He would never again set foot on the island of Kyushu.

He stayed in Osaka and Kyoto until the end of the tenth month, joining Maeda Toshiie and Hideyoshi at tea gatherings and generally socializing in and around the capital. When he returned to Edo on 1593/10/26, he held a banquet for his followers at Edo Castle and then returned to the business of deciding succession among vassals, finalizing enfeoffments, and issuing licenses and commendation letters, all banal, bureaucratic work that was actually far more important to the long-term success of his career than any of his more famous battles.[40] The year ended auspiciously; Ieyasu met in the twelfth month with the scholar Fujiwara Seika, who presented a lecture on the Confucian text, *Essentials of Good Government* (Ch: *Zhenguan zhengyao;* J: *Jōgan Seiyō;* Tang dynasty, 7th c.).[41] This meeting is the first sign in the extant documentary record of Ieyasu's interest in studying the governing practices of classical China, a hobby that would develop over the next decade into a serious passion and, one might argue, the foundation of a new social and political system.

In Korea nearly seventy thousand Japanese troops and laborers had been stationed in the southern part of the peninsula since the cessation of hostilities in 1593. High-ranking samurai and warlords passed the time pursuing various pleasures, hosting tea gatherings and practicing poetry exchanges, while lower-ranking soldiers and laborers engaged in the rituals of agricultural production with which they were familiar.[42] Ieyasu spent his time similarly in Fushimi and Kyoto, attending tea gatherings and socializing with nobles and warlords throughout late 1595 and into 1596. The stalemate and seemingly pointless mobilization of troops on the Korean peninsula could not last indefinitely, however, and in mid-1596 two new Ming ambassadors made their way to Japan to meet with Hideyoshi in person. The Toyotomi lord's plan was to host them in a grand reception hall newly built in Fushimi Castle. On 1596/7/13, however, the capital was wracked by an enormous earthquake.[43] As one diarist put it, "As for Fushimi, his lordship's castle and gate were destroyed or at least knocked down, and the central keep is completely leveled. A multitude of men, women, and inner guards are dead, of a number that is not yet known."[44] The damage spread all across Kyoto, knocking down pagodas, damaging temples, shrines, and residences, and injuring or killing many. Ieyasu's residence at Fushimi was also ruined, but he found time to travel with Hideyoshi to the Imperial Palace to check on the residents of the court.[45]

The inauspicious event, known as the Tenshō Earthquake, had destroyed Hideyoshi's new palace, a symbol of his authority and ambition, but he would not retreat from his planned meeting with the Ming ambassadors, which he seems to have mistakenly expected to result in Chinese acceptance of his demands for recognition as an equal. He therefore moved the reception of the Ming ambassadors to Osaka Castle while authorizing the reconstruction of Fushimi. Hideyoshi's high hopes that the Chinese emperor would bow down to Toyotomi stipulations were squashed when it was revealed that the Ming Son of Heaven would only recognize him as a king, or in other words, an inferior. The meeting resulted in a complete breakdown in relations. Though Ieyasu and others tried to dissuade him, Hideyoshi, nursing a bruised ego, was convinced by his most hawkish generals to order the resumption of hostilities against Korea and China.[46]

Ieyasu returned to Edo in the ninth month of 1596 and then joined Hideyoshi in Fushimi again at the end of the year for the Toyotomi heir's coming-of-age ceremony. Many of his peers were required to once again travel to Korea and engage with Korean and Chinese forces. These Japanese commanders enjoyed initial success but soon had to pull back to well-established centers of Japanese control such as Pusan. Ieyasu, meanwhile, socialized and engaged in politics in the capital. He ushered in the arrival of 1597, for example, with a gift of rice to the court noble Yamashina Tokisune.[47] He also made frequent visits to the residences of his peers, to the Imperial Court, to local religious institutions such as Yoshida Shrine, and to events held by Hideyoshi.[48] Furthermore, he played the role of host at his own residence in Fushimi, inviting warlords such as Oda Nobukatsu, Yamana Toyokuni, and Asano Nagayoshi to a banquet in the ninth month.[49] Additionally, in the tenth month, for example, he lent Hosokawa Sansai (also Tadaoki; 1563–1646) his copy of *Ancient Records of Izumo (Izumo fudoki),* the most complete of the early gazetteers of the provinces of Japan. In the eleventh month, he gave twenty-five volumes of the Chinese encyclopedia *Imperial Readings of the Taiping Era (Taiping yulan)* to the temple Shōkokuji, to fill in the gap left by an incomplete set offered earlier by Hideyoshi.[50] He continued to acquire art of various sorts, often during or after elaborate tea gatherings, including tea jars from Hideyoshi and Maeda Toshiie.[51]

Ieyasu was, however, acutely aware of the conflict in Korea. In the sixth month, for example, he wrote a letter of sympathy to Asano Nagayoshi's heir Yoshinaga, who was fighting in Korea under Katō Kiyomasa. The short letter is a rare glimpse at the concern Ieyasu felt for a young warrior who was forced to fight in a pointless war:

> The official situation has left you in an unclear position, so I write to you by messenger. This long deployment must have brought you many hardships, and I hope you will soon receive an order and be able to return home. I intend to send you five awnings, but I will tell you the details later.
>
> Very truly yours,
>
> 6/16 Ieyasu
>
> To: Lord Asano, Minister of the Western Capital[52]

Ieyasu drafted similar letters to warriors stationed in Korea during this period, as well as the usual commendation letters to temples and shrines in his home provinces and enfeoffment letters to warriors joining his ranks. In this fashion he maintained contact with individuals in his various networks while spending time away from both his home domain and the action on the continent.

Although Hideyoshi's war in Korea points to a kind of unstable megalomania, Ieyasu's relationship with the Toyotomi lord seems to have been as strong as ever. Ieyasu opened 1598 with a gift to Hideyoshi of oysters in the shell, for which Hideyoshi wrote him a letter of thanks on 1/21. In the fourth month Ieyasu hosted Hideyoshi at his residence in Fushimi and soon after traveled with Hideyoshi and his young son and heir, Hideyori, to Kyoto. In the capital Hideyori received a new court rank on 4/20, and on 5/01 Ieyasu accompanied the boy home to Fushimi while Hideyoshi stayed behind, beginning to feel the onset of what would be his final illness.[53] The court performed ceremonies for his recovery in the sixth and seventh months, but on 7/15 Hideyoshi assembled the various warlords at the residence of Maeda Toshiie and ordered them to swear fealty to his heir, Hideyori; they also signed written oaths, which were then deposited with Toshiie and Ieyasu for safekeeping. The promises continued in the eighth month, with more written oaths exchanged between the warlords pledged to serve Hideyoshi and with several visits to Hideyoshi's sickbed.[54] Ieyasu and Maeda Toshiie seem to have been the primary facilitators of this process; of the twelve written oaths produced on Hideyori's behalf in this period, eight were addressed to or authored by one of these two men, and two were authored by their heirs.[55] After weeks of desperate but ultimately fruitless preparation, with a full-scale international war ongoing and a single heir who was still a toddler, Toyotomi Hideyoshi died on 8/18/1598.

In the months after Hideyoshi's death, Ieyasu gradually emerged as the most likely successor to the position of national hegemon despite his apparent dedication to Toyotomi Hideyori, the heir. In 1600 the forces of those warlords opposed to Tokugawa hegemony clashed with the armies of Ieyasu and his allies, as well as a number of Toyotomi vassals whom Ieyasu convinced to join him on the field of battle at Sekigahara. That conflict is discussed in more detail in chapter 5. In the following section, I discuss the period immediately after Sekigahara, when Ieyasu campaigned to receive the appointment of shogun from the Imperial Court, a process that involved extensive residence in Kyoto and sustained engagement in the capital's practices of sociability.

IEYASU'S GIFT GIVING AFTER SEKIGAHARA

Not long after the end of hostilities, Ieyasu dispatched a number of retainers to Kyoto to begin the process of reporting on the financial holdings that could now be confiscated from the defeated generals of the army that had opposed Ieyasu and his allies.[56] Land enfeoffed to samurai who had died in battle, such as Ōtani Yoshitsugu, or who committed suicide after their defeat, such as Uda Yoritada, could now be reassigned, a process that would take years. Around the country, some pockets of resistance remained, but loyal warlords such as Katō Kiyomasa and Date Masamune engaged in various cleanup campaigns, toppling castles and defeating recalcitrant resisters.[57] On 10/2 Ieyasu met with members of the court who traveled from Kyoto to Osaka, an important sign of the growing recognition of Ieyasu as the preeminent politician in the nation.

Osaka and Kyoto were the focus of Ieyasu's activities for the next year, with Osaka Castle his primary residence for five months, until 3/23 of 1601. Writing as the guardian of Osaka Castle made Ieyasu's word the equivalent of law; when he informed Mōri Terumoto (along with Mōri Hidemoto and Kikkawa Hiroie)[58] that the majority of his lands would be confiscated, including the Mōri ancestral home territory, because of Terumoto's involvement with the Western Army, Terumoto's response was to take the tonsure and make his son Hidenari the new head of the Mōri house, a clear indication of the weight of Ieyasu's pronouncement.[59] Being in Osaka and then Kyoto also put him in close proximity to the Imperial Court. The court was not a military force, of course, but did appoint elite warriors to the court ranks; thus the court was empowered to perform certain political functions in the decentralized system that had dominated the archipelago since the collapse of Ashikaga authority in the late fifteenth century. Many shrine-temple complexes, themselves powerful landholders, political brokers, and occasional militant actors, also had headquarters in or around the Kansai region. When Ieyasu sent out prohibitions to temples around Japan, as he did on 10/3 in a letter to Hōryūji, his central position in the Kansai as well as his recent victory combined to make the document authoritative.[60]

Osaka and Kyoto were also the key sites for Ieyasu to enact a politics of sociability through gift giving, tea gatherings, falconry, and theatrical performances. On 10/7, for example, he sent fresh fish to the Imperial Court and on 10/25 a gift of some swans,[61] the kind of ubiquitous exchanges that served to remind his elite peers of his ongoing presence and munificence. Similarly, on 11/9 Ieyasu provided the funds for a Noh performance, a form of patronage with the familiar distinctive lineage of other forms of spectacular accumulation: Ashikaga Yoshimitsu and Yoshimasa, Nobunaga, and above all Hideyoshi had effectively made the patronage of the theater a form of pageantry, a tradition that Ieyasu continued.[62] Being in the Kansai also allowed him to participate easily in religious rituals and other forms of sociability in the capital and surrounding regions, though such outings are less frequently recorded in the documentary record. Lastly, his location gave him immediate access to the leaders of various social groups in the region who were also politically powerful, even if they did not have the might of samurai armies at their backs.

The New Year began inauspiciously, with Ieyasu canceling festivities because he was ill. Instead, he arranged for the various warlords to see him in Osaka on 1/15, after he had recovered, to offer their New Year's greetings.[63] Visits to the Imperial Court on the first day of the first month had long been a calendrical ritual in Kyoto, and many warlords held a smaller version of the ceremonial reception of vassals in their home domains through the sixteenth century. Hideyoshi, recognizing the political potential of this symbolically powerful and highly visible spectacle, had appropriated the practice by requiring warlords from across the country to attend him and perform increasingly elaborate rituals.[64] Ieyasu likewise began receiving guests from across the archipelago in this first year after his victory at Sekigahara, many of them bearing gifts. The long sword known as Torigai Kunitoshi (figure 20), for example, was originally made in the Kamakura period and passed down among various warriors until it was lost during the Battle of Sekigahara. It was recovered by the warlord Tomita Nobutaka and gifted to Ieyasu, who later bequeathed it to the Owari branch of the family.[65]

Soon after New Year's, Ieyasu began the work of transferring enfeoffments, a puzzle that would occupy much of his time over the next several years. It is often assumed that those who fought with Ieyasu at Sekigahara benefited and those who opposed him had their lands taken away, but the actual process of reassignment was far more complicated. Many transfers were small, such as the first one to occur in 1601, on the eighteenth day of the first month: Arima Yorinori, a warrior who had fought for Ieyasu, was moved from a small domain that earned just 10,000 *koku* of income per year to a larger domain that earned 20,000 *koku*. Ten days later, Katagiri Katsumoto, a warlord who was pledged to serve Toyotomi Hideyori and who had sided with the Western Army (though he didn't fight at Sekigahara), also received a larger domain, increasing from 12,000 *koku* to 28,000 *koku*. The next month, one of Ieyasu's closest retainers, Honda Tadakatsu, was transferred from the Ōtaki domain in Kazusa Province, worth 100,000 *koku*, to the Kuwana domain in Ise Province, also worth 100,000 *koku* (confiscated from the

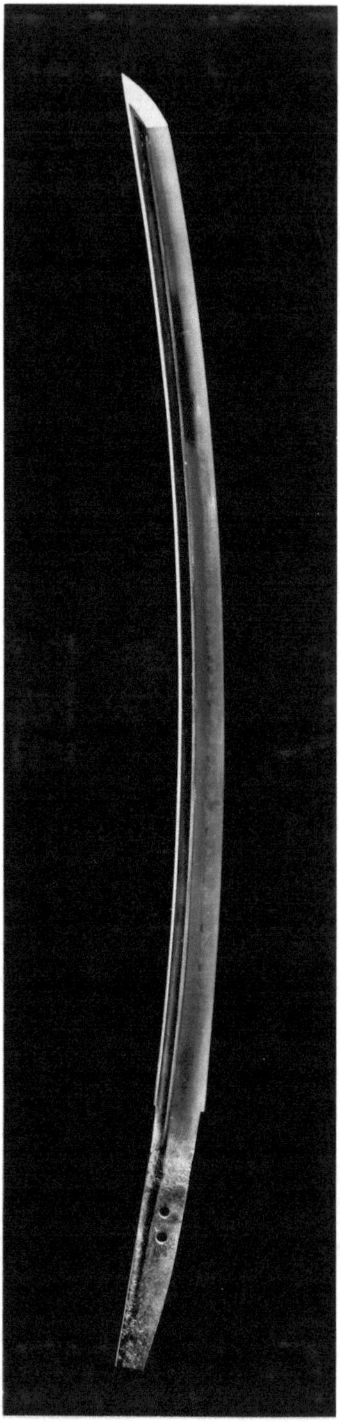

Figure 20. Sword (*tachi*) named Torigai Kunitoshi. Kamakura period, 13th century. Length 60.3 cm. Tokugawa Art Museum Collection, by permission of the Tokugawa Art Museum / DNPartcom

defeated Ujiie Yukihiro, who became a masterless samurai, or *rōnin*). This transfer may seem like a lateral move, inappropriate as a reward for one of Ieyasu's most faithful servants, but in fact it was a significant improvement in the material conditions of the Honda house because Tadakatsu's son, Tadatomo, was awarded the old fief of the Ōtaki domain at a reduced income of 50,000 *koku*. In other words, the income of the house as a whole rose from 100,000 to 150,000 *koku*.[66] These transfers are not conventionally treated as gifts within the Japanese historical literature, but they emerge from the same logic of obligation tied to self-interest.

The biggest loser in terms of confiscation of land was Uesugi Kagekatsu, whose opposition to Ieyasu in mid-1600 had precipitated, or perhaps triggered, the entire conflict. His massive domain of Aizu, worth 1,200,000 *koku*, was confiscated in the eighth month of 1601, and he was transferred to the much smaller, though still significant, domain of Yonezawa, worth 300,000 *koku*. Such moves were characteristic of Ieyasu's approach to reassignment: participants in Sekigahara were not simply rewarded or punished willy-nilly, without regard for rank, but rewarded or punished in a graded fashion that recognized the profound discrepancies in income and rank that dominated warrior society. So it was not unusual that one of Ieyasu's enemies, Uesugi Kagekatsu, would have ended up with a far more lucrative domain than one of his closest allies, Honda Tadakatsu, because the relative loss of Kagekatsu was greater (in recognition of his opposition to Ieyasu) while Tadakatsu's relative gain was greater (in recognition of his service). The differences in income, in turn, acknowledged the preexisting disparities in rank between the two men. Aizu, meanwhile, was divided among warlords whom Ieyasu wished to reward, with the main portion being transferred to Gamō Hideyuki, now half the original size at 600,000 *koku*. This same system was played out on a grand scale among dozens of warlords across the archipelago, with the first few months of 1601 standing out as a notably active period.[67]

At the end of the third month of 1601, Ieyasu departed Osaka Castle and moved into Fushimi Castle in Kyoto. His time in Fushimi Castle is rarely commented upon, as he is intrinsically associated with the establishment of Edo. But the period in which Ieyasu built upon his victory at Sekigahara, was appointed to the post of shogun, enacted the early policies of the new Tokugawa government, and then retired from the position in 1605 was spent primarily in Kyoto, not in Edo. In fact, in this period of roughly five years, less than one year was spent in Edo, while more than three years were spent in Fushimi, with the remaining time spent mostly on the road between the two centers (a trip that Ieyasu tended to make in about three weeks, with plenty of time spent hawking along the way).

In Kyoto, the administrative work that he had begun in Osaka continued apace, with letters of reassignment, enfeoffment, and other matters of feudal appointment and land occupancy going out almost every day to all corners of the archipelago. Some matters were attended to in person, as when the warlord Kuroda Yoshitaka, in 1601 nominally retired and known as Josui, came to Fushimi to see Ieyasu on 5/4. Yoshitaka had been a general under Hideyoshi, and had fought in Korea, where he reportedly took a disliking to Ishida Mitsunari that led him to side with the Tokugawa after Hideyoshi's death. Yoshitaka's son Nagamasa had faithfully served Ieyasu during the Battle of Sekigahara, and Yoshitaka had fought in the territories of his home island of Kyūshū on behalf of Ieyasu, joining forces with Katō Kiyomasa and successfully destroying several castles of warlords in the Western Army. Ieyasu tried, when he met with Yoshitaka in Fushimi, to convince the Kuroda lord to accept a transfer to the region of the capital. Ieyasu promised to speak to the emperor about a promotion in court rank as well, but Yoshitaka "flatly refused," preferring to stay out of politics.[68] Such a refusal would have been unlikely under Hideyoshi, so this is perhaps an indication that Ieyasu was not yet respected or feared to the degree of his predecessor.

Sociability of this sort, in which personal visits, cultural gatherings, and rituals were used for political purposes, was key to the expansion and solidification of Tokugawa authority. During the fifth month, to facilitate participation in Kyoto society, Ieyasu began constructing a residence in the city that would become a symbol of Tokugawa authority in the imperial capital, Nijō Castle.[69] He also left Fushimi Castle to visit with various elites who were resident in Kyoto, sometimes in their own homes, as when he called upon Kanamori Nagachika (Sogen) on 6/22 in the latter's residence in Kyoto.[70] Nagachika had fought on Ieyasu's side at Sekigahara, was awarded various fiefs, and became the first ruler of the Takayama domain as a result, but his main passion was the culture of tea. This predilection made him a good source of information with excellent access to art objects, particularly because he had been close to Nobunaga's and Hideyoshi's primary tea master, Sen no Rikyū.

Ieyasu's attempts to solidify his political authority and extend his social and cultural contacts were successful, and he increasingly received the kind of treatment normally reserved for a sovereign ruler. When Ieyasu became ill toward the end of the sixth month of 1601, for example, the Imperial Court issued a decree to all shrines and temples to conduct rituals for the improvement of his health. When the sickness persisted, the court performed a musical ceremony in one of the palace gardens as a supplication to the deities for his recovery.[71] Several court diarists noted Ieyasu's recovery in the early part of the eighth month in their records, and the court subsequently sent two courtiers to Fushimi Castle to offer the Tokugawa lord a gift of incense.[72] Ieyasu, in turn, sent a gift of fish to the court the following week.[73]

During this period of residence in Fushimi Castle, Ieyasu established new policies—or in some cases, revived old ones—that would come to characterize Tokugawa rule. In the third month of 1601, he ordered the provinces of eastern Japan to conduct land surveys (*kenchi*) of the sort that had been practiced by warlords for decades.[74] Hideyoshi's surveys, known as the Retired Imperial Regent's Land Surveys, are perhaps the best known because of the national scale of the investigations, but the Takeda and others had also carried out comprehensive surveys of land in their provinces that paved the way for new economic policies. In this sense, the land assessment policies of Ieyasu, and later the evolved policies of the Tokugawa shogunate, were very much rooted in the economic concerns of sixteenth-century warlords. In the eighth month, Ieyasu extended this directive to the entire archipelago. Other administrative developments in this period included regular prohibitions (which established Tokugawa authority) sent to temples and shrines,[75] the issuance of village regulations,[76] mining regulations and the establishment of a silver mint at Fushimi, and increased regulation of coinage.

In the tenth month of 1601, Ieyasu traveled to Edo for just two months, before returning to Fushimi on the nineteenth day of the new year. This pattern would be maintained for several years: long spans of time spent in Kyoto, punctuated by short visits to Edo. Few histories of Japan even mention this period, though in terms of documentary evidence, it is among the busiest of Ieyasu's entire career. The problem, perhaps, is the relentless monotony of the sources from this time, repeating the fief reassignments, the prohibitions, and the other administrative paperwork that Ieyasu began disseminating immediately following his victory at Sekigahara. The record for this period shows the banal but vital labor of establishing a new political system, overlooked and largely uninteresting but transformative in its long-term effects. Even biographies of Ieyasu, with the exception of Nakamura's encyclopedic works, tend to disregard this period and jump from Sekigahara to shogun.

However, a number of events and trends from this period stand out as significant elements in Ieyasu's construction of "good government," in addition to the points noted earlier. First of all, Ieyasu continued to actively engage in the politics of sociability and cultural patronage. His trips between Kyoto and Edo usually became opportunities to go hawking, and hunted birds in turn became gifts for the court.[77] Each return to Kyoto was a ceremonial occasion, with members of the court and representatives of temples and shrines visiting Ieyasu in Fushimi Castle to welcome him back to the capital, as on 1602/2/19.[78] In fact, cozy relations with some members of the court—as politically riven a group as could be found anywhere in Japan—are apparent throughout the records from this period, with courtiers such as Yamashina Tokitsune, who was both a doctor and a strong advocate for funding for the court, calling on Ieyasu at Fushimi with some regularity to discuss poetry or exchange gifts.[79] Furthermore, we must remember that in this period Edo was still little more than a fortified town, while Kyoto was the capital city and center of culture, with a legacy of visual and performing arts going back more than eight hundred years. Ieyasu had ample opportunities to partake in the fruits of this legacy, as when he attended at Fushimi Castle a performance of Kōwakamai (which involved recitation, dance, and a chorus, similar to but distinct from Noh theater) on 1602/3/28; or when he sponsored a Sarugaku performance at the Empress's Palace on 5/2 of the same year.[80]

The overwhelming picture that emerges from the sources in this period is that Ieyasu was, well before receiving the post of shogun, in complete control of the field of warrior politics. One sign of his preeminence was his demand that warlords financially support the construction and repair of the major castles used by the Tokugawa for administrative and residential purposes in Kyoto. On 1602/5/1, he instructed warlords from across Japan to support the construction of the new, massive fortress at Nijō, what Harold Bolitho called "a tangible intrusion of warrior power into the city of courtiers and monks."[81] The following month, he commanded the warlords to financially support improvements to his preferred residence, Fushimi Castle, just outside of the city.[82] In early 1603 he requisitioned payment for expansions to the streets of Edo and construction of Nihonbashi, the major bridge that spanned the Nihonbashi river.[83]At the same time, his short visits to Edo became opportunities for him to solidify the administration of the city well before the actual establishment of a shogunate, which implies that the region was starting to grow as the headquarters of the Tokugawa domain. In the twelfth month of 1601, for example, Ieyasu appointed his retainer Aoyama Tadamasa to be the city magistrate for Edo, as well as the general magistrate for the entire Kantō region.[84] In the sixth month of 1602, Ieyasu ordered the construction of a library in Edo Castle and transferred to it the collection of one of the most significant textual repositories in Japan, the Kanazawa Library, originally established during the Kamakura period (1185–1333). He placed this library under the curatorship of a Zen monk from the Ashikaga Academy. Books were to be among the foundation stones of his new administration, and the establishment of this library—with its centuries of Confucian texts and treasures of Japanese literature—would educate his successors for generations.

CULTURED RULE AND SOCIABILITY

The year 1603 began with the now familiar ritual of Ieyasu receiving New Year's greetings from warlords, courtiers, and temple and shrine representatives. He also extended his own offerings, sending a gift of fish to the Imperial Court and offering the fruits of his hunting expeditions as well. Toward the end of this opening month, he learned that this year was to be momentous: Emperor Go-Yōzei intended to name him to the position of shogun, news that obviously pleased him. He rewarded the messenger who brought this agreeable information with gold pieces and a *kosode* robe.[85] Early the next month, he went hunting, killed a wild goose, and promptly presented it to the Imperial Court.[86] These gifts seem almost like preemptive acts of thanks or perhaps continued encouragement of the court, in anticipation of the ceremonial process to come.

On 1603/2/12 Emperor Go-Yōzei dispatched a messenger to Fushimi Castle to inform Ieyasu, who at that moment held the aristocratic rank of minister of the center (*naidaijin*), that the court had promoted him to the rank of minister of the right; furthermore, the court had appointed him to the position of shogun.[87] This announcement quickly became known throughout the city—one sycophantic diarist recorded that it had been raining on the morning of the twelfth but the skies cleared after the appointment of the new shogun—and demanded some semipublic rituals to mark its significance. These occurred in the third month, when Ieyasu traveled into central Kyoto to stay at the newly completed Nijō Castle on the twenty-first. Four days later, he visited the court to offer thanks for his promotion. Soon after, warlords, courtiers, and temple and shrine representatives came to offer congratulations to him at Nijō.[88] He again invited members of the court to visit on the first day of the fourth month, and then from the fourth to the seventh, he sponsored Noh performances and banquets at the castle for warlords and aristocrats. On the sixteenth he returned to Fushimi, but two months later he was back at Nijō and again sponsored two days of Noh performances.[89] Gifts of fish, birds, and other prized foodstuffs continued to flow, usually from Ieyasu to the court, but occasionally in the opposite direction as well.

The concluding act of this ritualized performance of elevating Ieyasu to the highest position in the land involved Toyotomi Hideyoshi's heir, Hideyori, and Ieyasu's granddaughter, Senhime. On 7/28 Senhime—Hidetada's eldest daughter, though only seven at the time—traveled from Fushimi to Osaka Castle to participate in the marriage ceremony that would bind her to Hideyori.[90] This performance appears to have been intended to ameliorate the obvious tension between Ieyasu's stated commitment to protect Hideyori and preserve power for him and Ieyasu's own obvious rise to preeminence as the political leader of Japan: if the Toyotomi house and Tokugawa house were linked, the fortunes of one would profit with the other. This marriage is a notable example, as with many others earlier in Ieyasu's career, of young people and women, or in this case a girl, being used as pawns in the chess game of warrior politics. Such objectification would become one of the defining characteristics of the early modern system, which was more concerned about bodies and their movements (seen particularly clearly in the system of alternate attendance) than any other form of power: even ideology could be largely controlled, the system seems to argue, by keeping people in place, as international and domainal travel prohibitions demonstrated.

It would not have been particularly surprising if Ieyasu had immediately decamped for Edo, his work in Kyoto being, in effect, complete, but he stayed in the city for another eight months after his appointment to the post of shogun and the marriage of his granddaughter to Hideyori. This period of time is marked by the same forms of administrative work as the years immediately after Sekigahara, illustrating the monumental—and still ongoing—task of land reassignment and temple and shrine prescription and prohibition involved in setting up a new form of good government. In the ninth month, a regulatory code was issued to Kyoto courtiers that many historians have interpreted as a kind of first strike against courtly independence by the newly empowered Ieyasu. Lee Butler has shown, however, that this interpretation is an exaggerated attempt on the part of modern historians seeking to emphasize court-warrior conflict soon after Ieyasu's investiture. The code in fact originated in the plans of Emperor Go-Yōzei and represented his attempt to clamp down on his own guards, making it an internal courtly matter.[91] Also ongoing were Ieyasu's politics of culture and sociability, though less intensive than before his appointment to the post of shogun; it may have been less convenient, as his new position would have demanded considerably more pomp and ceremony, and thus may have been less inviting. In the tenth month, he did find time to visit the Fushimi residence of Yamaoka Kagetomo, who was unwell, but otherwise Ieyasu ventured out less often.[92] Soon after, on 10/18, he departed for Edo.

In Edo more pieces of the puzzle of his new administration began to fall into place. After arriving, Ieyasu received word from the court that his son Hidetada had been promoted to the post of right commander of the imperial guard (*u konoe no taishō*), a position that would come, in subsequent centuries, to function as a kind of ceremonial stepping-stone before each of Ieyasu's descendants was appointed shogun.[93] It elevated Hidetada's credentials among the population of elite warlords and also increased his authority in relation to the court. The same day, Ieyasu appointed his young son Yorinobu to be lord of the Mito domain to the north of Edo, with 200,000 *koku* in income—not bad for a boy just a year and a half old.[94] The notion that Yorinobu had any authority is of course a fiction, but Ieyasu's strategy of putting members of his own house in positions of authority and guaranteed wealth, protecting them from the violence of the civil wars that surrounded him as a child, was key to the long-term success of Tokugawa rule. And it cannot be overemphasized that, despite the victory at Sekigahara, such success was not guaranteed in 1603; after the rise and fall of so many rulers and governments in the previous century, it must have been impossible to imagine that a stable administration that would last for centuries could be implemented.

As Ieyasu settled into the new post of shogun, his work continued unabated: letters of commendation, prohibition, and so on continued to be issued on a regular basis, though more often from the brushes of magistrates or scribes than the Tokugawa lord himself. The ceremonial trappings of shogunal rule, however, became more dense, and his participation in gift exchanges rose accordingly; in fact, during the two years of his tenure as shogun, Ieyasu gave and received more gifts per year on average than at any point during his life. Some material remnants of these exchanges survive in the shrines to his deified avatar and in the collections of his descendants, such as the dagger known as Fudō Masamune (figure 21), given to him by Maeda Toshinaga, lord of the massive Kaga domain, a precious, heirloom weapon that Ieyasu passed down to the Owari branch of the family upon his death.

After returning to Kyoto in the third month of 1604, for example, Ieyasu received the entire array of Kansai warlords on 4/5 in an elaborate ritual of deferred New Year's greetings. Since Ieyasu had been in Edo for his first New Year's Day as shogun, these men had waited to mark the occasion until the Tokugawa lord's return. According to the *Diary of Tokitsune (Tokitsune kyōki),* this assemblage included key retainers such as Hosokawa Tadaoki, Ikeda Terumasa, Fukushima Masanori, and Katō Kiyomasa, as well as a few courtiers.[95] Then, half a year after the actual passage into the New Year, Ieyasu visited the court on 6/22 to offer his greetings to the emperor, and the following day members of the court visited him in Nijō Castle to reciprocate, which Ieyasu marked with a Noh performance.[96] The dance of sociability continued with a stream of gifts sent to the court, including

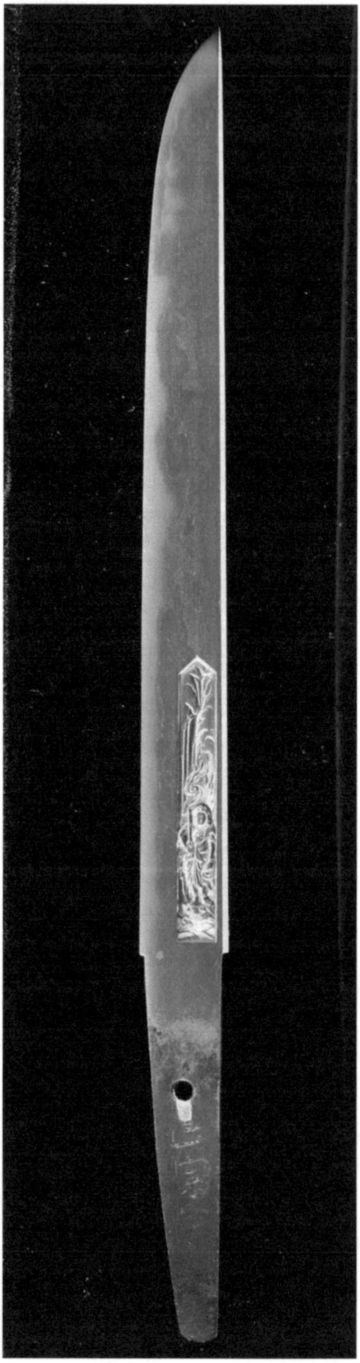

Figure 21. Dagger (*tantō*) named Fudō Masamune. Kamakura period, 14th century. Length 24.8 cm. Tokugawa Art Museum Collection, by permission of the Tokugawa Art Museum / DNPartcom

melons and candles.[97] In the eighth month, Ieyasu observed the festival dances of Kyoto City commoners from the front of Fushimi Castle, an almost kingly act of public pomp.[98] Even his movements back and forth between Kyoto and Edo became the pretext for gift exchanges: as he prepared to depart the capital for Edo in the eighth intercalary month (an extra month added every three years to align the regular calendar with the solar cycle), for example, the emperor sent two courtiers to Fushimi Castle to offer him parting gifts. Soon after, various members of the court and heads of temples sent him travel money (*senbetsu*), symbolic contributions of cash and other gifts furnished to mark a long trip.[99]

While engaging in the politics of sociability in 1604, however, Ieyasu also had to contend with the lingering ceremonial and cultural authority of his former liege, Toyotomi Hideyoshi. To mark Hideyoshi's thirteenth death anniversary, in the eighth month the Toyotomi sponsored a series of ritual events that reinforced Hideyoshi's legacy and also gave an opportunity for Hideyori, as well as the people of Kyoto, to celebrate. Some events were private, but most were public and well attended, including a Shinto procession on 8/14 that included priests, musicians, and theatrical performers; a public dance performance in front of Hōkōji on 8/15; and so on.[100] Ieyasu helped sponsor these events, but must have felt uneasy about the lingering symbolic authority of Hideyoshi, as well as the great enthusiasm with which the general public greeted these celebrations.

Ieyasu's trip to Edo at the end of 1604, which lasted from the intercalary eighth month to the beginning of 1605, was to be his last visit to Edo as shogun.[101] Upon returning to Kyoto, and after receiving the now usual ritual visits from the elites of the capital, he finalized arrangements that had probably begun much earlier, to retire from the post of shogun and pass the mantle of authority to his son Hidetada. Why would Ieyasu have wanted to pursue what appears to be a course of political deflation, at least as far as his own personal status was concerned, in 1605? First, we must remember the long tradition of retired emperors, retired shoguns, and even retired regents who continued to rule from (an ostensibly shadowy but in fact rather well-lit position) behind the screen of semipublic politics and to hold equivalent, if not superior, court rank. As John Brownlee has remarked, "The diffuse nature of legitimacy in the ancient imperial state, extending beyond the reigning Emperor to one or more Retired Emperors, is virtually incomprehensible in terms of the modern conceit of sovereignty."[102] In some cases such retired emperors established separate courts (*in-no-chō,* or *insei*), which did not so much replace mainstream organs of government as overlap with them. Retirement thus became a means of adding to or complicating the political authority and reach of a particular house at a given moment in history. By retiring, Ieyasu would thus increase the political authority of the Tokugawa—ample reason for him to pursue the matter.

In addition, however, we must remember that in 1605 Ieyasu was sixty-three years old. His first master, Imagawa Yoshimoto, had died at the young age of forty-one, Nobunaga died just short of forty-eight, Uesugi Kenshin died at forty-eight, Takeda Shingen died at fifty-one, Hideyoshi passed away around the age of sixty or sixty-one (depending on when we believe he was born), and Chōsokabe Motochika and Maeda Toshiie both died at the age of sixty. In short, although there were some exceptions, a warlord born in the early sixteenth century could not have reasonably expected to live much beyond the age that Ieyasu claimed in 1605. And the key problem that had to be dealt with before his death was the very nut that Nobunaga and Hideyoshi had failed to crack: the stable and reliable succession of an heir in his majority into a position of unassailable authority. This need would seem to have been the strongest of several compelling rationales for Ieyasu to nominally retire at what can only be called the height of his power up to that point in his career.

Hidetada arrived at Fushimi on 3/21 after a journey from Edo that took longer than usual because he was accompanied by an army of as many as 100,000 men.[103] Hardly a subtle statement, this army was rather a loud pronouncement using the vocabulary of the civil wars of the sixteenth century. Ieyasu and Hidetada wanted no opposition to their plan. The fourth month of 1605 was devoted almost completely to the transfer of power. On the first day of the month Ieyasu and Hidetada together received a number of courtiers at Fushimi Castle, probably in preparation for the negotiations to come.[104] On the seventh day, Ieyasu requested official permission from the emperor to step down from the post of shogun and transfer the position to Hidetada.[105] On the eighth day, Ieyasu and Hidetada processed to Nijō Castle, their usual starting point for any visit to, or ritual interaction with, the court, and predictably, the following day the two did indeed visit the emperor at court.[106] Two days later both Tokugawa lords received a group of courtiers and temple and shrine heads at Nijō Castle, ostensibly for another late exchange of New Year's greetings, but more likely for the purpose of preparing for Hidetada's new appointment. Soon after, the two returned to Fushimi Castle. Then on the sixteenth day, they received the official announcement that Ieyasu had been withdrawn from the shogunal appointment and Hidetada had been elevated to the post.[107]

CONCLUSION

It is often said in English histories of this period that Ieyasu, having retired as shogun, withdrew to Sunpu Castle to rule from afar, but this is incorrect.[108] First, Ieyasu spent an additional five months in Kyoto and then moved back to Edo. There was still much political work to do, specifically in the fields of socializing and cultural patronage. One problem that remained, of course, was the Toyotomi. Soon after Hidetada's appointment as shogun, Hideyoshi's widow, Kita no Mandokoro (known in 1605 as Kōdai'in because of her retirement and establishment of the temple Kōdaiji in Kyoto), urged Hideyori to go to Kyoto to see Hidetada and Ieyasu in person. However, Hideyori's mother and the former consort of Hideyoshi, Yododono, refused, recognizing that this would expose Hideyori to Tokugawa capture and also acknowledge the young Toyotomi lord's inferior position. Ieyasu therefore sent his seventh son, Matsudaira Tadateru (1592–1683), who was just one year older than Hideyori, to visit the Toyotomi in Osaka Castle.[109] Somehow this social dance illustrates the tension of the moment, in which Ieyasu was secure in his position as retired shogun, but insecure in the continued existence of a Toyotomi heir in Osaka. Perhaps it was the pressure of Hideyori's presence that inspired Ieyasu to remain in Kyoto and to practice, somewhat relentlessly, the politics of sociability in this period.

Ieyasu's remaining time in Kyoto was spent socializing and engaging in semipublic acts of ritual performance, freed now from the burden of the post of shogun. On 1605/6/16, for example, he invited local warlords to Fushimi Castle for a celebration of the annual calendrical ritual of *kajō,* which usually included consumption of pounded rice cakes (*mochi*) and a variety of sweets.[110] Beginning on 7/7, he held three days of Noh performances at Fushimi.[111] In the eighth month, Ieyasu personally toured the area to the west of the palace with members of the court and with Itakura Katsushige (the shogunal deputy in Kyoto) in preparation for an expansion to the imperial compound.[112] Such expansion and maintenance may have been needed, but the outing still seems like a quid pro quo for the court's support of the Tokugawa. Finally, after months of politicized socializing, Ieyasu left Kyoto in the ninth month of 1605. Having spent most of his time as shogun in residence in the capital city, the retired shogun now apparently felt secure enough in the authority of his house and the guarantee of succession of the position of shogun that he could finally journey to the city with which he is most associated: Edo.

CHAPTER FOUR

Lordly Sport

Raptors, Falconry, and the Control of Land

On the fourth day of the eighth month of 1615, two months after destroying Osaka Castle and extinguishing the threat of the Toyotomi house, Ieyasu departed Kyoto for the last time. He returned to Sunpu, his base as retired shogun, with just a few brief stops along the way. The Tokugawa founder continued to be involved in politics, of course, but a gift of five falcons received on 9/10 from Satake Yoshinobu (lord of the Kubota domain), Date Masamune (lord of the Sendai domain), and Mogami Iechika (lord of the Yamagata domain) hinted at what seems to have been his main passion in these final months, if not for much of his life.[1] In the words of one contemporaneous observer, Ieyasu was a "first-rate falcon fetishist" (*ichi dan taka suki*); another source reports that he employed as many as 150 falcon handlers.[2] Throughout the documentary record, in fact, indications of Ieyasu's passion for falconry are so constant as to become almost ubiquitous, part of the landscape that is easily ignored by modern historians because of its familiarity.[3]

It is difficult to know what kinds of birds of prey Ieyasu received in these gift transactions, as late sixteenth- and early seventeenth-century documents usually simply use the character *taka* for raptors, though the terms *tobi* (black kites or *Milvus migrans;* figure 22) and *washi* (eagle, a common name for several genera within the bird family Accipitridae) also can be found. In this book I usually gloss *taka* as falcon or hawk, but the term is perhaps most accurately rendered in English using the general term "raptor" or the scientific name for the entire order of birds of prey, Accipitriformes. Japan is home to many different groups and species of these birds, including both those that are native to the archipelago and those that seasonally migrate there from other locations around Northeast Asia and the Pacific. Perhaps the birds

Figure 22. Black kite (*Milvus migrans*), photograph by See-Ming Lee

that Ieyasu received from these northern warlords were Japanese golden eagles (*Aquila chrysaetos japonica*), native to northern Honshū and Hokkaidō, as well as some parts of the Korean peninsula. These birds have a modest wingspan of approximately 59–63 centimeters, and uniformly dark plumage with pale mottling on the upper wings. Or perhaps the birds were the rare eagles native to Sakhalin but also seen in Hokkaidō, known today as Steller's sea eagles (*Haliaeetus pelagicus;* figure 23), which possess a massive wingspan of 195–230 centimeters, white markings on the shoulders and tail, and a yellow bill. There are many additional possibilities, including mountain hawk-eagles (*Spizaetus nipalensis*), peregrine falcons (*Falco peregrinus furuitii* or *japonensis*), northern goshawks (*Accipiter gentilis fujiyamae*), and Japanese sparrowhawks (*Accipiter gularis*), among others.[4]

Ieyasu's love of falconry was more than merely a personal pursuit.[5] Walking and riding through the hills and mountains reinforced the imagined connection of warlords to the land while allowing for intelligence gathering. The birds themselves—both the raptors used to hunt and the birds they caught, including fowl and small mammals—were useful as high-status gifts. Hunted birds and animals could be presented at banquets and thus served as reminders of the feudal dependency built into the relationships of the warrior hierarchy. When Ieyasu sent hunted animals to his vassals or to allies for presentation and communal banquet consumption, he was lit-

Figure 23. Steller's sea eagle (*Haliaeetus pelagicus*), photograph by Anna Hesser

erally feeding his inferiors, as palpable a demonstration of benevolent authority as can be imagined.[6] Falconry also represented a field in which Ieyasu could demonstrate dominance and mastery, as when he engaged regularly in the sport during the buildup over several years to the confrontation with the Toyotomi. During a one-month period in 1612, for example, while traveling between Nagoya and Sunpu, Ieyasu reportedly caught more than seventy birds and sent all of them to Hideyori and the emperor, a complex message that was both respectful and profoundly political.[7] The Tokugawa lord could enjoy and work to strengthen his position, it seems, even in the final decade of his life. Or perhaps the distinction is a false one.[8]

The role of falconry in the larger politics of culture during these years of unification deserves our attention. When put in the context of the exchange of hostages and famous objects, the spectacles of banqueting and display, and the politics of sociability explored in previous chapters, falconry appears not to be the quirky devotion of a single powerful individual, but rather a key component in the hegemony of late sixteenth-century warlords. Similarly, falconry was a political and cultural tool, with additional utility because of its connection to rural land, isolated forests, and populations of animals—both the predators used to hunt and the game that was sought after as prey—all of which need further examination as part of the political, cultural, and environmental history of Japan.

What is falconry? Ancient written records, as well as the archaeological evidence of human populations hunting with raptors and using birds of prey in ceremonial practices, can be found in various forms in northern Africa, the Middle East, Central and East Asia, and the Americas. In general, falconry involved the capture or breeding of raptors—particularly hawks, falcons, eagles, and accipiters—followed by training to enable the birds to be used in hunting. As João Rodrigues noted of late sixteenth-century warlords:

> The lords and nobles breed in their houses many kinds of birds of prey, such as falcons, hawks, gerfalcons [gyrfalcons], and many other types, both big and small, so that they may go hunting with them. They have special houses where the birds are kept on wooden perches, tied by the leg with handsome cords of crimson silk. There are certain men appointed to breed, feed, and clean the birds, and this they do meticulously.[9]

The core practice of falconry was hunting with birds of prey, but the pursuit of this sport—which I have referred elsewhere as a "paramilitary pleasure," for its mixture of strategic goals and personal satisfaction—also required the securing and training of birds by professional falcon handlers (figure 24).[10] It also necessitated, as will be seen in this chapter, access to appropriate swatches of land for the hunting of game, particularly ducks, geese, and other birds. Lastly, the exchange of birds as well as the exchange of prey

Figure 24. A falcon trainer, photograph by Su Neko

became opportunities for sociability, with varying degrees of formality and institutionalization. In short, falconry was another realm in which the asymmetrical power relations of the late sixteenth century operated, with the dominance of a few individuals extending not only into the lives of human retainers but into the animal world and the local environment as well.

FALCONS AND POLITICAL AUTHORITY

References to falcons and falconry are found in the earliest written records in Japan, appearing in *The Record of Ancient Matters* (*Kojiki,* 712), *The Chronicles of Japan* (*Nihon shoki,* 720), and *The Collection of Ten Thousand Leaves* (*Man'yōshū,* 759).[11] Falcons seem to have been tied to notions of kingship and the authority of certain rulers over natural resources from these early times. Nintoku, the pseudolegendary emperor of the fourth century, reportedly enjoyed falconry. The historical veracity of Nintoku's reign is not of concern here; rather, the fact that the authors of *The Chronicles of Japan* linked falconry to kingship and articulated this connection is evidence enough of the early prominence of the practice. By the late eighth century, the right to engage in the sport emerged as the prerogative of the sovereign, as seen in prohibitions against nonimperial falconry in *Continued Chronicles of Japan* (*Shoku nihongi,* 797) and similar proscriptions up until the twelfth century.[12]

Literary works such as *The Tale of Genji (Genji monogatari)* indicate the manner in which falcons and falconry functioned in the court. In the first chapter of *Genji* ("The Paulownia Court"), for example, the Minister of the Left receives a gift of a horse and a falcon in the context of a coming-of-age ceremony at which he was officiating.[13] This passage shows the role of falcons in aristocratic gift exchanges, and indeed this practice would later be adopted by elite warriors as one of the most common forms of sociability. Later, in chapter 18 ("The Wind in the Pines"), the falconry expedition of a group of young aristocrats is mentioned, and when the group returns, "the young falconers offered a sampling of their take, tied to autumn reeds."[14] Here we see the prominence of the presentation of the prey captured by falcons during an outing. In some cases the hunters presented the caught birds or small mammals informally, as this passage indicates; in others, swans, geese, and other large birds were the centerpieces of large banquets that served to reinforce the hierarchy of rank while emphasizing the magnanimity of the emperor (and later the shogun) as a provider of sustenance. Such a banquet is seen in chapter 33 ("Wisteria Leaves"), in which "a brace of fowl" taken by the royal falcons is served at a banquet along with wine, all accompanied by music.[15] Lastly, in chapter 29 ("The Royal Outing"), the author describes the spectacle of a royal hunt, an event that the general public came out to witness, with carriages lined up along the streets of the capital city and all members of the court dressed in their finery. "The princes and high courtiers in charge of the falcons were in fine hunting dress. The falconers from the guards were even more interesting, all in printed robes of most fanciful design. Everything was very grand and very novel, and the carriages of the spectators fought for places."[16] The public and performative nature of these events, in which the wealth, power, and general cultural capital of the court were advertised to all, were deliberate and conspicuous statements. All of these elements that Murasaki Shikibu described in her literary account of the court—the instrumentality of the falcon and its prey as gifts, the ritual of the banquet, the display of authority performed in the public outing—adhered to the practice of falconry in medieval Japan. The dominance of the court in the field of falconry was not unrelated to their dominion over significant swaths of land, from which birds were attained and in which hunting occurred.

Warriors took to falconry, as well as other forms of hunting, in the provinces and in the more urban centers of power that developed in the twelfth and thirteenth centuries.[17] The first warrior government, established in Kamakura in 1185, proscribed falconry among warriors on numerous occasions, but the prohibition seems to indicate not the monopoly of falconry by the shogunate but rather its widespread practice among samurai. Falconry can thus be understood as a privilege and a pleasure associated with independence and authority, and as professional warriors gradually wrested much of that power away from the Imperial Court, the prerogative to engage in this particular form of hunting shifted as well. Some courtier falconry continued, as seen in the production and transmission of manuals of falconry practice by the Saionji house in Kyoto, though even these texts may represent attempts to concretize knowledge of practices that were fading from use among aristocrats.[18] The court gradually found itself on the receiving end of gifts of game and other prey hunted by warriors and their raptors, and no longer the protector of the tradition of falconry. By the Muromachi period, a pyramid-shaped system of gift giving had evolved in which rural communities captured falcons and gave them to local warrior leaders, who then presented them to the shogunate, often to mark calendrical anniversaries or in the context of certain rituals. Some of these birds were then passed on to the Imperial Court.[19] Having lost its direct control of estates, the court also had less ability to procure raptors and secure falconry grounds.

With the collapse of the authority of the Ashikaga shogunate in the late fifteenth and early sixteenth centuries, regional warrior leaders became more active in falconry, were less likely to give their finest raptors to Kyoto, and were more likely to use them for their own hawking. An unusual case was that of Asakura Norikage (also known as Sōteki, 1477–1555), a warrior of Echizen Province in the first half of the sixteenth century, who successfully raised falcons, rather than capturing them in the wild.[20] The poet Sōchō visited Norikage in 1524, writing, "In the garden of his residence, Norikaga had for four or five years set up nests for hawks. Last year for the first time two, one large and one small, hatched chicks. It was a very rare event."[21] More common was gift exchange among warlords, with those who lived in the northern area of Japan, particularly the region of the Ōu Mountains, having plentiful access to falcons. Date Terumune (1543–1585), for example, lord of Mutsu Province in the north, sent a falcon to Hōjō Ujimasa in the Kantō region.[22] The mountains of Kai Province were also home to populations of raptors. In 1579, the warlord Takeda Katsuyori sent Uesugi Kagekatsu a raptor, referring to it as a "famous product of this province" (*tōgoku meibutsu sōrō*).[23] Such "products" were carefully supported and subsidized by these eastern warlords because of their value in social exchanges of this sort. Warlords assigned retainer houses to maintain certain forests, providing payment in the form of tax exemptions, land protection, and other special treatment.[24]

The birds involved in these social exchanges had their own trajectories through the environment and indeed through the hierarchies of village and warrior power, though the practice of falconry was what brought the animals into the service of the samurai, or what we might think of as a form of "avian vassalage."[25] In the Kantō region of eastern Japan, for example, the lords of Koga (*Koga kubō*) in Shimōsa Province were at the center of networks of gift exchange that frequently involved falcons and their prey. They actively sought falcons from lesser warrior families, such as the Makabe house of warriors. The Makabe sent falcon catchers to Mount Tsukuba in the summer months to trap falcons in their natural environment and gave the acquired birds to the lords of Koga in the early autumn on a near-annual basis. In return, they received the favor of their superiors, as well as occasional gifts of swords, armor, or horses. Swans, geese, and in some cases cranes were also important presents, usually received by the lords of Koga in the first month of the year and often reciprocated by the gift of a sword.[26]

Like the other forms of spectacular accumulation examined in this book, falconry and the exchange of falcons intensified in the second half of the sixteenth century, particularly under the patronage of Nobunaga, Hideyoshi, and Ieyasu. According to the first chapter of *The Chronicle of Lord Nobunaga,* Nobunaga began to engage in the sport at a young age, usually in the company of his teacher in the arts of war, which implies that the practice was fundamental to his training as a landed warrior.[27] This same chapter gives an evocative description of the practice of falconry under Nobunaga's command:

> When Nobunaga goes hawking . . . he forms a group of twenty spotters and sends them two or three leagues ahead. One of them will keep an eye on the birds that have been spotted while another will report back, "In such-and-such a village there are wild geese, in this-and-that locality there are cranes." A single horseman . . . will slowly circle the place where the birds are, his horse's flanks covered with straw. Little by little he comes closer. Nobunaga follows in the shadow of the horse, so that the birds cannot see him, with a falcon on his arm. When he has come close enough, he runs forward and releases his falcon. A certain number of men will have been assigned as so-called receivers. Carrying hoes and acting like farmers, these men pretend to work the empty fields. When Nobunaga's falcon has caught its prey and is still struggling with it, the receivers will collect the bird for him. Nobunaga is very good at this. They gather in bird after bird.[28]

Falconry expeditions and falcon exchanges then appear repeatedly throughout the records of his life, as when he was presented with a falcon and a sword from the newly installed shogun Ashikaga Yoshiaki in 1568.[29] In 1575, during Nobunaga's second invasion of Echizen—this time to destroy the True Pure Land League that took over after Nobunaga's destruction of the Asakura in 1573—he issued the following item in a list of nine regulations for the province: "Do without falconry, unless it be to scout terrain; otherwise it profits you nothing. There is no objection to children's engaging in it." In this regulation, we see the tactical value of falconry in a society at war: developing an understanding of the lay of the land, the contours of the mountains, and the density of the forest would only aid a commander in battle. The practice of falconry for its own sake was, for Nobunaga's inferiors, perhaps not worth the expenditure of time and money. Contrast this view with the news ten days later that "the men whom Nobunaga had sent to the Far North for the purpose of obtaining falcons brought back fifty. Twenty-three of these Nobunaga bought for himself, and his men acquired the rest."[30] It seems that Nobunaga increasingly sought, if somewhat sporadically, to regulate the practice of falconry for pleasure, while vigorously pursuing the sport himself and in the company of his men.

What other functions did falconry play in Nobunaga's career? One purpose of the Oda lord's large falconry outings was, like the accumulation of an impressive collection of tea utensils, to impress onlookers with his wealth, military might, and skill in this respected practice. In 1577, for example, Nobunaga visited the Imperial Court at the beginning of a major outing and put on a show for the urban and aristocratic spectators. The group included more than one hundred archers, fourteen elders bearing falcons on their arms, and of course Nobunaga and his pages and horse guards. All were "dressed up as fancy suggested," and the retinue "drew an excited response form the crowds." Perhaps most impressive was the honor of the emperor himself offering gifts to the archers and then examining Nobunaga's falcon in person.[31] Early the next year, Nobunaga presented a crane to the emperor and another crane to the courtier Konoe Sakihisa, both caught by his own falcons. Giving such gifts to the emperor and members of the court stood out as a singular honor and marker of status and is a reminder that presenting a gift was by no means an acknowledgment or statement of inferiority, but in fact could express awareness of the giver's superior position, particularly within the warrior hierarchy.[32] To be sure, Nobunaga was usually the recipient of such gifts; the pages of the *Chronicle* are littered with accounts of his receipt of gifts of falcons from near and far. But in the case of gifts to the emperor, particularly that of a luxury food caught by hawking, the privilege of having the authority to perform this exchange was itself an expression of power.[33] A more public statement of his authority occurred in 1581, when Nobunaga presented large quantities of geese caught by his own falcons to the residents of Azuchi; they, to express their thankfulness, sponsored a Noh performance at a local shrine.[34] Through these exchanges, Nobunaga foregrounded the benevolence of the hegemon, as a provider both to the imperial sovereign and to the commoner residents of his own castle town.

The case of Nobunaga also illustrates that falconry was culturally adjacent to warrior control of both human subjects and symbolically significant objects such as tea utensils. Warlords like Nobunaga accumulated both birds and bird handlers to prepare for the large falconry expeditions previously described. The acquisition, training, and deployment of falcons, in particular, must have resonated for military commanders as being similar to the treatment of horses (another widely admired and exchanged vassal animal among elite warriors) and indeed soldiers.[35] The exchange of prized falcons among warriors, part of the complex gift exchanges examined in the previous chapter, was similar to the exchange of hostages as well as of tea utensils and other singular gifts. The presentation of game acquired through falconry, conversely, created opportunities for munificent and spectacular entertainment of the sort previously found only at court celebrations or shogunal banquets. Falconry thus worked to construct the authority of Nobunaga as hegemon while strengthening the hierarchy of the community of warriors that supported him, in a manner that reinforced a communal vision of the samurai as both predators and providers.

REGULATING FALCON HABITATS AND COLLECTING FALCONS

In 1588, while in Settsu Province, Hideyoshi enjoyed a few days of falconry. He wrote to his wife, Kita no Mandokoro, back in Jurakutei: "In this period I am engaging in falconry every day and am eating well. Please do not worry. Everything is forgotten but the falcons, and at night I sleep soundly."[36] Falconry for Hideyoshi thus served at times as a form of respite from the constant struggles of war and politicking, a means of relaxing and perhaps recovering. In the same letter he notes, "I have been staying up chatting for the burning of two candles," implying that these excursions allowed for convivial association with his men that might have been less common in more hierarchical and institutional contexts. However, the practice also was politically useful, providing opportunities for massive displays of wealth and power as well as explicit references to previous warrior regimes. In 1591, for example, Hideyoshi reportedly engaged in falconry for more than a month, working with one hundred fifty falcon handlers, using forty-eight falcons, and catching three thousand birds. When he led his outing back into Kyoto at the end of this campaign, he treated the event as if it were the return of a victorious military parade, setting up seating for members of the court to admire his and his huge procession's victorious arrival.[37]

Such spectacular displays of falconry required larger numbers of birds of prey, however, and Hideyoshi demonstrated a corresponding interest in the protection and control of land from which falcons were taken, particularly those with rookeries providing a reliable supply. Some warlords in the long sixteenth century had previously established rookeries, especially those in regions famous for their raptors, such as the Takeda in Kai Province. Hideyoshi followed this trend but pushed the institutionalization of falconry production and protection a step farther, establishing multiple raptor preservation regions that were secured by prohibitions against the removal or sale of birds from within. Perhaps the most significant example was the Hyūga Rookery (Hyūga hōsō) in southern Kyushu, a region home to several nesting and breeding territories (figure 25). In 1587, during the massive invasion of Kyushu, Hideyoshi's army occupied Hyūga in part to have access to its falcons, which were well known as prized birds. At the conclusion of the offensive, the hegemon appointed Shimazu Yoshihiro, younger brother of the family head Yoshihisa, to take on the role of Hyūga Rookery commissioner (a role that was added to the negotiated requirement that he send his fifteen-year-old heir and eight-year-old child to Osaka as hostages).[38] His role was to guarantee the protection of the territory within Hyūga in which falcons built nests and bred naturally and also to regulate the access

Figure 25. Illustration of hunting in Hizen Province, detail. Kizaki Moritaka (b. 1711), 1784. Original dimensions: 720 x 30 cm. National Archives of Japan

of approved falcon catchers to these nesting territories. It goes without saying that this arrangement primarily benefited Hideyoshi, giving him access to a regular supply of raptors.

Hideyoshi's falconry activities and his efforts to preserve raptor habitats increased during the Korea campaign, when he marshaled a truly spectacular assemblage of falcon handlers—reportedly 850 men—to take with him to the base of operations in Kyushu. It seems likely that his intention was to bring these handlers to Korea, though he did not end up making that voyage. Instead, he practiced falconry in northern Kyushu while his generals fought on the Korean peninsula, as indicated in a letter to Maeda Gen'i, and also in a record from a tea gathering that Hideyoshi attended, during which a wild falcon purportedly landed in a pine tree outside the tea house in response to Hideyoshi's call. Hideyoshi also went out hawking with Ieyasu and other generals who were stationed at Nagoya Castle in Kyushu and likewise received falcons that had been caught by his men in Korea.[39] Meanwhile, various warlords under Hideyoshi's command issued policies regarding the protection of falconry breeding grounds and the care of sick falcons in this period, including Asano Yoshinaga, the aforementioned Shimazu Yoshihiro, and Gamō Ujisato. The resulting birds were sent to Hideyoshi.[40]

In the end, the Toyotomi lord approached falconry with the same zeal and flare for spectacle that he brought to the practice of tea. One historian has noted the resonance between the hegemon's activities in perhaps these two most prominent fields of his cultural politics: "Famous tea utensils made their way into Hideyoshi's hands one after another, much as the superb falcons that had been raised at great pains by the various warlords entered his collection."[41] Hideyoshi himself acknowledged his attempt to monopolize these practices, and in particular, his accumulation of their prized objects in his interactions with his nephew and, for a time, adopted heir, Hidetsugu. The oath that Hideyoshi required Hidetsugu to sign is notable in this regard: in addition to demanding that the new imperial regent would be prudent in his oversight of military matters, strict in his attention to the law, and faithful in his service to the court, the Toyotomi lord insisted that his heir "not follow Hideyoshi's example in the tea ceremony, in hawking, or in the courtship of women."[42] Such practices, Hideyoshi's policies make clear, were too important, too pleasurable, and too powerful to be shared with others, at least on the scale demanded by the hegemon.

IEYASU AND THE POLITICS OF FALCONRY

Ieyasu's dedication to falconry is well documented. The earliest reference comes from the hagiographic text, *Tales of Mikawa (Mikawa monogatari),* and claims that his interest in and contact with birds of prey began at a young age, while a hostage of Oda Nobuhide.[43] His documented interest began in the 1570s, when he was allied with Nobunaga and increasing his territory in central Japan. Letters from this time between Ieyasu's retainers and the vassals of the Uesugi, for example, mention gift exchanges involving falcons during a period in which these two warrior houses were contemplating an alliance against their neighboring warlord, Takeda Shingen.[44] In 1574, after a series of victories against the Takeda in the wake of the unexpected but welcome death of Shingen, Ieyasu wrote a letter to Nobunaga expressing his pleasure that the Oda lord would be visiting him to engage in falconry and reporting that they could pursue many first-rate fowl that had been gathering in his territory. In 1577, Ieyasu sent a letter to an ally thanking him for a present, which was itself reciprocating Ieyasu's gift of a falcon trainer from the previous year.[45] Early the following year, Nobunaga paid an "official visit" (*onari*) to Ieyasu in his home domain and the two engaged in the sport together.[46] Its recording as an official visit rather than merely an outing implies that the hierarchical relationship between Ieyasu and Nobunaga—in which the former was a junior ally, though not strictly speaking a retainer—was ritually manifested in the performance of the reception of the Oda lord and the journey of the two into the fields. Falconry in this period of Ieyasu's career thus seems to have functioned as an instrument of alliance building and relationship maintenance.

Ieyasu and his peers also engaged in falconry in seasonal contexts. The diary of Ieyasu's retainer Matsudaira Ietada, for example, shows that falconry often occurred before and after the New Year's celebration. In the period from 1577/11/2 to 12/11, Ietada records his own falconry on ten occasions; between 1579/12/3 and 12/16, he records seven instances; and between 1580/1/7 and 3/11, he records fourteen excursions.[47] Likewise, Ietada's diary indicates that Ieyasu also went hawking more regularly in the winter months, particularly around New Year's, and that these trips may have been connected to traditions of annual renewal, with gifts of cranes and other game dispensed to celebrate the arrival of the first day on the first month. Ieyasu's hawking expeditions took him to hunting grounds within his domain—Kira, Nishio, and Tahara while he was based in Hamamatsu, and Nakaizumi during his time in Sunpu—where his magistrates had official residences.[48] His annual visits to these magistrates served to reify the hierarchical bonds that defined the relationship between a lord and his retainers, not unlike the tea gatherings that Nobunaga and Hideyoshi (among other warlord tea practitioners) hosted for their vassals to mark annual holidays. Conversely, when Ieyasu invited retainers or allied warlords to his castle to engage in falconry, similar, if less hierarchical, relationship building ensued.

Acquiring raptors was a concern for Ieyasu during this period, especially as his participation in the politics of sociability increased in the final years of Nobunaga's reign and immediately after his assassination. In 1579, Ieyasu sent two letters to the Date family in northern Japan that mention his dispatch of an agent to arrange the acquisition of falcons.[49] Like Nobunaga, therefore, Ieyasu was actively engaged in attempts to acquire raptors from northern climes, and then to maintain them in his home domains, as letters that discussed the seasonal care requirements of the birds from this same period reveal.[50] He also received hawking paraphernalia as gifts, as his correspondence with a representative of Enryakuji in 1585 indicates, in this case the leather straps (known in English as "jesses") used for tethering.[51] The following year, Ieyasu received a falcon as a gift from Hideyoshi in an intensely political situation, after the visit of Hideyoshi's mother as a hostage to Okazaki Castle and Ieyasu's concomitant sojourn at Osaka Castle to acknowledge Hideyoshi's suzerainty.[52]

Under Hideyoshi, Ieyasu engaged in falconry both independently in his home domain and in the company of the Toyotomi liege. For example in 1587, having recently moved his headquarters, Ieyasu spent much of the year overseeing the reconstruction of Sunpu Castle by Matsudaira Ietada while Hideyoshi was completing his campaign to conquer western Japan. Ieyasu seems to have found time to go hawking multiple times in the first three months of the year. He also took a trip to Kyoto in the fall to visit Hideyoshi, receive a new court rank, and do some sightseeing on Mount Hiei to the east of the city, the home of one of the capital's major temple complexes that was still being rebuilt after Nobunaga's attack in 1571. Then in the third month of 1588, Ieyasu wrote several missives to Mogami Yoshiaki regarding his ongoing conflict with Date Masamune, a correspondence that would soon result in falcon exchanges as well.[53] Ieyasu then traveled to Kyoto, where he met with Hideyoshi. On 3/29, the two went hawking in the suburbs of the capital, and Hideyoshi marked the occasion by giving Ieyasu a falcon.[54]

These types of interactions imply that falconry was a major component of Ieyasu's work as an ally of Hideyoshi. A closer look at the records of the exchanges of the Tokugawa lord with Mogami Yoshiaki in the late 1580s, for example, shows numerous thanks for presents of falcons (some intended for Ieyasu but others intended for Hideyoshi), gifts that were part of the Toyotomi lord's attempts to bring the hostilities between Yoshiaki and Date Masamune to an end.[55] Ieyasu also dealt with the other side in this conflict, exchanging letters with one of Date Masamune's retainers in 1588 regarding the peace negotiations and mentioning his own annual attempts to acquire falcons from those northern territories.[56] In fact in 1591, Ieyasu wrote to Masamune to thank him for the falcons he had received.[57] Also in 1591, Hideyoshi summoned Ieyasu to Kyoto to help negotiate with Masamune after the northern lord had been slow to heed Hideyoshi's call to arms for the siege of Odawara, a job that may have been aided by the existence of a preexisting relationship—mediated by the exchange of falcons—between Ieyasu and Masamune.[58] Later that year, a rebellion in Mutsu Province required Ieyasu to launch his armies out of his new territory and travel for the first and only time in his life to the north, where he joined Gamō Ujisato, Date Masamune, Asano Nagayoshi, and other Toyotomi vassals who were called to unify this last unsettled region of Japan. Ieyasu returned home victorious and with all of Japan unified under Toyotomi rule, at the end of the tenth month.[59]

After Hideyoshi's death in 1598, Ieyasu's falconry was both more frequent and less explicitly in the service of politics. Or perhaps since his actions were increasingly those of an independent actor, his falconry was no longer in the service of a third party's political ambition, despite the intentions of Hideyoshi that Ieyasu and the other major Toyotomi generals would wait patiently for Hideyori to come of age. The tension surrounding New Year's Day of 1600 is a good illustration of this. The major warlords of the archipelago observed the holiday by visiting Osaka Castle to offer greetings to Hideyori in the main Honmaru residence. They then made their way to the Nishinomaru residence to offer similar greetings to Ieyasu, who was living there for a brief period. This procession is a striking illustration of Ieyasu's position. He was, on the one hand, at this moment the most powerful individual in Japan, "Lord of the Realm," and yet he was still unable to surpass Hideyoshi's heir, Hideyori.[60] Soon after, Ieyasu attended a Noh performance in Osaka Castle with many of his fellow warlords before they returned home. He found time to go hawking and also planned to pay a visit to the Imperial Court before coming down with a cold.[61] At the end of the second month, he ordered an Ashikaga Gakkō printing of *Essentials of Good Government* (Ch: *Zhenguan zhengyao;* J: *Jōgan Seiyō;* Tang dynasty, 7th c.), the text that Fujiwara Seika had taught him about in 1593. In the third month Ieyasu interviewed William Adams, the English member of the ship *Liefde*.[62] All of these actions fall outside of the conventional understanding of politicking and institution building of the sort associated with the reunification of Japan, yet they were unquestionably part of the buildup to the Battle of Sekigahara.

Ieyasu became aware in this same period that Uesugi Kagekatsu, one of Hideyoshi's vassals in eastern Japan, was busy restoring the defenses of his castles and fortifications in Aizu, which may have been the motivation for Ieyasu's request that Kagekatsu visit him in Osaka in the fourth month.[63] Kagekatsu refused, which put some pressure on Ieyasu as he contemplated the post-Hideyoshi landscape of political power and personal alliances. In the fifth month he began to make clear his plan to attack Kagekatsu at Aizu, which is seen, for example, in letters to warriors such as Iono Sukenobu of Iono Castle in Shimotsuke Province that instructed him to fortify and hold his position in the northern part of Ieyasu's territory, close to the perimeter with Aizu.[64] This instruction ensured that the northern border of the Kantō provinces was secure and on alert.

Next, in the opening days of the sixth month, Ieyasu wrote to vassals and allies whose domains were located between Kagekatsu's territory and the capital region, and informed them of his intent to attack Aizu around the seventh month.[65] On the sixth he assembled his main commanders and organized the approach and attack plan, for which he received approval from the court two days later.[66] He also made preparations for his own absence from Osaka, meeting with Toyotomi Hideyori and leaving Sano Tsunamasa in charge of the Nishinomaru residence. On the sixteenth (in what is widely seen as the opening move that would lead to the Battle of Sekigahara) Ieyasu departed Osaka Castle to lead the attack on Aizu. He traveled with his personal force of approximately three thousand hereditary retainers from his days in Mikawa Province, as well as significant numbers of Toyotomi retainers who either felt obligated to Ieyasu or hoped to gain from an invasion of Aizu.[67] After a brief stopover at Fushimi Castle, in which he stationed Torii Mototada as caretaker, he headed east toward Edo, engaging in falconry along the way even as he prepared for the coming conflict.[68] Ieyasu's eventual victory over those opposed to Tokugawa hegemony would have a substantial impact on the practice of falconry and indeed on the ecosystem within which falcons lived.

TOKUGAWA INSTITUTIONALIZATION OF FALCONRY

Moving forward, for now, to the period immediately after the Battle of Sekigahara, Ieyasu was increasingly acknowledged as the most powerful military and political figure in Japan. Having defeated Ishida Mitsunari and the anti-Tokugawa league, Ieyasu began his sustained campaign to build up the political and cultural capital necessary to be appointed to the post of shogun. As discussed in the previous chapter, his embrace of the politics of sociability and his close interactions with warlords and the members of the court in this period were central to this process, and falconry and falcon exchanges played their part as well.[69] As shogun and later as retired shogun, Ieyasu became even more involved in the economy of gift exchanges, receiving falcons and hawking paraphernalia on multiple occasions. For example, as shogun, Ieyasu received offerings of falcons from the Matsumae, attested to by a "red-seal letter" sent to Matsumae officials in 1604.[70] Such offerings of raptors to the shogunate became increasingly ritualized under later Tokugawa rulers, part of the larger system of gift exchange and political pageantry that buttressed the authority of Edo for centuries. Similarly, in 1607 Ieyasu sent several personal letters to Nakagawa Hidenari, ruler of the Oka domain in Bungo Province (present-day Oita Prefecture, Kyushu), expressing his thanks and pleasure for receiving paper fabric (*kamiko*) garments, which were used during cold-weather falconry, and for the enquiries about his falconry.[71] Around the same time, Ieyasu sent a letter of thanks to Matsura Takanobu, ruler of the Hirado domain (present-day Saga Prefecture, Kyushu), in response to the gift of a falcon.[72] A letter of thanks sent to Hachisuka Yoshishige in 1609 uses nearly identical language to the letters sent to Nakagawa Hidenari, offering thanks for the inquiry about Ieyasu's falconry and for the gift of ten braided cords used to tie falcons' legs.[73] As the Tokugawa period progressed, a massive system of falcon gift exchange developed, which has been thoroughly chronicled in the work of Okazaki Hironori and Nesaki Mitsuo.[74]

The context for these exchanges was Ieyasu's demarcation of policies, often through reviving or expanding previous late-medieval institutions, that would come to characterize Tokugawa rule, including the protection of falconry habitats and the regulation of those who could practice the sport.

As noted previously, in 1601 Ieyasu ordered land surveys, followed by proscriptions for religious institutions,[75] land surveys and assorted, related administrative instructions,[76] rules for the increasingly profitable mining operations, the formation of the silver mint at Fushimi, and better control of specie production. In the ninth month of 1601, he issued two edicts that demonstrate the role of what can be thought of as cultural policy in these early days of his national administration. First, Ieyasu ordered the printing of numerous Chinese works using movable wooden type at the Fushimi temple academy press.[77] Second, he acted to protect falconry and the regular supply of falcons (as the Takeda had done in Kai, and Hideyoshi had done at Hyūga) by establishing a rookery in Higo Province on the island of Kyūshū, an area that bordered the aforementioned Hyūga rookery and was also well known for its falcons.[78] Like Hideyoshi, Ieyasu recognized that falcons, key to the gift economy and politics of the sociability of warlords, were too valuable to go unprotected and unregulated.[79] It also is no coincidence that these rookeries were located at the peripheries of the archipelago; protecting and controlling the land at these spots reinforced the reach of the Tokugawa.

After retiring from the position of shogun, Ieyasu worked to strengthen the protection of and indeed monopolize the practice of falconry. In 1612 he issued a short set of regulations for the court, now lost, which notably included the prohibition of falconry by courtiers.[80] These regulations were supplemented by a 1613 letter from Yamashina Tokitsune, a courtier with whom Ieyasu had a close relationship, to his fellow aristocrats, in which Ieyasu's interdiction of falconry by members of the court is again clarified.[81] Similarly, in a list of prohibitions that the retired shogun sent to Iwashimizu Hachimangū, a shrine located just outside of Kyoto with a deep historical connection to the imperial family, falconry is explicitly demarcated as forbidden in the passage banning the taking of life in general.[82] In the same period, Ieyasu institutionalized the practice, previously engaged in by Nobunaga and Hideyoshi in an ad hoc fashion, of giving particularly high-quality prey caught during falconry to the court on an annual basis. Also, when warlords gave this prey to the shogun, the birds were often then regifted to the Imperial Court. Within the court, complicated rules for the exchange of birds and the expected comportment at banquets involving birds became a significant form of the politicized socialization in the Tokugawa period.[83] In a sense, then, the court continued to participate in the larger culture that emerged out of the practice of falconry, and the emperor continued to exert influence over this field of cultural practice, though with more constraints than in previous periods.

The practice of falconry was thus increasingly the prerogative of elite warriors and their retainers, one of the hereditary rights of this group that was limited by cost to a class-based subset of higher ranking, elite samurai. In the tenth month of 1614, leaving his son Yorifusa in charge of Sunpu Castle, Ieyasu with his son Yorinobu led an army toward the first confrontation with Toyotomi Hideyori in Osaka Castle. Falconry was a marker of his dominance over both his fellow warriors and over the lands of the archipelago as much as it was a paramilitary pleasure, a means of preparing for the work of war.[84] He made his way leisurely along the Tōkaidō, stopping occasionally to hunt, and arrived at Kyoto after a sedate journey. The ability of a landed warlord—or in the case of Ieyasu at this moment, a retired shogun—to engage in falconry while traveling made it a particularly useful pursuit for surveying land while engaging in the politics of culture.

Indeed, although the discussion thus far has focused largely on the procurement and exchange of falcons and actual hawking outings, equally important was access to areas of land where falconry could be pleasurably and effectively practiced. Control of land was of course at the heart of the political and economic system of late sixteenth-century Japan, so attempts to restrict land for falconry use were also part of the power dynamics of the period. Hideyoshi had previously set up restricted falconry grounds (*takaba*) in strategically located spots that both provided him with good hunting territory and allowed him to keep an eye on neighboring warlords. Ieyasu continued this practice when he was transferred to the Kantō region in 1590, prohibiting bird hunting and gun usage in certain forests (perhaps based on precedents established by the Hōjō before him). He also established facilities for the care and training of falcons (*takabeya*) and assigned family retainers to their management and administration. The best example is Matsudaira Ietada, whose diary of course serves as an important record for late sixteenth-century warrior life, as well as many details of Ieyasu's career. However, historians who focus on falconry estimate that Ietada, who Ieyasu did charge with various falconry-related tasks and the management of falcon facilities, was by no means alone in this regard, but rather was an unusually well-documented individual within a class of elite retainers who helped Ieyasu and other warlords control the land designated for falconry.[85]

After Sekigahara, Ieyasu's new authority gave him additional powers in the field of falconry. He could allocate falconry grounds as part of the larger process of land confiscation and reassignment. For example, he granted new falconry grounds to Date Masamune in 1601, one of several such grants from this period.[86] He was also able to continue the process of institutionalizing Tokugawa falconry grounds in the Kantō. In Musashi Province, for example, the Oshi region (present-day Saitama Prefecture, Gyōda city) was managed by intendants, many of whom were also falcon trainers, and the land is referred to in contemporaneous documents as falconry grounds set aside on the orders of Ieyasu. In 1615 Ieyasu intended to go hawking in the area around Koshigaya, but was prevented from doing so by flooding of the falconry grounds; the intendant in charge of the area was rebuked as a result, perhaps for his failure to notify the retired shogun of the state of the grounds.[87] Other eastern provinces such as Shimōsa, Kazusa, and Sagami also contained falconry grounds that shogunate-appointed intendants worked to protect and manage. These lands became part of Ieyasu's collection, accumulated for personal use and thereby removed from the public domain. In western Japan, falconry grounds had long been protected for the use of the court, of various warlords, and under Hideyoshi, of the Toyotomi. After Sekigahara, Ieyasu gave some of these parcels of land and also the work of administering them to his retainers in the region, warlords such as the Ii family in Hikone, the Kanamori in Takayama, and the Ikeda in Himeji, as well as his half-brother Matsudaira Sadakatsu, the keeper of Fushimi Castle. The Tokugawa also retained numerous falcon handlers and trainers with whom they worked when visiting western Japan, with some maintaining residences in both Kyoto and Edo.[88]

Eventually, the Tokugawa extended regulations regarding the protection of falcons and falconry grounds beyond the confines of these established parcels of lands and into the daily lives of villagers. In 1626, for example, the shogunate issued regulations through the "five household" (*gonin gumi*) system regarding the discovery of raptor nests by rural commoners, clarifying that leaders were to protect and manage any such nests as part of their hereditary duties. In other words, the right to engage in falconry, as Nesaki Mitsuo has argued, was solely the prerogative of members of the warrior status group and controlled centrally by the shogunate.[89] The protection of falconry grounds and rookeries and the prohibitions against hunting in certain lands that Ieyasu and the other early Tokugawa rulers established were, of course, dwarfed by the deforestation that resulted from the massive lumber usage through building projects in the early years of the seventeenth century.[90] However, the early Tokugawa attention to the fate of raptors and their environment, not out of a sense of environmental altruism but rather in the spirit of spectacular accumulation, is a reminder that the asymmetrical power dynamic of the wars of the late sixteenth century extended beyond the battlefield and into the lives of commoners and indeed the ecosystem of the archipelago.

MATERIAL CULTURE, HISTORY, AND THE EPHEMERAL

What is missing from the records of Ieyasu's trips into the fields with his birds and his falcon keepers is a description of the details of the experience. The sensory experience of the hunt, the textures of the woodlands, the felt impact of the weather; all these particulars are absent in the dry notations of Ieyasu's activities in his final years, such as the following excerpted entries from 1615 in the *Record of Sunpu (Sunpuki)*:[91]

> 9/14: Everyone is saying the lord went into the mountains early to do falconry.
> 9/18: His lordship headed out early for some falconry. He caught four wild geese.
> 9/21: His lordship headed out early for some falconry. He caught a crane, four wild geese, six wild ducks, and in addition a heron.

Like the absence of records that shed light on Ieyasu's inner life, the ephemeral nature of the falcons and their prey makes it hard for us to understand the texture of these moments of embodied experience. The bodies of the birds decay into desiccated and unwanted corpses; unlike the Chinese ceramics and swords that are exchanged with equal enthusiasm among elite warriors and which then are protected over the centuries by these men's descendants, the birds that they prized disappear. We are left with the dry and bureaucratic records of a ruler, not the living and breathing encounters of a historical subject with the world around him.

One rare exception was the memo (*oboegaki*), a genre of writing that appeared with increasing frequency in the documentary record in the final years of Ieyasu's life. Ieyasu scribbled notes for himself with some regularity, writing down the names of things to aid his memory or perhaps as part of his writing habit. Tokugawa Yoshinobu goes so far as to call him a "memo maniac," implying an almost unhealthy obsession with recording the minutiae of daily life.[92] While these texts reveal nothing of Ieyasu's emotions or inner thoughts, their regularity and relative banality point to what may have been the constant tug of the need both to know and to remember, to categorize and to consolidate. In two documents from 1613–1615, both titled "Incense Matching Memorandum," for example, the retired shogun notes in his own hand the fragrance of various types of incense. Ieyasu is known to have enjoyed incense connoisseurship and collected rare woods from around Asia, as well as metal and ceramic incense burners from China.[93] Two similar memos (one from 1616 and the other undated) record the names of tea jars (*chatsubo*), including many of the prized possessions of

Ieyasu's collection such as Daihan'ya (Chinese, Southern Song-Yuan dynasties, Tokugawa Art Museum), and Hōgan (Chinese, Yuan-Ming dynasties, Tokugawa Art Museum).[94] Other lists from this period record textiles, gold and silver coins, night watchmen, poetic words (*utamakura*), and Noh plays.[95] Perhaps the longest memo, indicating a subject that was well and truly an obsession, listed falcon handlers and low-level menials involved in Ieyasu's hawking activities.[96]

This evidence paints a picture of a leader who indeed exploited his power over both people and land to pursue the practice of falconry as frequently as possible. It is thus not surprising to learn from the extant documentary record that the retired shogun's final pleasurable act seems to have been a falconry trip. In early 1616, Ieyasu headed into the Tanaka region close to his home base of Sunpu Castle. He became ill the same evening, and his son sent a retainer to verify his condition.[97] He rapidly deteriorated, so the shogun traveled from Edo to Sunpu, followed in quick succession by messengers bringing enquiries of concern from temples and shrines, the assorted warlords, and the Imperial Court.[98] The Tokugawa lord's condition remained serious, so the emperor offered to engage in rituals and ceremonies beseeching the gods for Ieyasu's improvement.[99] The court increased his aristocratic rank to imperial grand minister (*daijō daijin*), and he made some improvement.[100] Over the course of the following two months, however, as he made plans for the probate of his collection of objects, his significant monetary resources, and other powerful forms of his legacy, his condition worsened. He died on 4/17 in the morning at the age of seventy four.[101]

Ieyasu left behind a transformed political and cultural landscape. A significant component of his legacy was the huge collection of art and other durable works that had resisted the ravages of late medieval time and would continue to survive under the stewardship of his early modern descendants and the shrines established in his honor. I have argued throughout this book that these objects possessed a kind of agency in the society of late sixteenth-century Japan, influencing and having an impact on the people they came into contact with through the value and values ascribed to them. I continue to demonstrate that this body of material culture played a role in shaping and defining our understanding of the period, and of Tokugawa Ieyasu in particular, in the remaining chapters of this book.

However, one category of material culture that has failed to mold our conception of the past is the falcon. Raptors are inherently ephemeral, like people, which was surely part of the attraction for warriors, who captured, raised, and trained them, then watched them hunt. The falcon's graceful pursuit of prey served as an idealized substitution for the messy reality of war, a kind of theatrical restaging of the potentially fatal work that defined war-

Figure 26. Image from album of hawks and calligraphy. Kano Tsunenobu (1636–1713). Edo period. 27.3 x 23.9 cm. Metropolitan Museum of Art

rior identity. But in the end both the actors in this idealized play and their audience died and turned to dust. The falcons left behind no material legacy and could not be reified and fetishized beyond their short lifespan. Paintings of falcons (figure 26) entered the pantheon of visual culture and became two-dimensional signifiers of painterly skill and decorative intent rather than palpable, physical records of the lived experience of falconry. There is evidence that some warlords named their favored birds, with Nobunaga's remarkably titled falcon, Randori (plunder), being perhaps the best example: a clear linkage of the social entertainment of hunting with the violent conquest and acquisition of property in warfare.[102] But raptor taxidermy of the kind found in Europe, it seems, was not practiced in early modern Japan.[103] Later Tokugawa shoguns, with a few exceptions, lost interest in falconry. The gifts of falcons and their prey became annual ceremonies, part of the rhythms of Tokugawa power, rather than components in a larger system of hawking practice; this marginalization is one of the ways in which falconry was quite distinct from tea culture, which diffused not just through the population of early modern warrior elites but across much of the Japanese archipelago.[104] Rather, the tracts of land set aside for the exclusive use for falconry by the Tokugawa and other feudal lords became environmental symbols of the inherent inequity of the early modern status system,[105] and these preserves were quickly and thoroughly absorbed for other uses after the fall of the Tokugawa. Most significantly, unlike the swords, suits of armor, Chinese ceramics, and other weighty pieces of material culture that Ieyasu bequeathed to his descendants, which by their very existence in storehouses, shrines, and modern museums have shaped latter-day attempts to imagine the past, the falcons that Ieyasu intensively accumulated disappeared from the flow of things into the present.

Historians have perhaps not been sufficiently attentive to the role that material culture plays in shaping our present-day horizon of expectations when examining records of the past. While we judiciously scrutinize documentary evidence and the context for its production and dissemination, we may accept or even ignore the impact of things on our historical imagination. How do we come into contact with such material culture, which subconsciously shapes our perception of the past? Many people encounter old things first in the home, but inherited objects represent particularly subjective versions of history, edited by individuals who carefully craft a material narrative for future generations. Large-scale material edifices, such as architectural and environmental monuments, are equally ideological, less objective records of human culture than forms of local heritage or national patrimony that are preserved or destroyed depending on the balance between economic need and political necessity. Most powerful of all, museums—be they family, history, or art museums—are filled with objects that seem to make history concrete. The illusion that we are encountering a natural sample of the lived experiences of human actors who are otherwise distant from us in time and space is both one of the greatest strengths and greatest dangers of the museum. All of these cases make clear that the old things that still surround us in the present did not arrive here through a random pattern of sedimentation; they were filtered, shaped, rearranged and in some cases literally remade to suit the needs of historical subjects along the way.

The absence of falcons from the material record of the late sixteenth century, and the corresponding lack of attention to the significance of this practice in the politics of unification, stands as a useful example. Some small remnants of the practice did endure; later registers of the material culture associated with Ieyasu and inherited by subsequent generations of the Tokugawa house reference some of the paraphernalia of hawking, including jesses and the very same "silk cords" mentioned by João Rodrigues at the beginning of this chapter.[106] But overall, these ephemeral birds are lost to us, a striking metaphor for the lived experiences of our historical subjects and a useful counterexample to the durability of other types of things and the illusory implication they provide that the past lives on without complication in the present.[107]

CHAPTER FIVE

Severed Heads and Salvaged Swords

The Material Culture of War

More than any other phenomenon of the late sixteenth and early seventeenth centuries, Tokugawa Ieyasu is associated with war, particularly the titanic conflict of 1600 that is often seen as the tipping point between medieval and early modern: the Battle of Sekigahara. Likewise, the 1614–1615 Tokugawa assault on the remaining forces of the Toyotomi house, ensconced in the formidable fortress of Osaka Castle, represents in some sense the victory of the Tokugawa over history itself, the final step from the Sengoku age of war to the Pax Tokugawa of stability; or, in the eyes of Toyotomi loyalists, the final act of betrayal in a series of Tokugawa perfidies. But these two massive military battles—which collectively involved armies of samurai the likes of which had never previously been mustered in Japan, more than 450,000 total—can be read alternatively as ritual and performative acts, as encounters between things, or as exercises in the management of warrior labor through the well-tested politics of sociability explored in previous chapters. The glorification of acts of bravery over the reality of the slaughter of human bodies is all too typical an example of militaristic ideology, of Tokugawa historicism refined in late-nineteenth and twentieth century discourses of national crisis and national unity.

This chapter considers the history of these two massive conflicts at the end of Tokugawa Ieyasu's career while paying attention to two parallel and related acts: taking heads and collecting swords. More broadly, I consider war as a semiritualized act through which warrior society is unmade and reconstituted, an inherently social process bounded by culture rather than a dramatic encounter between heroic individuals. Historians of medieval Japan have demonstrated that struggles over political authority were as likely to occur in the realm of ritual practices as in martial conflicts.[1] More broadly, the hierarchy that defined warrior status distinctions and that allowed warrior bands to function both as units that waged war and as organizations that engaged in governance was *activated* by ritual rules and practices, ranging from the rubrics that governed seating order at meetings to the regulations that determined proper letter-writing.[2] The rituals of war and the associated ceremonies of collecting and display—both of heirloom treasures and of body parts—were likewise collectively a means of control, an attempt to "dominate nature and the natural violence within human beings."[3]

This chapter also calls attention to the relationship between the sword, a symbol of samurai culture that has been romanticized and aestheticized in complex ways in both the early modern and modern periods, and beheading, a regular ritual practice in Japan's culture of war. In the link between the sword and the severed head, we see resonances that are similar to the exchange of art in the culture of tea and the exchange of hostages in the politics of détente. Hostage exchange and beheading as practices of war are widely seen as atrocities in the world today, but both appear frequently in the documentation of premodern Japan. The ritualized taking of heads, in particular, is startlingly common. In war epics such as *Tales of the Heike,* beheading often serves as a synecdoche for war itself, as when Taira no Tomomori says to Munemori, "Now that the good fortune of your house has run its course, beheading a hundred or a thousand men would do nothing to make you again the master of the world."[4] It is also a signifier for martial prowess, as when Minamoto no Yoriyoshi was claimed to have beheaded "sixteen thousand men and more."[5] Also notable is the use of beheading and the spectacle of the displayed head as a means of communicating power, as when Taira no Noritsune ordered two hundred archers beheaded and "hung their heads in menacing view."[6]

It is this last understanding of the utility of decollated heads that is the most striking in *Heike* and that serves as a useful reminder before examining the material culture of war in Ieyasu's career. In the chapter titled "The Parade of Heads," Minamoto Noriyori and Yoshitsune argue that a grand, public display of the heads of defeated Taira was necessary to bring stability to the land: "If we may not parade these Heike heads through the streets, what warning hereafter will serve to deter evildoers?"[7] The spectacle of taken heads was thus a form of ritual politics, a means of articulating not just military might and victory in battle but a threatening form of ethical righteousness. A public was required for the message to be effective; as Patricia Palmer put it, displays of severed heads "enunciated the triumph of violence and the threat of more to come."[8] In the case of the Minamoto presentation of their victory over the Taira at Ichinotani, "The parade of heads went forward. The onlookers could not even count them. Past attendance at the palace now caused many to quake with fear."[9] Similar performances of power were key to the attempts of the hegemons in the late sixteenth century to pacify Japan, and indeed to the stability of the Pax Tokugawa, a polity built in part on the threat of violence.[10]

THE BATTLE OF SEKIGAHARA

The death of Hideyoshi in 1598 created a conundrum for Ieyasu, who was the wealthiest and most powerful of the generals who had sworn fealty to the Toyotomi lord and promised to look after his heir, Hideyori. There is no indication in the documentary record that Ieyasu intended from the beginning to go against Hideyoshi's wishes and establish a new military government. Rather, the Tokugawa lord seems to have bristled against the small restrictions that made sense when the charismatic Hideyoshi was alive but that were inconvenient after his death, such as the requirement that marriage alliances be approved by committee.[11] Ultimately it was the hostility between Ieyasu and several of his primary vassals and the warlord Ishida Mitsunari, lord of Sawayama in Ōmi Province and one of Hideyoshi's most trusted followers, that increased the likelihood of a military conflict. Although Mitsunari was significantly weaker and poorer than Ieyasu as a ruler, he wielded significant influence among the generals who had been loyal to Hideyoshi and was able to rally many to the anti-Tokugawa cause. By late 1599, most of the major warlords who had served Hideyoshi in Korea or in Osaka Castle had returned to their home domains and were preparing their troops for war.[12] Ieyasu reached the same conclusion, and after returning to Edo from Osaka in mid-1600, he issued a fifteen-article military code that outlined the formation of the troops into an advance force to be led by Tokugawa Hidetada and a main force led by Ieyasu himself, as well as the protection of Edo in their absence.[13] Their goal initially would be an assault on Uesugi Kagekatsu, but the ultimate conflict would be with Mitsunari. Ieyasu set brush to paper and began his usual preparation for battle, writing letters with instructions for vassals, demanding participation in the upcoming attack, or providing information to those already involved in the lead-up to the conflict.[14]

Mitsunari moved quickly to transform his own personal quest to oppose Ieyasu into a rallying cause for the wobbling Toyotomi regime. He traveled to Osaka, to be close to Hideyoshi's heir Hideyori, and appealed personally to his fellow warlords. His petition must have been successful, as the result was support for his cause. Mōri Terumoto, one of Hideyoshi's trusted generals and the second most powerful warlord in Japan after Ieyasu, arrived in Osaka on 7/16 with ten thousand men, and assumed the role of chief commander of the anti-Tokugawa forces. The following day, Mitsunari and his confederates issued a thirteen-article document impeaching Ieyasu, which was sent to warlords across Japan.[15] This impeachment document is notable for its inclusion of issues that are ostensibly social rather than political. Some of the charges relate to affairs that are commonly associated with institution building in late sixteenth-century Japan: military action, enfeoffment, state affairs, and land surveys, and the repeated claim that Ieyasu violated the regulations left by Hideyoshi. Other items charge Ieyasu with violating Osaka Castle, the home of Toyotomi Hideyori and in many ways the architectural symbol of Toyotomi authority, which Ieyasu had occupied before returning to Edo. Also notable are the accusations concerning relationships: the letter accuses Ieyasu of ostracizing two warlords, subjugating another, and forming new alliances. Lastly, numerous charges concern Ieyasu's manipulation of the late sixteenth-century bodily surplus, through the use of hostages, the related practice of marriage arrangements and alliances, and the agitation of youth—an intriguing accusation that implies that Ieyasu had a youthful following of eager samurai.

Fortunately for Ieyasu, by the time this document reached him and Hidetada, they had already decided to turn away from the assault on Uesugi Kagekatsu and to separately launch their armies toward a confrontation with Ishida Mitsunari. It was particularly significant that a large group of Toyotomi vassals traveling with Ieyasu had already declared their loyalty to the Tokugawa lord before the arrival of this document, making it more difficult for them to change their positions.[16] Ieyasu soon returned to Edo, while the main Tokugawa force of forty-three thousand headed to the west and began taking actions against Mitsunari's allies in the area around the Nōbi plain;[17] soon after, Hidetada led another force along the Nakasendō, the historic highway that cut through the central, more mountainous regions of Japan. Eventually, this move would lead Hidetada and the forces under his command—estimated to have consisted of roughly thirty-nine thousand men—to join up with the main army now waiting in the Gifu region (although Hidetada was famously delayed along the way and arrived late to the battle). On 9/1 Ieyasu finally departed Edo with a force of approximately thirty thousand men. In a revealing but somewhat unusual move, however, he hid the strength and the intention of his force by rushing his advance along the Tōkaidō and avoiding the usual pomp and ceremony of a large, marching army. For example, the large flags called horse insignia (*uma jirushi*), which were decorated with gold fan motifs and that usually marked such a procession, were not displayed. This modification made the large force less conspicuous and, more importantly, allowed it to move more quickly from Edo to Fujizawa, then to Odawara, and so on until the entire army arrived in Kiyosu just eleven days later.[18]

The conflict unfolded in the narrow, box-shaped valley that was home to the Nakasendō post station town of Sekigahara in the early morning hours of 9/15. Mitsunari and his anti-Tokugawa forces—known as the Western Army—occupied the key positions in the valley to block passage toward Kyoto and Osaka.[19] Ieyasu's forces—the Eastern Army—began to arrive in the valley amid rain and mist. Reportedly visibility was so poor that the troops in the Tokugawa vanguard unintentionally skirmished with Mitsunari's lead troops when they stumbled into them in the dark. The Tokugawa commander pulled back slightly and set up his men facing the enemy. Both forces waited until the fog, which one contemporaneous document describes as "lying thick between the mountains," began to lift.[20] As the air started to clear, the battle began when the front lines began to clash, and a Tokugawa troop of arquebusiers started shooting volleys toward the Western Army.[21] The combined sound of these two aggressive acts signaled to all those gathered in Sekigahara that hostilities had commenced (figure 27).

Most of the Eastern Army commanders on the field craved a direct encounter with Ishida Mitsunari, knowing that killing him and bringing his head to Ieyasu would represent the greatest victory of the day. The warlord Kuroda Nagamasa took a small group of soldiers to the north and turned at the foot of the mountain toward the Ishida camp, flanking the troops of Shima Sakon and Mitsunari that were fighting on the front line. They rained gunfire down upon the troops of the Western Army, causing many casualties, and, more importantly, the collapse of the front line protecting Mitsunari.[22] Seeing this break in the line, the Eastern Army commanders in the vicinity urged their troops to charge, and Ishida's large force looked close to capitulating. Mitsunari, however, had brought some large hand cannons (*ishibiya*) from Osaka Castle and quickly ordered that they be fired on the advancing forces of the Eastern Army. These weapons, used primarily for ceremonial purposes, are unlikely to have done much damage, but did reportedly contribute to the halt of the advance of the pro-Tokugawa forces, perhaps simply because of the loud noise they created. The Eastern Army troops also perhaps encountered screens of sharpened bamboo and other temporary fortifications that stopped their momentum.[23] The failure of this push to reach Mitsunari must have been disappointing for Ieyasu; on the other hand, significant damage had been done to the Western Army, and the weakness of the deployment of the various anti-Tokugawa troops, despite their superior positions, had been exposed.

It was now midmorning, and Mitsunari decided to launch the next phase of his plan to crush Ieyasu and his allies. He ordered that a signal fire be lit

Figure 27. Folding screen illustrating the Battle of Sekigahara, detail. Edo period, 17th century. Osaka Castle Museum

on the mountain behind him, which was a prearranged message to two of the generals stationed outside of the valley—Kobayakawa Hideaki to the south and Mōri Hidemoto to the east—that the time to enter the field of battle had arrived. Hideaki's large force and the four units positioned in front of him would swoop down from the southwest, while Mōri Hidemoto's large force would attack Ieyasu (who had yet to enter the battle) from behind, destroying the progress of the Eastern Army and surrounding them with fresh, hostile forces. The Tokugawa troops would be caught in a trap, surrounded on all sides and unable to escape.

Despite the clear signal sent by the fire, neither warlord moved or responded. Mitsunari, surely with some sense of trepidation, quickly sent a messenger to Hideaki, who was nearer to him, urging him to act, but received no reply. The reason for the Kobayakawa lord's silence was his decision to change sides and support the Tokugawa, which would not become clear until he ordered his troops to enter into battle in support of the Eastern Army. Most primary sources and modern historians credit Hideaki's treachery to the secret messages that Ieyasu had reportedly been sending him to convince him to change sides.[24] Though the actual process by which these messengers would have reached Hideaki the night before is hard to imagine (with so many troops on the move and the area around his camp dominated by Western Army forces), still, it is not impossible to believe that some form of surreptitious communication transpired. Hideaki may have been unsure of how to proceed, or afraid; he was reportedly a drunkard and not particularly brave, and on one occasion had to borrow money from his adopted mother-in-law, Hideyoshi's widow (and the Tokugawa sympathizer) Kita no Mandokoro (also known as Nei, Nene, and Kōdai'in).[25] It seems equally likely, however, that Hideaki was biding his time to see which side would have the advantage. At this point, the answer to this question was not yet apparent. The Western Army held superior positions around Sekigahara, but the Eastern Army had the momentum.

A similar if somewhat more dramatic scenario was playing out below Mount Nangū to the east, where Mōri Hidemoto's large army was camped at the base of the mountain, and Kikkawa Hiroie—a vassal of the Mōri house and the leader of the Mōri vanguard—occupied the main route down from the mountain to the main road into Sekigahara. Hiroie was well known as a politician and commander, having played a key role in the survival of the Mōri house during a period of upheaval and having acquired a reputation on the field of battle during the Imjin War. However, he had been contacted on 9/14 by two of Ieyasu's vassals, Honda Tadakasu and Ii Naomasa, and given an oath to switch to Ieyasu's side in exchange for protection from "undeserved penalties." Hiroie thus believed that siding with the Tokugawa—despite Mōri Terumoto's position as one of the Toyotomi elders and Hidemoto's determination to take part in the battle—would save the Mōri house in these times of civil war.[26] Accordingly, Hiroie used his position as leader of the vanguard troops of the Mōri forces stationed on Mount Nangū to block access to the battlefield and acknowledged neither the signal of Mitsunari nor the entreaties of Hidemoto. The other units stationed around Mount Nangū were similarly bound to follow the lead of the vanguard and thus were also prevented from marching to the road, turning to the west, and joining the conflict.[27] Even in war, ritual could serve as a weapon, and in this case the ceremonial order of attack prevented a major force from participating in the battle. Mōri Hidemoto and his men couldn't even see the conflict that they could hear.

Kobayakawa Hideaki, on the other hand, occupied a position from which he could view the entire field of battle as he waited and decided how to act.

Camped on the side of Mount Matsuo, he could see directly below him the ongoing struggle below, but still made no move to act. Finally, Ieyasu decided to force the issue and ordered some of his arquebusiers to fire their guns in the direction of the Kobayakawa troops, not as an attack but as a forceful invitation. In response to this communication and perhaps his own internal calculus, Hideaki decided the time had come to support the Tokugawa cause and ordered his troops to swoop down into the flank of the Western Army below him, and these troops were soon overwhelmed.[28]

Seeing this development, Ieyasu finally ordered his own troops to enter the battle. As Kasaya Kazuhiko remarks, it is strange to think that the men under the Tokugawa lord's immediate command didn't even participate in the Battle of Sekigahara until it was almost over, but perhaps this hesitation was a sign that he recognized the great peril his forces were in when they entered the box-shaped valley of Sekigahara.[29] Too many variables were in play, and if anything had gone wrong—if Kobayakawa hadn't defected, if the Mōri had indeed joined the combat—then we can hypothesize that he would have needed those men to protect his own retreat.

The entry of both Kobayakawa Hideaki's forces and Ieyasu's troops inundated the Western Army after just a few hours and can be seen as the major tipping point in the battle. Mitsunari's coalition was crumbling everywhere on the battlefield. One veteran general of the Western Army, Ōtani Yoshitsugu, receiving reports that his forces were being decimated by the Kobayakawa, assessed the situation and opted not to flee but rather to commit ritual suicide, perhaps because he was sickly (he suffered from leprosy) or perhaps because of the futility of his position.[30] The Western Army forces stationed on and around Mount Nangū—all of those blocked, in effect, by Kikkawa's refusal to lead them into battle—learned of the defeat of Mitsunari's forces and fled toward their own home provinces as well.[31] All that remained were the troops of Ishida Mitsunari, who found themselves besieged by the combined forces of the Eastern Army, betrayed by Kobayakawa and Kikkawa, and one by one, abandoned by their allies. Mitsunari had, however, chosen his position on the field of battle well. He was able to retreat into the forested cover provided by Mount Ibuki on the northern side of the valley.[32] Five days later, Ieyasu's soldiers captured Mitsunari in the hills north of Lake Biwa.[33] Less than two weeks after, on the first day of the tenth month, Ishida Mitsunari and two of his confederates were executed at the Rokujō-gawara execution grounds in Kyoto. Their decapitated heads were displayed at Sanjō Bridge in the heart of the city, a long-standing tradition of publicly exhibiting this most identifiable body part as a signifier of power.[34] "It was a clear day," according to one diarist; "More than ten thousand came to look," claimed another.[35]

TAKING HEADS AND PERFORMANCE REVIEW

Let us return to the day of the battle. Ieyasu's army had, through a combination of planning and a great deal of luck, prevailed. That same afternoon, the Tokugawa lord next turned to a key ritual of war, as important in terms of the sociopolitical connections that sustained his authority as the awarding of land or the tides of battle: the "examination of heads" (*kubi jikken*) of the vanquished enemy. This rite was a chance to quantify and qualify acts of valor in a semipublic setting, naming accomplishments and congratulating allies in a kind of performance review that was key to the cementing of bonds of fealty. The examination of heads was no euphemism, though; actual, decapitated heads, cut off of enemies in the field using swords (while the battle was mostly fought with guns, pikes, spears, and other weapons), were washed if necessary and then placed before Ieyasu so he could verify the identities of vanquished commanders.[36] (The heads of common foot soldiers were neither taken nor examined, but piled into mounds.)

This practice originated in the necessities of warfare going back as far as the Heian period. Later, in the early medieval period, head collecting was useful because warrior aristocrats who wore substantial layers of makeup could only be identified through careful cleaning of the head followed by close examination.[37] Afterward the heads were typically buried, though in some cases they were displayed publicly.[38] Over time, the emphasis shifted to the ability of individual warriors to document in material fashion their work. Chroniclers commented that the taking of heads gradually became a means of providing evidence of one's accomplishments, "tangible proof of battle service."[39] In the early medieval period some commanders tried to curtail the practice because of the danger it posed to soldiers who became preoccupied in the midst of battle, but the practice persisted. By the second half of the sixteenth century, it had again become standard practice, and records such as *The Chronicle of Lord Nobunaga* are filled with references to heads being taken in the hundreds and even thousands.[40]

Sekigahara's version of this grisly process is recorded in several sources, though the physical act of the examination is glossed over and the emphasis instead is put on the performance review. The early modern history/hagiography *War Tales of the Keichō Era (Keichō gunki)* notes that "When the battle was over, his Lordship put on his helmet, sat on a camp stool on the bank of the Fuji River, and summoned his generals to discuss the accomplishments of each." He praised various vassals for their actions. He stood up from his stool and took Ii Naomasa's hand, saying that the victory was the result of his meritorious actions. He gave many of his generals gifts and thanked all of them for their participation in the day's "work" (literally known as *hataraki,* the term that would later come to mean labor).[41] Then Kobayakawa Hideaki, the turncoat, entered the gathering and bowed down before Ieyasu's chair, apologetic for his previous support of Mitsunari despite the fact that his switch had in effect guaranteed victory. Ieyasu rewarded him by giving him the honorable position of leading the vanguard in the next battle, the attack on Sawayama Castle, the hereditary headquarters of Ishida Mitsunari.[42] The ritualistic examination of severed heads at the end of a battle is thus a transformative moment in warrior society, in which a set of social bonds and a hierarchy that has just been unmade through acts of brutality is stitched together again in a meeting that resembles the tea gathering, the banquet, or the reception.

We do not know if the heads were specially prepared before this inspection or if they were brought straight from the battlefield. A warrior woman who lived in Ōgaki castle, where Mitsunari had taken up residence before the final battle, reported the following in a much later chronicle known as *O-an's Tales:*

> The severed heads taken by our side also were collected in the Keep. We attached name tags to all of them, to keep track of whose they were. Then we would carefully black the teeth of each head. Do you know why? In the old days, a head with black teeth was prized as the head of a man of rank, so they asked us to blacken the teeth of any head that had white teeth. We weren't frightened of the heads. We would lie down and sleep with blood-stinking heads all around us.[43]

Though not recorded in the primary sources, two physical relics can be seen in Sekigahara to this day that mark the taking of heads. The two "head mounds" (*kubizuka*) are called the Eastern Head Mound and the Western Head Mound, which refer to the two geographical locations of the burial sites of Western Army heads. They are reminders of the physicality of this battle that would come to redefine the political landscape. Though exact casualty figures have never been determined, it is clear that thousands of men died. (Some primary sources claim casualties in the tens of thousands, but such high numbers seem unlikely considering the military technologies that were employed.) The Head Mounds stand as solemn memorials of the violence of this battle, small hills that are literally filled with skulls, decollated heads that have been crushed of life in the course of yet another war.

THE WINTER AND SUMMER SIEGES OF OSAKA CASTLE

Let us turn now to the last major military conflict of Ieyasu's life, the twin sieges of Osaka Castle that marked his last outing as a commander as well as the final gasp of the Toyotomi regime. The conflict was precipitated by a disagreement about ceremony that had its roots in the Tokugawa attempt to regularize ritual power. One example of such an attempt occurred in 1613, when Ieyasu issued a short set of regulations for courtiers, which he sent to Kyoto deputy Itakura Katsushige.

Regulations for Courtiers

Item: Courtiers are to pursue their family studies day and night without negligence.
Item: Whether old or young, anyone who disobeys the regulations or acts in an unbecoming manner will be exiled. The length of punishment will vary according to the seriousness of the crime.
Item: Those on day and night guard duty, old or young, are to serve with diligence. Their deportment must be proper, and when attending the emperor, they must do so according to traditional stipulations.
Item: Whether night or day, it is prohibited to loiter about back alleys and other places where one has no business.
Item: Those who privately engage in inappropriate competitions or associate with vulgar attendants and the like, except [at times of] public festivals, will be punished, as stipulated in preceding articles.
These articles are now in effect. When word [of transgressions] arrives from the regental families or court envoys, the warriors will take appropriate actions.
Keichō 18/6/16 [Ieyasu's red seal]

Overall, these 1613 prohibitions do not seem to be particularly onerous. Instead they prompt us to question the context for their issuance. Ieyasu had already worked to deny the court the power to independently award warriors new rank or promotions in rank, one of the few explicit ways in which the court could involve itself in national politics. These rules, by contrast, seem to focus primarily on livelihood—the instruction that aristocratic families should pursue their studies day and night—and, more importantly, comportment. This proclamation was in response to the increasing frequency of conflicts between Kyoto townspeople and a kind of early Japanese *flâneur:* the ruffians (*kabukimono*), young people of various backgrounds who flaunted outrageous styles and behaviors and in some cases engaged in criminal behavior. Even young men of the aristocracy had been drawn to the style and bravado of this trend, which helps to explain why the issuance of these regulations was well received by conservative members of the court.[44]

More of a blow to courtly independence, and therefore the possibility that aristocrats could influence national politics by supporting the Toyotomi cause, was Ieyasu's issuance of a new set of regulations aimed at eight prominent Buddhist temples in Kyoto. These institutions served as places of residence and, in effect, employment for many retired members of the Imperial Court, and also as conduits through which the court influenced Kyoto society. Known as *Regulations Governing Court Approval of Purple Robes,* these documents essentially curtailed the ability of the eight temples to name priests to the rank of abbot without prior shogunal approval. It is possible, as Lee Butler notes, that the intention of this regulation was not only to weaken the court.[45] Other Buddhist temples around the country were also subjected to a range of regulations during this period, and Ieyasu seemed to have been more interested in Buddhism than ever before, meeting regularly with priests and arranging debates among teachers from different Buddhist schools.[46] In the end the effect, at least, was to create the appearance of a Tokugawa administration that was less and less tolerant of forms of independent political agency, and increasingly concerned with monopolizing authority for itself. This development was in keeping with the growing power of the shogunate, which in early 1614 demanded oaths from Edo city magistrates, elders, and other officials.[47]

Considering this regulation of temples in 1613, or what we might see as the attempt of a secular institution to control a sacred one, it is perhaps not surprising that the spark that ignited the final conflict between the Tokugawa and the Toyotomi was a ritual object produced and deployed in a Buddhist mortuary context. It is well established that the Toyotomi used the visual, material, and sacred realms to expand and to perpetuate the influence of their house even after Hideyoshi's death, building, in part, on Hideyoshi's own masterful awareness of the hybrid religious and political power of art. Hideyori's dedication to rebuilding Hōkōji Temple, located adjacent to the Toyokuni Shrine that housed the deified spirit of his father, was a continuation of this practice. Hōkōji was one of many grand Hideyoshi building projects; this one was dedicated to providing a Great Buddha and Great Buddha Hall to Kyoto that would rival the famous one at Tōdaiji in Nara.[48] Despite numerous setbacks and enormous costs, Hideyori succeeded in sponsoring the building's reconstruction and notably the recasting of the huge Great Buddha statue by 1612; by 1614, the final pieces of the puzzle—the bell tower and gates—were ready to be unveiled. All that remained was the dedication of the temple itself, which required permission from the shogunate to proceed.

The resulting knot of letters of request, disagreements about ceremony and propriety, accusations, and counteraccusations is difficult to untangle, but is best understood as a kind of turf battle over religious ritual. Ieyasu was working hard, through his own conversations with experts in Shingon and Tendai Buddhist ritual as well as through the many prohibitions issued to temples and shrines in this period, to tame the plethora of religious conventions so as to make them, one suspects, more easily manipulated by the Tokugawa. Hideyori, through a kind of independent willfulness or perhaps a deliberate attempt to undermine such Tokugawa monopolies, resisted, repeatedly suggesting that the dedication ceremonies proceed according to his particular demands and vision.[49] In the seventh month, Katagiri Katsumoto—a warlord who had served as chamberlain to Hideyori and his mother since Sekigahara, and who was one of the primary Toyotomi negotiators with the Tokugawa—sent another in a string of letters to Ieyasu with detailed information about various aspects of the proposed ceremonies, including the text of the inscription on the huge bronze bell that was intended for the bell tower at the temple. The text of this inscription inspired ire on the part of Ieyasu's advisers, who read the particular Chinese characters as subtly implying Toyotomi parity with the Tokugawa.[50] Historians have interpreted this event in varying ways, with the two most common interpretations being that it was a legitimate Tokugawa critique of sloppy and offensive work by the Toyotomi; or alternatively, that it was a manufactured crisis, a kind of personal pretext for Ieyasu to go to war. The truth is that we cannot know, based on extant reliable evidence, if either of these readings is accurate, though throughout this book I have attempted to argue for the political and social significance of ritual as well as of material culture.

However, a crisis it was. On 1614/9/7 the Tokugawa required the major warlords of western Japan, including the Mōri, the Nabeshima, and the Shimazu, to sign documents swearing fealty to Ieyasu and Hidetada (or "both lordships" [*ryō gosho sama*]) in person in Edo, apparently in anticipation of the conflict to come.[51] By the end of the ninth month, it became clear that both sides were headed for a violent confrontation. The Toyotomi had a falling out with Katagiri Katsumoto, and he and many others who had worked to facilitate a compromise left Osaka Castle to return to their home domains.[52] On 10/1 Ieyasu decided that an attack on Osaka was necessary, and he instructed Hidetada to order the warlords of eastern Japan to prepare their armies for battle.[53] For the next week, Ieyasu and Hidetada both worked their various political channels to prepare for the coming conflict. Many of the western warlords, who had historically supported the Toyotomi cause, were now in residence in Edo, and therefore were essentially held hostage by the Tokugawa. Likewise, a constant stream of generals made their way to Sunpu during this period to be interviewed by Ieyasu in preparation. Decisions about the management of the assault were made as well: Ieyasu would travel with the army to Osaka to direct the battle, and shogun Hidetada would stay behind in Edo for a while before traveling separately with the main Tokugawa force to the west.[54]

Toppling the Toyotomi would be no easy task. Hideyori had attracted huge numbers of disenfranchised samurai (*rōnin*) as well as the forces of warlords who had decided to throw in their lot with Hideyoshi's son.[55] Some historians estimate the force inside and around Osaka Castle to have numbered more than one hundred thousand, while the combined Tokugawa forces are estimated to have been nearly twice that number. Additionally, Osaka Castle was one of the most impressive fortresses in the landscape of premodern Japanese history, a compound consisting of a main keep with an impressive tower, an inner bailey (*honmaru*), an outer bailey (*ninomaru*), an outermost bailey (*sannomaru*), and an outermost citadel (*sogamae*). The Jesuit Luis Frois reported that sixty thousand people worked on the original excavation of the outer bailey's moat, and thousands of boats were used to transport stone to the castle, which was protected not only by moats but also by the Yodogawa River. The compound was sturdily built but also lavishly decorated. The main tower was adorned with motifs of paulownia, chrysanthemum, peony, herons, and tigers in gold, and the roof glittered with gold foil along the rafters that contrasted with the blue ceramic roof tiles. The bridge connecting the inner and outer bailey was known as the Bridge to the Pure Land (*Gokurakubashi*) and was notable for its elaborate roof and watchtower.[56]

After arriving separately in Kyoto, Ieyasu and Hidetada launched their armies south toward Osaka on 11/15, and several days later set up their headquarters on appropriate hills that would afford strategic vantage points of the region. This engagement would prove to be an entirely different sort of conflict from the Battle of Sekigahara, which involved huge numbers of men but which was decided in a mere afternoon. What Ieyasu and Hidetada faced in the fortress of Osaka was a siege that could go on for years, an outcome that the aged Ieyasu no doubt wanted to avoid. Therefore, the Tokugawa approach was slow and deliberate by comparison with Sekigahara, but sharply determined to attain a result. On the morning of 11/19, Ieyasu met with his generals to study maps of the region. He then led his men in a successful attack on a fort at the mouth of the Kizu River.[57] This was followed by several small battles over the next few days,[58] which went the way of the Tokugawa and gave their forces control over the various small fortified structures surrounding the main Osaka Castle compound. However, initial attempts to assault the fortifications surrounding the castle were unsuccessful.[59] Ieyasu next turned to his artillery, calling forward a range of guns to fire on the castle, including some heavy cannons of European manufacture and others procured locally, in Sakai.[60] This approach, which began on 1614/12/16, is not believed to have done any significant damage to the keep itself, but rather to have produced a psychological effect among the castle residents that, combined with enormous battle cries from the Tokugawa forces, prevented those inside Osaka Castle from relaxing or sleeping.[61] A description from the aforementioned *O-an's Tales* conveys the disturbance of cannon fire in this period (though not in this particular battle): "When they fired those cannon, it was horrendous; the turrets would shiver and sway, and the very earth seemed as if it would split open. For the frailer-spirited sorts of ladies, that was enough to make them faint on the spot."[62] This assault on the minds of the Toyotomi supporters, along with a number of small skirmishes, continued with little real progress, even though gunfire "fell like rain" upon the castle.[63] However, the bombardment did lead to the beginning of discussions within the castle, led by the women around Hideyori who had significant influence over him, regarding the possibility of conditionally accepting Ieyasu's peace overtures. Various proposals were made, modified, and rejected, until agreement emerged around the following points, many of which were in response to initial Tokugawa proposals:

> The various disenfranchised samurai (*rōnin*) gathered in Osaka Castle would be allowed to disperse peacefully (without interrogation).
> Hideyori's landed income would be guaranteed.
> Hideyori's mother Yodotono would not be required to go to Edo as a hostage.
> If Osaka Castle were to be turned over to the Tokugawa, some other suitable territory would be assigned to the Toyotomi.
> Hideyori's welfare would be protected without any double-dealing.[64]

Noticeably, these common points of agreement did not include details about the immediate aftermath of the siege, the treatment and occupation of Osaka Castle, or the specific responsibilities of either the Tokugawa or Toyotomi side in the months ahead. Still, both sides called off hostilities and began limited drawdowns of forces. Ieyasu returned to Nijō Castle in Kyoto, where he met with courtiers who must have been relieved by the end of hostilities.[65]

Shogun Hidetada, however, did not leave Osaka and return to Edo as might have been expected, but stayed for some time in the city. Notably, on 12/27 he sent a vassal to examine the condition of the moats around Osaka Castle.[66] To truly pacify the fortress, these significant obstacles would have to be filled in. This step was surely part of Ieyasu's and Hidetada's plan for the immediate post-siege settlement, but the degree to which it entered into the negotiations between the Tokugawa and Toyotomi is difficult to ascertain. Later accounts of the winter siege claim that the Tokugawa engaged in subterfuge about their plan or, perhaps, decided after the fact that this weakening of the castle defenses was necessary. It appears from contemporaneous documentation, however, that the Tokugawa planned all along to fill in the moats of the second and third compounds of the castle, while leaving the innermost moat untouched. By the end of the first month of 1615, much of this work was completed, and it cannot have gone unnoticed by the residents of the keep.[67] Hidetada only left for Kyoto on 1/19, and then for Edo on 1/28. A messenger brought Ieyasu the news that the filling of the moats was completed on the first day of the second month.[68]

The irruption of the siege did not allow a simple return to normalcy, however. Throughout the second and third months of the year, Hidetada and Ieyasu met secretly, sent messengers to each other for confidential conferences, and otherwise continued, in a cloak-and-dagger fashion, to plan for the next stage of the conflict with the Toyotomi.[69] A palpable tension gripped everyone involved: in the middle of the second month, a rumor circulated among the western warlords that Ieyasu and Hidetada were planning to suddenly return to Kyoto, perhaps to renew the assault on Hideyori.[70] In the third month, a similar rumor circulated in Kyoto.[71] Furthermore, messengers arrived at Sunpu with regularity from Hideyori, and from various parties in Osaka and Kyoto, delivering news, gifts, and requests.[72] Perhaps the most important message received in this period, however, came from Itakura Katsushige, the Tokugawa deputy in Kyoto. Katsushige informed Ieyasu that the Toyotomi were reinstalling many of the defensive measures around Osaka Castle, and this process included dredging the moats, storing foodstuffs, and rallying (and paying) disenfranchised samurai.[73] By the beginning of the fourth month, Ieyasu and Hidetada were ready to confirm the rumors and to return to Osaka.[74] Ieyasu left Sunpu on 4/4 and Hidetada departed Edo six days later. They issued military codes, they commanded their military commanders to gather in Fushimi Castle, and otherwise prepared for battle as they had less than half a year earlier.[75] Ieyasu arrived in Kyoto on 4/18 and took up his usual residence in Nijō Castle. Three days later, Hidetada arrived at Fushimi Castle, and a cavalcade of visitors—members of the court, warlords duly summoned to battle, vassals, and messengers—streamed through the reception halls of both men.[76] The profoundly communal nature of war, the centrality of the politics of sociability in the gathering of forces intended to destroy such relations, was never more apparent.

The Tokugawa launched their forces on 5/5, and despite various attempts by Hideyori's generals to slow their advance, successfully pushed through

Figure 28. Folding screen illustrating the Summer Siege of Osaka. Edo period, 17th century. Osaka Castle Museum

to the city itself by 5/7. Hideyori and his generals decided to meet them in the area to the south of the castle, around Tennōji Temple, rather than succumb to a siege of the castle with its compromised defenses (figure 28). This move amounted to a kind of suicide mission, as Ieyasu's army is said to have numbered at least 150,000, while the Toyotomi forces at this point amounted to around 50,000, making this one of Japan's largest—and most lopsided—battles.[77] The result was entirely predictable; despite a brave plan and several hours of valiant effort, the Toyotomi forces were obliterated by the main Tokugawa force at Tennōji and also at Okayamaguchi where Hidetada protected the Tokugawa flank. Hideyori's men began to retreat toward the castle before he could ride out to glory with his own personal guard. Furthermore, a fire had somehow erupted inside the castle, purportedly in the kitchen. By the late afternoon of 5/7, Ieyasu's forces were shooting at the keep as they had during the winter campaign, and the situation was rapidly descending into complete chaos. Hideyori's generals began committing ritual suicide in anticipation of the imminent collapse of the inner defenses.

This war was perhaps more destructive than any preceding battle in Ieyasu's career. The battle occurred not in a rural valley, as had been the case with Sekigahara, but in the middle of a thriving urban center that was home to an unusually large and elaborate castle. Men and women of different status groups and occupations were directly threatened by the outbreak of hostilities, and those that were trapped in the keep had no choice but to flee, desperately, while the structure collapsed around them. Genre screens representing the battle illustrate the desperate attempts of women to swim across the river while troops, hell-bent on looting and pillaging, chase them from the shoreline. Civilians beg for their lives as samurai tower over them, swords raised. Bodies float in the water. In one particularly arresting scene, a weeping woman from the castle is forced to hand over her gowns to a poor footsoldier wielding a pike. In another, soldiers escort a young woman prisoner who is looking back at her destroyed home. And in another example of the resonance between the traffic in bodies and the collecting of objects, one scene shows a samurai from Ieyasu's army standing guard over a significant pile of confiscated treasures: swords, suits of armor, lacquered boxes, and other famous objects of the defeated Toyotomi.[78]

Early the following morning, Hideyori ascended to the top of the keep to kill his mother, his wife, Senhime, and himself, but was stopped by a vassal.[79] Senhime—Shogun Hidetada's daughter—was sent outside to the Tokugawa forces, and Hideyori and Yododono ended their own lives, though the exact details are not known and rumors that Hideyori had escaped haunted the Tokugawa for years.[80] Richard Cocks, head of the British East India Company trading post in Hirado, provides a useful summary:

> They say the taking of this fortress hath cost above 100,000 mens lives on the one parte and other, and that on the Prince Hideyoris parte no dead man of accompt is found with his head on, but all cut ofe, because they should not be knowne, to seek reveing against their frendes and parents after. Nether (as some say) can the body of Hideyori be fownd; soe that many think he is secretly escaped. But I cannot beleev it. Only the people of these sothern parts speake as they wold have it, because they effect the yong man more than the ould.[81]

Though it may not have numbered one hundred thousand lives, the victory over the Toyotomi resulted in the collection of a huge number of decapitated heads, and a head examination ceremony was held, though the details are not recorded. Stories of Tokugawa Ieyasu examining the head of the Toyotomi vassal Kimura Shigenari, who died while leading his troops in a direct assault on the approaching Tokugawa forces, circulated in the Tokugawa period and are represented in the Meiji-period woodblock print found on the cover of this book (figure 29). Even more interesting is the existence of a range of documents that record some of the details of head taking in this conflict, documents that would have been submitted to officials for recognition after the battle was completed.[82] It was vital that a witness be present at a head taking to verify the identity of the vanquished warrior.[83] When a witness was not present, warriors seeking reward for their labor had to lodge special requests and were not likely to be successful. This requirement was, of course, to prevent warriors from taking credit for the actions of others by taking the heads of corpses on the battlefield or by otherwise

Figure 29. Print of Tokugawa Ieyasu Examining a Head. Tsukioka Yoshitoshi (1839–1892). Meiji period, 1875. 16.3 x 22.7 cm. Los Angeles County Museum of Art

claiming kills that were not their own. Another item in the text noted the importance of taking both the head and the helmet in the case of particularly high-ranking foes; it was an embarrassment to take the head but ignore or discard the helmet. Battlefield collecting thus focused both on body parts and material culture, another clear linkage between acquisition and the violence of war in the late sixteenth and early seventeenth centuries.[84]

SALVAGED SWORDS

Ieyasu returned to Kyoto on 1615/5/8 amid a torrential downpour and began the process of administering the aftermath of the battle, a task that would require him to remain in Kyoto for a further five months.[85] The first visitor, the day of Hideyori's death and Ieyasu's own arrival in Kyoto, was Nabeshima Katsushige, a former Toyotomi vassal who had fought for Ishida Mitsunari before Sekigahara but who joined Ieyasu and led troops for the Tokugawa in both the Winter and Summer Sieges of Osaka Castle. Nabeshima could provide Ieyasu with a different account of the battle, from the point of view of the field, and allow him to start gaining a broader perspective on the huge conflict that had ended surprisingly quickly.[86] Although Ieyasu and Hidetada had prepared assiduously, eviscerating the defenses of Osaka Castle and assembling an army that was too large to fail, the speed of the victory, compared to the month required to complete the first siege, was still startling. On 5/10 Ieyasu assembled the major warlords in Nijō Castle and presented awards to various commanders for their actions in Osaka, including gifts of tea utensils and other treasures.[87]

After holding confidential talks with Hidetada about the outcome of the battle on 5/11, he then began meeting with the various elites of Kyoto: temple leaders and courtiers all made their way to Nijō in the following days to meet with Ieyasu and, notably, on 5/15 to witness a religious debate among Tendai priests.[88] Three days later, another debate followed at Nijō, this time on the topic of Buddhist logic (J: *inmyō;* Sanskrit: *hetu-vidyā*) and in front of a larger audience including courtiers, temple and shrine heads, and numerous warlords.[89] Three days later, yet another debate occurred among Shingon priests.[90] Two days later, after a meeting with the shogun, Ieyasu sponsored another debate, this time among Tendai priests.[91] These debates point to a shift in Ieyasu's attention away, perhaps, from temporal affairs and more and more toward the problem of his own mortality. The business of government was mostly out of his hands at this point, though he still took responsibility for major decisions and was clearly the primary authority of the family and the shogunate. The bureaucracy had developed sufficiently, however, for him to be able to pursue other matters. Religious debates continued with great regularity alongside the politics of sociability, with Ieyasu giving and receiving gifts—to the emperor, from Shimazu Iehisa, and so on—in a systematic fashion.

In the sixth month he also invited Oda Uraku—a former priest, a prominent tea master, and the younger brother of Nobunaga—to Kyoto, and asked him to investigate what had happened to the ceramic tea caddies that were lost in the destruction of the Osaka fortress.[92] Other sources record that Ieyasu similarly asked two lacquerers to repair tea caddies broken in the blaze.[93] A week later, he commanded a sword maker to reforge famous swords that had also been damaged when the castle burned.[94] Ieyasu's attention to the material culture possessed by the Toyotomi is usually ignored in accounts of his life and of the long sixteenth century because the policies issued around this time are widely seen as providing the legal framework for the Tokugawa social and political system that would dominate Japan for the next 250 years.[95] But Ieyasu's insistence that his underlings find and reclaim the most precious things associated with the Toyotomi regime serves as a reminder that art objects, too, had the power to affect their society. By excavating, repairing, and then keeping these things associated with the now-vanquished Toyotomi, Ieyasu and his heirs controlled, to some degree, the memory of Hideyoshi and his line.

One of the best-known objects rescued and rehabilitated from the destruction of Osaka Castle is the tea caddy known as Nitta. Like First Flower (discussed in chapter 2), this small ceramic container (8.6 cm tall and 7.9 cm in diameter at the widest point) dates to around the thirteenth century in the Southern Song dynasty in China. The pot is simply thrown and trimmed, and decorated with an iron-brown glaze that covers the top portion of the vessel and drips down onto the dark clay on one side.[96] The pedigree of the piece is one reason that Nitta was so highly valued. According to the tea diary *Record of Yamanoue Sōji,* this tea caddy was once owned by Murata Jukō (1423–1502), an early merchant tea practitioner from Sakai who is credited with beginning the tradition of rustic (*wabi*) tea that became dominant in later centuries.[97] The next known owner was Miyoshi Masanaga (1508–1549), a warlord and tea practitioner from Shikoku. Later Oda Nobunaga owned Nitta, followed by Ōtomo Sōrin (1530–1587; also Yoshishige), another warlord and tea practitioner who also is well known as one of the more prominent Christian converts of the sixteenth century. Sōrin was an avid collector of tea utensils, and only parted with this piece when his increasingly dire political and economic circumstances demanded it. The Jesuit Luis Frois recorded this sad moment in 1585:

> King Francisco (Otomo Yoshishige) became poor after the people of four kingdoms (Buzen, Chikugo, Chikuzen, and Higo) rose in rebellion and refused to obey his son, the prince (Yoshimune). And so he ordered that a utensil, very highly prized in Japan, should be sold in the city of Sakai. This was a small glazed porcelain cup shaped like a pomegranate, and it was used to hold certain leaves ground into a powder, which they drink with hot water on every occasion. Faxiba Chicugendono (Hideyoshi), lord of the greater and more important part of Japan, heard about this precious jewel and he yearned to obtain it for it was a very famous piece in Japan. He gave him fifteen thousand crowns for it, and to show his special favor, he ordered that the money should be carried overland, via the kingdom of Yamaguchi, to Bungo, which is a very long route.[98]

The piece stayed with the Toyotomi until the destruction of Osaka Castle, which gave Ieyasu the opportunity to finally obtain another of the three best tea caddies in Japan. Today, it is impossible to see the fine lacquer repairs to the piece that allowed it to be reassembled.

Many of the additional surviving, reclaimed heirlooms from Osaka Castle are swords. The dagger known as Ebina Kokaji (figure 30), for example, was made by the renowned Heian-period (794–1185) smith Sanjo

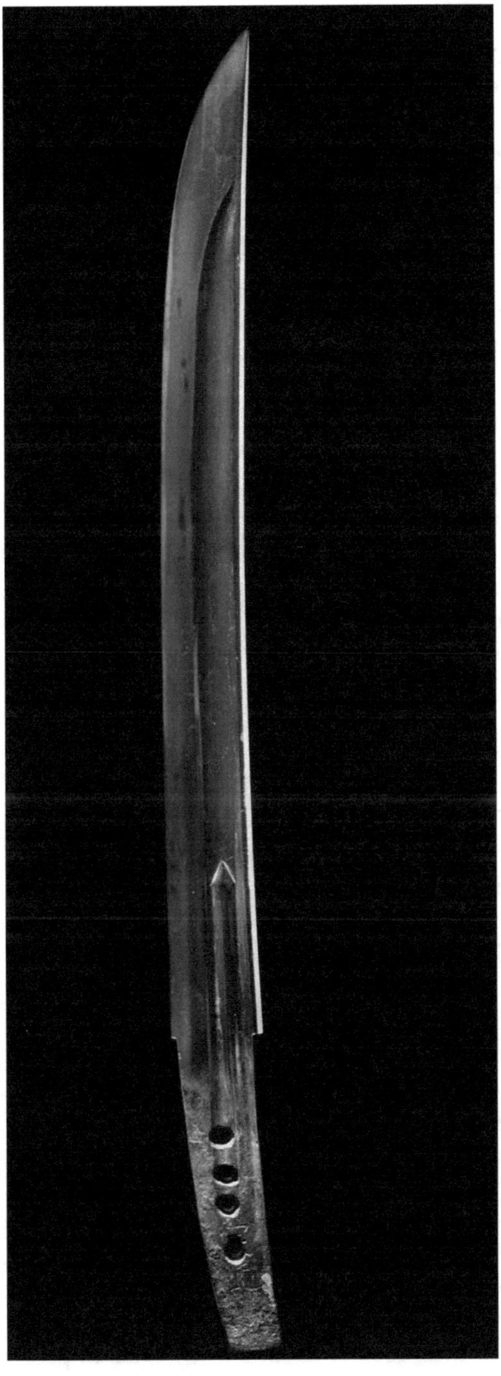

Figure 30. Dagger (*tantō*) named Ebina Kokaji. Sanjō Munechika. Heian period, 12th century. Length 29.7 cm. Tokugawa Art Museum Collection, by permission of the Tokugawa Art Museum / DNPartcom

Kokaji Munechika (who himself is the subject of much mythologization, including a Noh play in which he is assisted by a fox spirit in forging a blade for the emperor).[99] This prized weapon is 29.7 centimeters in length and was reportedly once owned by the Ashikaga shoguns. Other examples from the Kamakura period (1185–1334) include the long sword Ichigo Hitofuri by the sword maker Yoshimitsu and the long sword Nansen by the sword maker Ichimonji. Such swords were vital components of social rituals that helped maintain warrior society—as gifts that were exchanged with great regularity; as symbols of both masculinity and patrimony, as Elizabeth Oyler reminds us; and as practical tools that could be brandished to strike opponents or remove heads at the end of a battle.[100] Indeed, stories that circulated throughout Japan in the Tokugawa period associated Ieyasu with the lethality of his impressive collection of blades, such as the legend of the Miike Sword. According to this hagiographic tale, Ieyasu on his deathbed ordered that this heirloom weapon be tested on a convicted felon, a practice known as "trial cutting" that was not uncommon in the age of Pax Tokugawa.[101] After learning that "it had cut though him all the way down to the block without a problem," he placed the weapon at his side and vowed that "with the power of this sword he would protect his descendants of all generations to come."[102] This description explicitly links the violent potential of the blades collected and worn by the warrior class to the power of the Tokugawa to continue ruling Japan.

Ieyasu's salvaging of both swords and ceramic tea caddies from the ruins of Osaka Castle casts both types of objects into the same category, as things that are both symbolically significant enough and durable enough to be rescued. More broadly, however, the differences between swords—and the larger category of material culture explicitly associated with warfare, including armor, helmets, and other heirloom weapons—and tea utensils such as tea caddies are considerable. Famous tea caddies of the sort acquired by Ieyasu, as we have seen repeatedly, often had names, biographies, and fairly fleshed out genealogies of ownership. Heirloom swords, on the other hand, were usually known by the name of their maker or perhaps a place name and carried less documentation of their trajectory through various collections. For some particularly well known tea utensils, we can trace their appearances at multiple tea gatherings and other semipublic events, punctiliously recorded in the tea diaries (*chakaiki*) and other forms of documentation that became increasingly significant among commoner tea practitioners in the sixteenth century. Such careful record keeping was central to the emerging identity of tea practitioners as a distinct social and cultural group. No such record exists for swords; a register that similarly recorded not just the name and origin of a sword but its record of kills and beheadings on battlefields, not to mention its journey from the hands of one warrior to another, and its exchange in rituals of obeisance and appeal over a period of several hundred years is absent from the known archival collections in Japan. Perhaps the reason for the lack of a record was that the identity of warriors as a distinct social group was firmly established in the practical skills, the martial accomplishments, the social rituals, and the cultural practices that this book explores.

Although these salvaged swords were only a drop in the bucket of Ieyasu's collection, which included more than one thousand heirloom pieces when he died, their reclamation and reforging represented a concerted effort not just to defeat the Toyotomi but to literally accumulate and own the treasured weapons of their now vanquished foe.[103] Like the return of the heirloom sword to Minamoto Yoritomo in *Tale of the Soga Brothers,* the acquisition of these weapons represented Ieyasu's authority and, indeed, were a symbol of the "quieting of swords" or the pacification of the realm, of the Tokugawa's right to rule.[104] This attempt to tidy up after the destruction of the Toyotomi is elided in accounts of the founding of the Tokugawa period and overviews of the beginning of the early modern age in Japan, but, like the destruction of Osaka Castle and the issuance of legal codes, the repossession of these powerful works of art was a fundamentally political act.

CONCLUSION

During Ieyasu's last two months in Kyoto, the shogunate issued several pieces of significant legislation that would become foundational policies for the early modern state. On the thirteenth day of the intercalary seventh month, the shogunate issued the "one province, one castle" policy, which limited each province—but effectively, each notably landed warlord—to one castle, to prevent military buildups and the proliferation of defensive structures of the sort that were so important throughout the sixteenth century.[105] The following month, on 7/7, Hidetada assembled the various warlords in Fushimi Castle, where the adviser to the Tokugawa, Konchiin Sūden, read the new *Code for All Warrior Households.* The group of warrior leaders, perhaps stunned by this new list of limitations to be placed on them and their progeny, then had to sit through a long Noh performance.[106] It is notable that this semipublic piece of political pageantry was hosted not by the retired shogun but by Hidetada, perhaps signaling the full transfer of this-worldly authority to the younger Tokugawa lord. Although historians have frequently referred to this document as a kind of constitution for warrior rule in the Tokugawa period, it was hardly a radical document; rather, it was "ostentatiously traditional," as Harold Bolitho put it, referring to precedent and Chinese texts on government in a relentless use of the past—real and imagined—to prescribe present practices.[107]

This performance was quickly followed by a similar recital on 7/17, in which the Shogun invited members of the court to Nijō Castle for a presentation of *Regulations for the Palace and Nobility.*[108] Ieyasu had ordered various Zen monks in Kyoto to begin work on copying key passages from a number of Chinese and Japanese texts in 1614 to prepare for the issuance of codes, a process that took far longer than he had expected. He also instructed his adviser Sūden to work on this document for months, studying various forms of precedent and citing a number of Chinese texts.[109] The final text explicitly cites *Essentials of Good Government* (Ch: *Zhenguan zhengyao;* J: *Jōgan Seiyō;* Tang dynasty, 7th c.), which Fujiwara Seika had discussed with Ieyasu so many years before and which he had ordered printed through the Ashikaga Gakkō in 1600; as well as the fifty-volume *Essentials of the Many Books* (Ch: *Qun shu zhi yao;* J: *Gunsho chiyō*). Historians have typically interpreted this code as a strong Tokugawa attempt to separate the court from the sphere of politics. Lee Butler, however, has convincingly argued that the code in fact upholds the influence of certain court administrative positions and in general empowers the court, which is consistent with Ieyasu's interest in the power of precedent. All evidence points to Ieyasu's intention to support the interaction between the court and Kyoto's population of commoners and warriors, and also to support their mastery of traditional arts and other family practices. The code also pays scrupulous attention to the politics of court ceremony, detailing seating arrangements, clothing, and other practices that were at the heart of the court's claim to symbolic authority in Japanese society. Ieyasu's overwhelming goal with the issuance of these regulations was not suppression of the court but rather improving—through the regulation of ritual—its order and stability, marred as it had been, like much of Japanese society, by factions and internal politics.[110] Like the two titanic wars that marked the triumph of the Tokugawa in warrior society, these attempts to stabilize the field of symbolic politics relied on rituals to make sense of the messiness of social groupings and their hierarchical relations. Both acts contributed to the making of a society and the defining of a polity that would rule Japan—through the threat of violence and the performance of ritual—for more than 250 years.

CHAPTER SIX

Apotheosis

Ieyasu's Early Modern and Modern Afterlives

In December 1999, the World Heritage Committee of the United Nations Educational, Scientific and Cultural Organization (UNESCO) inscribed the shrines and temples of Nikkō, Japan, on the World Heritage list. The committee acknowledged in its decision that the temples and shrines of Nikkō represent works of architectural and artistic genius; that they are perfect examples of the decorative styles and building designs of the Edo period (1603–1868); and that the entire site of Nikkō is an outstanding instance of a Japanese religious site in which the natural environment informs the sacred meanings of the religious institutions and their objects of veneration. The mountainous region of Nikkō, located eighty-seven miles north of Tokyo, has long held religious significance, with a major shrine that dates back to the eighth century. The primary focus of the site since the seventeenth century, however, is the mausoleum complex known as Tōshōgū (figure 31), which houses one of the most important deities of early modern Japan: Tōshō Daigongen, "Great Avatar Who Illuminates the East," more commonly known as Tokugawa Ieyasu.

This chapter considers the early modern apotheosis of Ieyasu in the magnificent conifer forest of Nikkō as a continuation of the phenomenon of spectacular accumulation. It focuses on the seventeenth-century deification of the Tokugawa founder, the establishment of multiple ritual centers for his worship, the use of material culture in these and other acts of memorialization, and the proliferation of cultural and architectural products related to Ieyasu's memory over the course of the early modern period. The chapter then turns to the modern period, particularly the activities of Tokugawa Yoshichika (1886–1976)—the head of the Owari branch of the Tokugawa family and

Figure 31. Nikkō Tōshōgū, photograph by author

an active politician, scholar, colonial administrator, and philanthropist—who worked to preserve the material legacy of the Tokugawa in wartime Japan. He founded the Tokugawa Art Museum in 1935 and thereby guaranteed that a significant portion of Ieyasu's collection would continue to be displayed, to dynamically changing audiences, becoming a kind of visual substitute for the history of the late sixteenth century.

This chapter also argues that the representation of Ieyasu's life at key moments after his death established discursive conventions that define our understanding of his role in the founding of the early modern state. A genealogy of discourse and representation is at work in the seventeenth-century deification of Ieyasu, the popularization of his cult, and the modern rehabilitation of the founder of the Tokugawa regime after that government was destroyed. This connecting fiber—one that links biography to hagiography to historiography—reveals the diachronic progression of history's making, unmaking, and redeployment according to the needs and interests of historical subjects who operated in changing cultural and socioeconomic contexts. It connects the history of Tokugawa Ieyasu's spectacular accumulation during his life and the circulation of his collection during his afterlife to the story of Japanese national identity and the politics of the display of visual and material culture in museums domestically and abroad, issues that continue to inform scholarly and public debate and, on occasion, stir controversy.[1]

EARLY MODERN APOTHEOSIS

Ieyasu ostensibly left behind a set of final instructions in the last days of his life: "Bury my body at Mount Kunō and have the funeral service at Zōjō Temple. Place the Buddhist mortuary table at Daijū Temple in Mikawa. After a one-year period of mourning, build a small hall at Mount Nikkō and invite the deity. I will become the tutelary deity of the eight provinces of the Kantō."[2] While the deification of humans was extremely rare in practice in medieval Japan,[3] there was an important precedent in Ieyasu's own lifetime: the apotheosis of Ieyasu's former liege and political predecessor, Toyotomi Hideyoshi, from whom the Tokugawa founder undoubtedly appropriated a great deal in his own attempt to pacify, unify, and stabilize the archipelago. Hideyoshi had arranged for his own deification as a Shinto deity—Toyokuni Daimyōjin, or "Most Bright God of Our Bountiful Country"—at a shrine in Kyoto next to Hōkōji, a project that was successful in terms of the grandeur of the visual and material results, as well as the impact on the population of Kyoto, which took part in the Toyokuni festivals with great enthusiasm.[4] Ieyasu was never as gratuitously ambitious as Hideyoshi, but the model of apotheosis as a means of marrying secular and sacred authority with the added value of increasing the family influence through popular ritual practice was surely appealing. On the other hand, Hideyoshi had failed to protect his legacy for his heir, and Ieyasu needed to prevent a similar outcome for his own children. A version of apotheosis that followed upon, but was also distinct from, Hideyoshi's deification was required.[5]

Ieyasu's initial hope was for a simpler, more local process of deification, in which he would be enshrined at Mount Kunō near Sunpu Castle, with his vassal Sakakibara Teruhisa to act as the shrine's priest. When Shogun Hidetada heard of Ieyasu's plan, however, he commanded the Rinzai Zen monk Konchiin Sūden (1569–1633) and the Tendai monk Tenkai (1536–1643), both shogunal advisers, to discuss the deification with Ieyasu, to ensure that it was ritually and politically proper. The "conspicuous proliferation of testamentary stipulations" that ensued was a result of Tenkai's and Sūden's attempts to ensure that their and others' religious and institutional interests were appropriately involved.[6] The decision to build some sort of structure at Nikkō was probably a concession to Tenkai, who had been given the responsibility of supervising the preexisting temple complex on the mountain several years earlier. Later, another religious adviser, the Shinto and Buddhist priest Bonshun (1553–1632), counseled Hidetada on the differences between Buddhist and Shinto funerary practices and between enshrinement as an avatar (*gongen*) and as a god (*myōjin*). Two days after Ieyasu's death, Bonshun officiated at the ceremony (in the tradition of Yoshida Shinto) held in the newly constructed shrine on Mount Kunō, installing Ieyasu's spirit in the main building. Three days later the shogun visited along with other members of the Tokugawa family.[7] This seemingly hastily constructed ritual structure was the "Shrine That Illuminates the East," originally called Tōshōsha but later changed to Tōshōgū.[8]

Rather than representing the end of Ieyasu's biography, however, his enshrinement at Mount Kunō represents the beginning of a new stage in what could be considered as his early modern afterlife. "For the theologians, Tenkai, Sūden, Bonshun, their finest hour had just arrived. Hardly had Ieyasu been enshrined than Tenkai started to object."[9] As the master of the temple complex at Mount Nikkō, Tenkai seemed determined to arrange not a secondary shrine in the Kantō but a complete reconfiguration of the deification of the Tokugawa founder, with nothing less than the removal of Ieyasu's body to Nikkō and the relocation of the worship of this new deity to Tenkai's religious domain. Quarrels among the religious advisers ensued, letters were dispatched to those who might influence the shogun, and as a result, rumors circulated in Kyoto about the conflict. A power struggle over his legacy was surely something that Ieyasu, always attentive to the importance of stability, would have wanted to avoid. Fortunately for the Tokugawa, within a matter of months Tenkai had achieved his victory and emerged as perhaps the most influential Buddhist leader in eastern Japan. He managed to keep Sūden out of the mourning ceremony that Tenkai oversaw at the private family temple of the Tokugawa, Zōjōji, in Edo; likewise, he successfully convinced Hidetada to allow Ieyasu's body[10] to be moved in the tenth month of 1616 to Nikkō, "where, on the seventeenth of the fourth month, exactly one year after his demise, Ieyasu was installed as *daigongen*."[11] Hidetada visited the shrine at that time to mark the anniversary of his father's death, though the structure was still under construction. It was mostly completed in 1619, in time for Hidetada's second visit, and the shogun visited again in 1622 to mark the seven-year death anniversary of Ieyasu.[12] Visiting Nikkō became a ritualized performance of the politics of the Tokugawa state for many later shoguns, a means of demonstrating publicly the shogun's faith to the founder and deity enshrined in the mountain's Tōshōgū.[13]

Within a year of his death, Ieyasu was thus the object of ritual worship and veneration at two separate sites as a result of the rivalry among the Tokugawa's religious advisers. This multiplication illustrates an obvious point about Ieyasu's deification: worshipping the deity that was Tokugawa Ieyasu was a symbolically powerful practice with overt political overtones that could be beneficially appropriated. Constructing a Tōshōgū shrine in which to engage in this ritual form of politics soon emerged as a useful means of arrogating Ieyasu's memory for contemporaneous purposes. Tenkai established a Tōshōgū at the headquarters of his Tendai school in 1617, while the shogunate built a Tōshōgū in Edo Castle in 1618. The heads of the three branch Tokugawa houses likewise constructed Tōshōgū in their domains in 1619 (Nagoya) and 1621 (Mito and Wakayama), a decision followed by various temples and warlords. By the mid-seventeenth century, Tōshōgū had spread to domains and cities across Japan, looking less like a form of familial worship and more like a kind of state-sponsored religion.[14] This expansion does not imply that the worship of Tōshō Daigongen was monolithic. Nakano Mitsuhiro has catalogued the variety of Tōshōgū sites and ritual practices that emerged over the course of the early modern period and argues that the cult's activities (and, though largely unverifiable, beliefs) were heterogeneous in terms of status, geographic region, period, and calendrical context.[15] Even this diversity of practices, however, represented a victory for the Tokugawa, who managed to install their founder not only as an object of veneration but as a nationally significant figure who was celebrated and worshipped in manifold ways: in terms of the legitimacy of the regime, the mode of reverence was perhaps less significant than the fact of reverence.

This nationalization of the worship of Tōshō Daigongen was an incremental process. Perhaps the key period in the expansion of the Tōshōgū as a sacred institution was the reign of the third Tokugawa shogun, Ieyasu's grandson Iemitsu. As has often been noted, Iemitsu was the first Tokugawa shogun to lack experience leading troops into battle and was certainly the first early modern shogunal ruler to have been raised almost entirely within the confines of Edo Castle. Born in 1604, Iemitsu was appointed ruler—despite reportedly being sickly and withdrawn—in 1623 in a repetition of the process by which Ieyasu had retired and forced his contemporaries to accept Hidetada as their next ruler. On 1623/9/27 Hidetada stepped into the position of retired shogun and arranged for the court to appoint his young son to the post of shogun. Iemitsu proved himself to be an active and activist administrator who rather ruthlessly eliminated his talented younger brother and worked in every field to solidify his authority as shogun. Many of the policies that came to be thought of as characterizing the Tokugawa regime—the bureaucratic reach of the shogunate, the severe suppression of Christianity, the system of alternate attendance, and the seclusion policies that kept most foreigners out of Japan and prevented all Japanese from traveling internationally—were his innovations.[16] And, not surprisingly, Iemitsu was the central figure in expanding the worship of Tōshō Daigongen and indeed the actual Tōshōgū structure at Nikkō to a previously unimagined scale.

Iemitsu began his reign with a major renovation of Nijō Castle in Kyoto, the most obvious and central symbol of Tokugawa authority in the imperial capital. The project was "designed to enhance the sophisticated image of the third shogun and to make explicit Iemitsu's function as imperial surrogate."[17] It was part of a larger early Tokugawa culture of architecture-as-politics, or "the psychology of architectural intimidation."[18] This successful building project may have inspired Iemitsu to create a monument for his father Hidetada in 1632, a project that avoided deification but produced a mausoleum in Edo near Zōjōji that "inaugurated the era of Iemitsu's personal power with its bold architectural statement of authority and that set the pattern for the architectural design at Nikkō."[19] This structure, Taitokuin, was separated from the city by impressive walls and large, ornate gates. The worship hall in the center of the compound was accessed by a particularly sumptuous gateway demonstrating "unprecedented rhetorical flourish" and "curvilinear exuberance."[20] This successful project served as the model for Iemitsu's reconstruction of a number of structures at Nikkō, transforming the complex into one of the most elaborate shrine and temple assemblages in Japan.

In 1634 Iemitsu launched this project in Nikkō, which would end up consuming 568,000 *ryō* of gold, 100 *kanme* of silver, and 1,000 *koku* of rice from the treasury of the Tokugawa by the time it was completed two years later.[21] Iemitsu had previously visited Nikkō six times,[22] perhaps felt a great fondness for the place, and also may have understood its potential as a ritual and political site par excellence. The result was a sprawling landscape of temple and shrine structures with connected paths, gateways, and gardens, set amid a towering and awe-inspiring conifer forest (*Cryptomeria japonica*), or, as the UNESCO report puts it, set in a context in which "mountains and forests have a sacred meaning and are objects of veneration."[23] The magnificence of the structures and their surroundings was matched, or perhaps surpassed, by the extravagant decorative programs on the outside and inside of the gates and halls, which collectively amounted to a kind of visual database of more than five thousand Buddhist, Confucian, and Daoist symbols, motifs, and figures carved into the Tōshōgū structure. These included, for example, 644 sacred animals such as Chinese lions (*shishi*) and dragons; 950 birds, including phoenixes and hawks; and 1,423 plants, including peonies, chrysanthemums, and other symbolically significant plant motifs (figure 32).[24] The buildings themselves, which have been fairly well documented in English, are still standing and, thanks to the support of the Japanese government, as well as the UNESCO designation, continue to count as one of the most visited tourist destinations in Japan.[25]

This new site was used almost immediately to mark the twenty-first anniversary of Ieyasu's passing on 1636/4/17. Kobori Enshū (also Masakazu, 1579–1647), a construction magistrate and garden designer who worked for the Tokugawa as a tea master, attended the ceremony organized by Iemitsu on this occasion and in a letter, recorded a poem:

Hi no hikari	[The light of the sun
azuma o terasu	illuminates the east
kamikaze wa kyō yori	a divine wind as of today,
kimi no bandai no koe.	His lordship's infinite voice.]

According to Enshū, after the initial opening of the structure on the seventeenth, two days of ceremonies followed.[26] The desired effect was the draw of this site as a ritual complex, as a natural wonder, and as a powerful statement of Tokugawa authority that marks Nikkō as such a significant transformation in the afterlife of Ieyasu. Through the site, rather than functioning merely as a tutelary deity or intensively worshipped ancestor, Tōshō Daigongen became the keystone of shogunal power, seen particularly clearly in the visits of foreign embassies to Nikkō Tōshōgū. Iemitsu attempted to press this idea upon the Korean ambassador Im Kwang: "If you Three Ambassadors were to make a sightseeing trip [to Nikko,] We would consider it

Figure 32. Nikkō Tōshōgū, photograph by author

a glory for the entire nation. We should be unable to restrain our joy."[27] Although the Korean ambassador could perhaps make sense of this visit as a form of sightseeing, the Tokugawa understood it as a more ritualized journey that demonstrated obeisance. The *Record of the Tokugawa* noted that Im and his entourage "were permitted to make a pilgrimage to Nikkō, just as they had requested."[28] Ryūkyūan embassies and Dutch embassies were similarly required to visit the site.

> By giving the appearance that it was the spontaneous desire of these envoys from abroad to pay homage to 'Gongen sama,' by obtaining gifts and "articles of tribute," such as the Korean bell sent in 1643 or the Dutch chandelier which faces the bell before the Yōmei Gate, to decorate the shrine and further exalt Ieyasu's sanctity, such foreign pilgrimages could not fail to serve as a mechanism for extending the numinous range of the cult of Ieyasu beyond the immediate geographic boundaries of Japan.[29]

The resulting "illusion of Japanese centrality and primacy" was at the heart of shogunal policies regarding status, the control of religion, and travel. These policies claimed to protect and to empower Japan, they emanated from the Tokugawa administration, and they were reinforced and legitimated through the rituals and spectacle of the worship of Tōshō Daigongen.

Another significant aspect of the early modern afterlife of Tokugawa Ieyasu was the production, circulation, protection, and deployment of documents and objects associated with his life and memory. Ieyasu took some pains to protect his material heritage with instructions to divide his enormous accumulation of visual and material culture after his death. Though the exact process of this division is not known, some documentary evidence has survived that demonstrates that probate dictated that certain objects and set amounts of cash[30] passed to each branch Tokugawa house, as well as to the main shogunal branch in Edo and probably to the Tōshōgū on Mount Kunō and Nikkō as well. The most important record of probate is preserved by the Owari Tokugawa, *The Record of Utensils Inherited from Sunpu Castle* (*Sunpu owakemono odôgû chô*, figure 33).[31] This text was compiled according to Ieyasu's prior instructions over a period of two years from 1616 to 1618 at Sunpu Castle, and lists objects in eleven registers:

Register of swords 御腰物之帳
Register of handle ornaments 目貫かうかい帳
Register of gold and silver utensils 金銀之帳
Register of various utensils 色々御道具帳
Register of various utensils 色々御道具帳

Register of clothing 色々絹布帳
Register of medicine 御薬種之帳
Register of hardware 色々かな物帳
Register of various furnishings 色々細物帳
Register of various banquet utensils 色々御振廻道具
Register of horse fittings 御馬具之帳

Some of these categories are self-explanatory, such as swords, (sword) handle ornaments, clothing, medicine, horse fittings, and a separate but related register that listed money. Others, such as "various utensils," are less clear. Examination of the lists of objects, however, indicates that these contain most of the familiar objects that Ieyasu received as gifts, acquired through intermediaries, or confiscated from defeated enemies in his career as a warlord, shogun, and retired shogun. "Various utensils," for example, includes implements used in the preparation and serving of tea according to the *chanoyu* tradition so beloved by Ieyasu's predecessors and only barely engaged in by Ieyasu himself. Despite his lukewarm attitude toward tea, he still managed to amass one of the most impressive collections of tea utensils of his era, many pieces of which are still extant.[32]

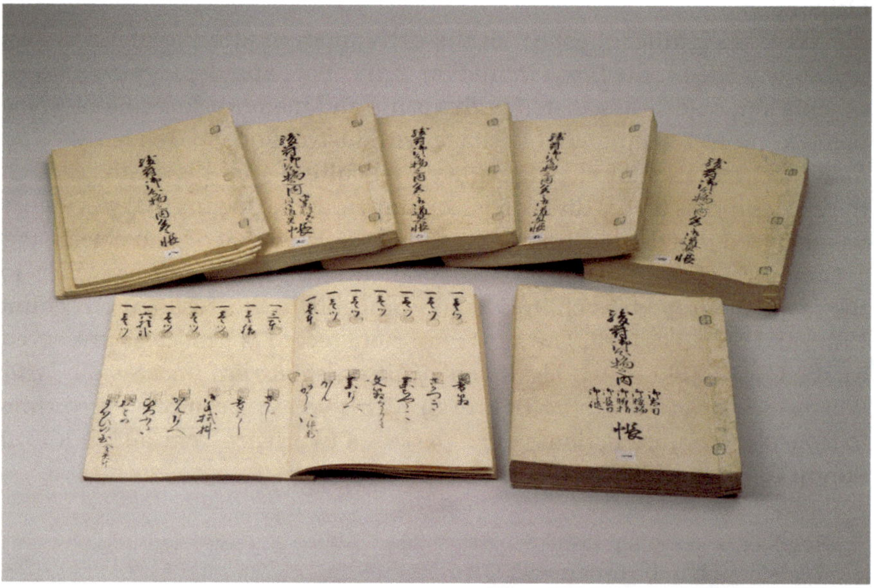

Figure 33. Record of probate from Sunpu, Owari Tokugawa family. Edo period, 1616–1618. 28.3 x 21.8 cm. Tokugawa Art Museum Collection, by permission of the Tokugawa Art Museum / DNPartcom

A few examples will illustrate the quality of the objects passed down as part of Ieyasu's inheritance. One impressive piece is calligraphy by the Chan (Zen) priest Yuanwu Kezin (Chinese, Southern Song dynasty, 1128; Hatakeyama Collection, Tokyo). It is interesting to note that this work became highly valued in the early modern and modern periods not only because of its connection to one of the most respected luminaries of the Chan tradition, but because it had been owned by Ieyasu himself. He bequeathed it to his son, the founder of the Owari Tokugawa house, Tokugawa Yoshinao, and his son, Mitsutomo, gave it to the fifth Tokugawa shogun, Tsunayoshi. This work is but one of many pieces of calligraphy and many tools used in the practice of calligraphy that Ieyasu preserved and passed down to his descendants. As I have argued elsewhere, Ieyasu's collection became a kind of template for model cultural practices for members of the Tokugawa house and by extension for elite warriors in general.[33] His interest in calligraphy and other cultural practices from China had far-reaching consequences. This pattern is analogous to the *iemoto* tradition in the performing arts, in which the aesthetic preferences of the grandmaster, the head of the pyramid-shaped schools that dominated the world of tea and other arts in Tokugawa Japan, were spread throughout the school through standardized curricula and through practices of repetition and reproduction, which made the "gaze" of the grandmaster the standard against which all other tea practitioners measured themselves. In some ways, the tiered hierarchy of vassalage and familial relations that Tokugawa Ieyasu employed as the foundation of the early modern political system in which his sons and close family members were given the positions of highest authority is similar to the *iemoto* system seen in the arts. We have evidence that many of Ieyasu's sons and grandchildren venerated and replicated Ieyasu's cultural practices, taught their sons and vassals to do the same, and thereby spread interest in the objects and the practices they represented, such as this sample of Chinese calligraphy.

The collection of paintings that Ieyasu handed down is similarly exceptional in quality. One piece, known as Budai (attr. to Hu Zhifu, Southern Song dynasty, 13th c., Tokugawa Art Museum), shows Budai (J: Hotei), one of the Chan sages, seeming to pull away a sack on which a child is just starting to fall asleep, a clear metaphor for awakening by ridding ourselves of attachments.[34] The work brought considerable symbolic power as a piece previously owned by both Ashikaga Yoshimitsu and Ashikaga Yoshimasa, the most famous and infamous Ashikaga shoguns, respectively. Another example is *Returning Sailboat from a Distant Shore* (figure 34), from the series Eight Views of the Xiao Xiang Region, by Yujian (hanging scroll, Southern Song dynasty, 13th c., Tokugawa Art Museum). This marvelous landscape painting was passed down in the Ashikaga family, owned by both Yoshimitsu

Figure 34. Painting of a returning sailboat. Yujian (n.d.). Chinese, Southern Song dynasty, 13th century. Important Cultural Property. 30.6 x 77 cm. Tokugawa Art Museum Collection, by permission of the Tokugawa Art Museum / DNPartcom

and Yoshimasa, and later by Imagawa Yoshimoto, Ieyasu's former captor and liege. As if that were not a significant enough personal connection, the painting had also previously been owned by Hideyoshi before entering the collection of Ieyasu.

Arms and armor were plentiful in Ieyasu's material legacy as well. Many examples of swords have been mentioned previously, but among armor, a particularly interesting example is the "laced rising-sun suit" (figure 35). This armor appears in *Record of Utensils Inherited from Sunpu Castle*. The entry reads as follows:

> A suit of armor worn by his Lordship:
> Item: Cuirass with full lacing, rising sun
> Tassets with full lacing
> Ornamental bows (*agemaki*) in crimson
> Item: Helmet with raised ridges
> Item: Hoe-shaped (*kuwakata*) helmet crest (*tatemono*), without *ken*
> Item: One nose cover [from the face mask]

Figure 35. Suit of armor (*gusoku*) with rising-sun design. Momoyama-Edo period, 16th–17th century. Tokugawa Art Museum Collection, by permission of the Tokugawa Art Museum / DNPartcom

Item: Armored sleeves with shoulder guards
Item: Thigh guards lacquered black
Item: Greaves with matching crests

This description closely matches the extant components. The armor consists of black-lacquered plates (of thick rawhide) held together by vertical blue lacing to form the cuirass, shoulder guards, and four-tiered skirt. Bright orange laces in a circular pattern in the middle of the breast plate and shoulder guards create three vivid representations of the rising sun (*hi no maru*). Exposed, black-lacquered plates at the top of the shoulder guards and breast plate, the "sleeves" (*kote*) or forearm guards, and the shin guards display crests in gold *makie* lacquer, including the chrysanthemum, paulownia, sacred Buddhist wheel, wood sorrel, seven treasures, water plantain, *tomoe,* and other motifs. The black-lacquered helmet is shaped like a lobed melon (*akoda*), and is marked by raised parallel lines in gold lacquer. At the front, two round medallions on the upturned rim frame a central hoe-shaped crest (*maedate*), all carved with patterns of chrysanthemum branches and decorated with gold lacquer. The flared neck guard is fastened using blue and orange lace.

The dispersal of this collection[35] to the Tokugawa shogunal and branch houses became an opportunity for new uses of the spectacular accumulation associated with Ieyasu: Tokugawa houses donated objects to the proliferating Tōshōgū, particularly those in the Tokugawa branch domains—Owari, Kii, and Mito—as well as to the main shrine at Nikkō. Thus large portions of Ieyasu's former collection were transferred to various Tōshōgū holdings. The circularity of the movement of these objects is striking. On the one hand, Tokugawa donations of Ieyasu-associated objects to the Tōshōgū represented a kind of spiritual reunion of the material culture with its previous owner; on the other hand, the transformation of these things from inherited goods to ritual objects can also be understood as the "return" of the collection as a new encounter in the social lives of Ieyasu's material heritage. Such a "resocialization," as Philip Fisher has put it, allowed the objects from Ieyasu's collection to continue to have some agency and a new sort of instrumentality long after their original functions had been effaced.[36]

In the case of the Tōshōgū in Wakayama, for example, home to the Kii branch of the Tokugawa house, Ieyasu's son Yorinobu donated many Ieyasu-owned objects after establishing the shrine in 1621. To take just one category of object—military items that are still held in the shrine today—Yorinobu gave four long swords, a set of Nanban armor and a Nanban helmet, a set of "body round" armor, a lacquered saddle and stirrups, a gold *makie*-decorated saddle and stirrups, and conch shells (blown in battle).[37] Similar offerings were made by almost every subsequent generation of Kii Tokugawa house leaders, with long swords in particular being donated by the third-, fifth-, sixth-, seventh-, eighth-, ninth-, tenth-, eleventh-, twelfth-, and fourteenth-generation lords of the domain. Inherited objects associated with Tokugawa Ieyasu were thus deployed by Tokugawa branch heads to reinscribe their own connection to the founder through a ritual of giving that itself represented a return, a circular process of both worship and legitimation that served the additional function of preserving and protecting this robust visual and material legacy from the long sixteenth century well into the modern era. And, as will be seen later in this chapter, shrines such as the Wakayama Tōshōgū were actively involved in the perpetuation of the mythology of Tōshō Daigongen through various ritual practices.

Another facet of the early modern afterlife of Ieyasu was his reanimation in a series of new cultural productions commissioned by Iemitsu. First, in 1635 Iemitsu commissioned a textual hagiography that would serve as a form of "political propaganda," aimed at the most elite members of the Tokugawa family and the Imperial Court. This scroll, completed in 1636 and known as *Origin of the Shrine That Illuminates the East (Tōshōsha engi)* was, like the enshrinement of Ieyasu at Nikkō itself, a product of the centenarian Tendai priest Tenkai. The Chinese calligraphy of the scroll was written by the retired emperor Go-Mizunoo (r. 1611–1629), and the substance was nothing less than Ieyasu's growing interest in and awareness of Tendai Buddhism as practiced by Tenkai, with some attention paid as well to Ieyasu's life in general. The scroll was presented to Tōshō Daigongen as part of the opening ceremonies of the new shrine, but "Tenkai's very formal language and Chinese characters, coupled with an absence of illustrations, made the 1636 version difficult and tedious to read, and the text itself, replete as it was with religious intricacies, was complex and not generally appealing."[38]

Unbowed, Iemitsu planned a second set of scrolls, this time written in mixed Chinese and Japanese characters and with considerably more attention paid to Ieyasu's biography, particularly his military prowess and victories in battles, as well as lavish illustrations by the painter Kano Tan'yū (1602–1674). The new scrolls, *Origins of the Great Avatar Who Illuminates the East (Tōshō Daigongen engi)* narrated and visually represented Ieyasu's life as a tale of divine emergence, with holy visions foretelling an auspicious and godly birth, unnatural wisdom in Ieyasu's youth, foreordained talent and military skill, references to mythical Chinese heroes, and other tropes of divine destiny. Though never displayed publicly, the scrolls were undoubtedly successful in establishing a discursive and representational narrative of superhuman accomplishment to legitimize the Tokugawa administration and the commissioning shogun in particular. The text also is related to the large corpus of "sayings of Ieyasu" that were transmitted orally and eventually collected in massive, multivolume books for study by the samurai and commoners alike. Though not causally connected, both represent the production and circulation in very different circles of a narrative of divine wisdom that characterized Ieyasu's early modern afterlife.

Both of these texts were part of a broader reinvention of the long sixteenth century that could only occur when most of those who had actually lived through the period had passed, extreme cases such as Tenkai aside. By the 1640 ceremonial dedication of *Origins of the Great Avatar Who Illuminates the East,* the process of reinventing and reimagining the age of Nobunaga, Hideyoshi, and Ieyasu was well under way. Even sources that are generally considered to be earlier and therefore more reliable, such as *The Chronicle of Lord Nobunaga (Shinchō kōki)* that is usually dated to 1610, were rearranged and edited by later seventeenth-century authors precisely in this period of reinvention, which not coincidentally begins around the time of Iemitsu's reign. Jurgis Elisonas' and Jeroen Lamers' description of Gyūichi's account applies well to much of the writing about the long sixteenth century in the middle and second half of the seventeenth century: "The general tenor of this book is anecdotal—not necessarily untrustworthy, but storified."[39] The hagiography of Ieyasu, or what could be called the unproblematized conflation of the historical subject with the deity, is clearly on display in Iemitsu's and Tenkai's two sets of handscrolls, perfect distillations of the challenge of reclaiming a pre-apotheosis Ieyasu when the understanding of him as Tōshō Daigongen became so widespread after 1636.

Another example of this newly produced iteration of Ieyasu was the series of dream portraits of the deity that Iemitsu commissioned Kano Tan'yū to paint in this same period (figure 36). As mentioned previously, Iemitsu was sickly as a young man, and a new and unexplained illness emerged in 1636 that tormented him until his death in 1651.[40] Throughout his life but particularly during his sickness, Iemitsu claimed on numerous occasions to have been visited by his grandfather in his dreams and as a result commissioned at least nine, and possibly more, dream portraits of Ieyasu. It was particularly important that Iemitsu commissioned many of these dream portraits not only in response to visions but to deploy during ritual activities. Oddly, we do not have a body of portraits of Ieyasu that were painted before his death and deification. One unusual portrait of Ieyasu (figure 8) in the collection of the Tokugawa Art Museum purports to show him at the 1573 Battle of Mikatagahara, obviously distraught by the Takeda advance as he sits on a camp stool and stares into the eyes of the viewer, but this is the sole exception and is such an unusual painting that it is hard to situate it in the known tradition of warrior portraits.[41] All other portrait represen-

Figure 36. Dream portrait of Tōshō Daigongen. Kano Tan'yū (1602–1674), inscription by Tenkai (1536–1643). Edo period, 17th century. 64 x 46 cm. Rinnō-ji.

tations of Ieyasu, particularly those that we see on the covers of books and museum catalogs about the Tokugawa lord, are best understood as representations of Tōshō Daigongen. Even the few that seem to show him in secular settings were of course produced in the context of the Tōshōgū worldview, mainly by Kano Tan'yū, and cannot therefore be seen as reliable pieces of evidence regarding the visage of Ieyasu as a historical subject. The dream portrait, and the other evidence in this chapter, suggest the following questions: Is it possible to reclaim a pre-apotheosis version of Ieyasu? Can the hagiography be separated from the biography? Should it be?

These are significant queries, in part because Iemitsu's historical reinvention was not limited to the subject of his grandfather (who clearly served not merely as a tool of legitimation but also as a source of personal inspiration and perhaps religious devotion for the third shogun), but also extended to government-sponsored policies that had an impact on the public and private recording and understanding of history.[42] In 1641 Iemitsu ordered Ōta Sukemune, a warlord and Tokugawa vassal who had some responsibility for scholarly affairs, to manage the massive project of compiling the genealogies of all warrior households. Sukemune in turn relied largely on the scholar Hayashi Razan and his son Shunsai (also Gahō; 1618–1688) in the massive endeavor that involved the tracing (and, in some cases, the inventing) of lineages for all but the lowest of samurai: warlords (*daimyō*), defined as direct vassals of the shogun with domains assessed at 10,000 *koku* or more; direct retainers (*hatamoto,* sometimes called "bannermen") of the shogun, with a stipend of less than 10,000 *koku* and more than 500 *koku;* and housemen (*gokenin*), a term that referred primarily to shogunal retainers.[43] The result, speedily compiled in merely two years, was ready in 1643. Consisting of 186 volumes in two sets, one in Chinese and one in Japanese, *Genealogies of the Houses of the Kan'ei Period (Ken'ei shoka keizuden)* contained the lineages of 1,419 warrior houses mapped, documented, and categorized to conquer the potential rivals of the Tokugawa through the power of knowledge and organization. Wars, betrayals, and other crises of the past were acknowledged in this graphed and delineated history of warrior families, but as Mary Elizabeth Berry put it, "It altered the portrayal of the Tokugawa shogun[s], who became not just predestined inheritors of lineage rights but masters of their troubled times. They were victors."[44] Iemitsu presented the text to Tōshō Daigongen in a ceremony at Nikkō Tōshōgū later that year, part of the accumulation of images, objects, and texts that occurred in service of the worship of the deified Tokugawa lord.[45]

Many of the facets of the early modern afterlife of Ieyasu as Tōshō Daigongen are private, hidden from the public in the shadows of closed-off rituals or in the sacred and therefore sealed repositories of shrine objects and documents. But other aspects of the larger politics of culture under Iemitsu—the reliance on the Nikkō Tōshōgū as a kind of keystone of Tokugawa legitimacy, paired with the administrative policy of historical and familial reinvention as a political zeitgeist—makes the significance of Ieyasu's transformation into the Great Avatar more than simply a Tokugawa family affair. Major death anniversary rituals, which routinely involved objects already in the shrine's collection as well as the receipt of new Ieyasu-associated objects from Tokugawa donors, were held and stand out as early modern iterations of the notion of spectacular accumulation: in 1640 to mark the 25th year since Ieyasu's passing; 1642 for the 27th year; 1648 for the 33rd year; 1665 for the 50th year; 1715 for the 100th year; and 1745 for the 130th year. Documents recording the ceremonies and attendees list numerous warlord participants, as well as the organizing shogun and various family and religious advisers.[46] Visiting the Tōshōgū became part of the ritual duty of each Tokugawa shogun, both a public and private act of devotion that doubled as a form of legitimation. Large shogunal processions to the Nikkō Tōshōgū were semipublic, of course, but the regular visits of each shogun to his more local Edo Tōshōgū—one in Ueno, one in Shiba, and one in Edo Castle—were often more private, occurring on the seventeenth day of most months.[47] Such repetition is a powerful form of historical production.[48]

A public version of this repetition developed as the Nikkō shrine and temple complex became a pilgrimage site for warlords and even lower-ranking warriors over the course of the early modern period, and attracted significant numbers of pilgrims from other status groups as well.[49] The presence of a preexisting temple and shrine and a new shrine to Ieyasu as avatar on Nikkō meant that pilgrims could engage in a kind of spiritual one-stop shopping, praying to three divinities rather than just one.[50] One account tells the story of a government official who traveled to Nikkō to pray to Ieyasu's avatar after falling out of favor with Shogun Tsunayoshi; also known are examples of scholars who turned to the worship of Tōshō Daigongen as "a divine power on par with the other gods and Buddhas."[51] Other pilgrims visited the shrine out of a broader desire to travel to the famous and historical spots of Japan. The scholar Kaibara Ekiken (1630–1714) received permission to travel to Kyoto in 1684 along the Kiso highway, an alternative to the bustling Tōkaidō route that would also have the added benefit of bringing him to Nikkō. In his journal about the journey, *A Record of the Eastern Road (Azumaji no ki),* he described his arrival in the village of Nikkō, the place where travelers like him would typically stay the night, as well as his ascent up the hill toward the shrine. He was particularly impressed by the accumulation of various stone monuments and pagodas donated by different warlords and the Korean bell donated by the 1636 ambassadors from Korea

Figure 37. Painted handscroll of the Nagoya Tōshōgū festival. Mori Takamasa (1792–1864). Edo period, 1822. 34.5 x 1267.8 cm. Tokugawa Art Museum Collection, by permission of the Tokugawa Art Museum / DNPartcom.

(which is still visible in the shrine precincts), as well as a lantern that was donated by Dutch visitors.[52] He was also struck by the grandeur of the site, particularly the height of the *Cryptomeria* trees that surround and tower over the buildings of the complex. The Tokugawa strategy of using the natural beauty and ritual sites of Nikkō Tōshōgū as a marker of their dominance over international relations seems, on this evidence, to have been successful.

Ekiken was not alone. Nikkō became one of the centers of religious discourse in the archipelago, part of a trend that expanded "the range of options available to prospective, nonofficial travelers."[53] So many travelers made their way to Nikkō that female pilgrims were discouraged, through complicated regulations, from overnight stays at Nikkō's temples and shrines. Already by 1655, the document *Stipulations for Mount Nikkō* needed to spell out some rules to keep the many female visitors away from compromising interactions with the temples' monks: "Women and nuns may not access the monks' quarters. It goes without saying that they may not be given shelter. Pilgrimage routes going through monks' quarters are an exception."[54] Clearly women were going to Nikkō with great regularity and frequently interacting with monks in ways that were seen as unseemly, which necessitated the production of the stipulations.[55]

It is also worth noting that the Tōshōgū continued to spread across the archipelago throughout the Tokugawa period, with warlords, temples and shrines, and even common villages setting up shrines to Tōshō Daigongen.[56] In some cases, festivals and other forms of public worship were held as well. A late seventeenth-century scroll of the Waka Festival in Wakayama, for example, shows dances, sumo contests, and huge processions occurring in the castle town and headquarters of the Kii branch of the Tokugawa house (figure 37). This festival marked the death anniversary of Ieyasu and began in 1622. It is still held today in the fifth month each year and is sponsored by the Tōshōgū in Wakayama.[57] The procession involved hundreds of performers and was widely known during the Tokugawa period as one of the "three great festivals" of the archipelago. Although the Waka Festival was one of the more famous public celebrations affiliated with Ieyasu, others occurred at Tōshōgū across Japan, and many are still (or newly) active today.[58] Central to the spread of the cult of Ieyasu's avatar was a focus on the shrines and their holdings, particularly objects associated with Ieyasu that came to have ritualistic value in the context of shrine ceremonies.

MODERN APOTHEOSIS

The fall of the Tokugawa government in 1868 has been well documented, though the fate of the Tokugawa and their holdings is less well known. Tokugawa Yoshinobu, the last shogun, retired to Sunpu as had the founder of his line, but found life difficult in the years of early Meiji, as some Tokugawa vassals blamed him for their own fallen fortunes. For many in the newly modernizing Japan, the Tokugawa name was associated with all that was backward and wicked about the past;[59] yet the family was used as a scapegoat far less than they might have been, and notably they kept their heads. Many of the Tokugawa branch house leaders stayed active in politics and managed to keep some of their fortunes intact.

The Tōshōgū continued to be active as sites of worship, but also became popular as parks and tourist attractions. Nikkō, in particular, became internationally famous as a tourist destination through the writings of many adventurous Westerners who visited and praised the site's natural beauty and architectural grandeur (figure 38). The determined Victorian traveler Isabella Bird, for example, wrote in her *Unbeaten Tracks in Japan,* "This is one of the paradises of Japan! It is a proverbial saying, 'He who has not seen Nikko must not use the word kek'ko' (splendid, delicious, beautiful)."[60] The reputation of the shrine and its environs soon spread among Westerners, until it became one of the required stops for any well-to-do visitor to Japan in the late nineteenth and early twentieth centuries. Although it has continued to actively propagate the worship of Tōshō Daigongen, somehow it has been transformed in the eyes of most visitors into a park, literally so with the establishment of Nikkō National Park in 1934.

By contrast, the public rehabilitation of the Tokugawa began with the emergence of a kind of nostalgia for an idealized past that was above all a reflection of alienation in the face of the challenges of modernity. A prime example occurred in 1889, when former Tokugawa retainers organized the three-hundred-year celebration of Edo's founding in Tokyo's Ueno Park. This park, part of a larger plan to transform Tokyo into a European-style city, had been built on the grounds of Kan'eiji, a Tokugawa-constructed temple that had been destroyed during the conflict that toppled the shogunate. The park included (and still includes today) a Tōshōgū. The organizers hoped to use the celebration as an opportunity to articulate their understanding that the Tokugawa had laid the foundations not just for the city of Tokyo, through the founding of Edo, but for Japan's modern prosperity, by naming the event "the tricentennial of Ieyasu's founding of the shogunal government." This proved to be too much for the imperial government, which insisted that the event be called "Tokyo tricentennial celebration." A newspaper editorial responded to the government's intervention:

Figure 38. The Tomb of Iyeyasu Tokugawa. John La Farge (1835–1910). 1888. Watercolor, 27 x 23.2 cm. Metropolitan Museum of Art

The Imperial Household has nothing to fear from Tokugawa Ieyasu, who completed the great task of bringing about order and stability, and who has loyally served the imperial family. We cannot at all understand why the protestors so detest the name of Ieyasu that they advocate a Tokyo tricentennial festival, but will not allow us to call it the Ieyasu tricentennial commemoration. Since this matter has already been decided, there's perhaps no reason to even mention it. Still, the city's residents who have enjoyed

> the benefits and prosperity of Ieyasu's rule should, regardless of what it is called, celebrate the event as a commemoration expressive of their adoration for the merits of Ieyasu's three-hundred year legacy as a military commander and political leader.[61]

The celebration involved numerous Tokugawa family members, with festival-like displays of "archery, swordplay, dancing, music, and fireworks."[62] Notably, it also included what may have been the first public display of objects associated with Ieyasu in modern Japan, organized by the Japan Fine Arts Association (Nihon Bijutsu Kyōkai),[63] a new, conservative Tokyo organization dedicated to an imported high-modern understanding of artistic preservation. The exhibition included armor, swords and other weapons, and even letters and other examples of Ieyasu's calligraphy.[64]

This ceremony and exhibition began, and in many ways charted the future progress for, the larger rehabilitation of the Tokugawa house, a process that was built on a distinctly modern version of the notion of spectacular accumulation. The key player was Tokugawa Yoshichika (1886–1976), who had a significant influence on the modern understanding of both Tokugawa Ieyasu and the legacy of the samurai, but whose unusual career is largely unknown. Yoshichika was adopted into the Owari Tokugawa family in 1908 and soon became the nineteenth head of the lineage with the title of "marquis." Trained as a historian and a botanist, Yoshichika became a member of the House of Peers in 1911. In 1918 he made the first of several philanthropic contributions when he founded the Tokugawa Institute for Biological Research. In 1923 he established the Tokugawa Institute for the History of Forestry. After traveling extensively—to Hokkaido, to China and Southeast Asia, and to Europe—in 1931 he established the Tokugawa Reimeikai Foundation as a preservationist organization, to which he donated the collection of the Owari Tokugawa family. Finally, in 1935, Yoshichika founded the Tokugawa Art Museum on the site of the former detached residence of the Owari Tokugawa in Nagoya.[65] Such philanthropy was widely praised and also had the added benefit of providing tax protection for heritage-rich, elite families.

Part of the context for Yoshichika's activities as a philanthropist and museum founder was his activity in radical politics. In 1931, through his friendship with the nationalist Ōkawa Shūmei, Yoshichika donated family funds (500,000 yen, a considerable amount) to the informal nationalist group, the Cherry Society (Sakurakai), for the infamous, aborted coup known as the March Incident.[66] In his memoir, Yoshichika claims that "I had no objection to revolution, but it would be unpleasant to kill people or be killed, so I insisted that 'kill no one' should be a precondition."[67] In 1936 Yoshichika was involved in plans for another coup—the February 26th Incident—as one of the elite politicians who would be willing to visit the emperor to try to convince him of the merits of reforming the government.[68] Yoshichika was uniquely suited to these tasks, as he was wealthy, a peer, and an acquaintance of the emperor's through their occasional gatherings to discuss natural history. Like many of his compatriots, Yoshichika avoided serious punishment after both of these events and soon became intimately involved in the planning of the Pacific War at the highest levels of government.[69]

An intrepid traveler, Yoshichika had taken a series of trips to the Malay Peninsula in the interwar period. On one of these sojourns, he had hunted tigers with the Sultan of Johore and subsequently became known in the Japanese media as the Tiger Hunting Lord (Toragari no Tonosama).[70] His interest in Malaya rose and he began seriously studying the language, even going so far as to coauthor a Malay textbook, *Learning Malay in Four Weeks (Maraigo yon shūkan)*, that was reprinted thirty times and was still in print in the 1980s.[71] After the 1941 invasion of Singapore, he used his connections in the government and military to suggest that his knowledge of Malaya might be useful for the empire. As a result, from 1942 to 1944 he served as supreme consulting adviser to the military administration of Singapore (specializing in sultan affairs) and civil governor of Malaya. He also became honorary president of Singapore's Raffles Museum and Botanical Gardens.[72] The dominant theme in Yoshichika's account of his time in Singapore in his autobiography, as well as in sympathetic accounts, is preservation, and in this area we start to see the connection between his political and philanthropic activities. One of his goals in accepting the assignment in Singapore, he claimed, was to ensure that Japanese forces would not "molest the mosques and palaces of the sultanates."[73] He also wrote in his autobiography about his growing obsession with collecting ephemeral texts and objects while living in Singapore, particularly his delight upon discovering later that one publication preserved while abroad was—in the wake of the firebombing of Tokyo and other cities—the last remaining example. In his writings he claims that he was acutely aware that the warrior nobility (*daimyō kizoku*) was a dying breed, making him a kind of last remaining example as well. Yoshichika's attempts to conserve the past while remaking the present therefore seem to have been two sides of the same coin of self-preservation.[74]

The establishment of the Tokugawa Art Museum (figure 39) was conceived in 1931 with the founding of the Tokugawa Reimeikai Foundation, which protected the material assets of the Owari Tokugawa in a tax-protected, nonprofit organization (*zaidan hōjin*).[75] The museum itself opened its doors in 1935. The original building was divided into three galleries, representing major genres of art from the lives of the Owari Tokugawa.[76] Exhibitions and catalogs from the period immediately after the opening of the

Figure 39. Tokugawa Art Museum. Photograph by author

museum include diverse genres of art from the Owari Tokugawa holdings, but also reflect the pro-imperial, nationalist ethos of the day. In 1936, for example, the museum organized an exhibition that included calligraphy by the seventeenth-century emperor Go-Mizunoo; the nineteenth-century emperor Kōmei; the last Tokugawa shogun, Yoshinobu; the progressive and innovative last lord of the Echizen Domain (and the birth father of Yoshichika), Matsudaira Shungaku; and the last domainal lord of Owari (and the adopted grandfather of Yoshichika), Tokugawa Yoshikatsu.[77] The exhibition thus carefully narrates the cultural production of the imperial family and of the daimyo class as one unified heritage (seen also in the relatively recent designation of *kizoku,* or "modern nobility"). On August 3, 1937, Emperor Hirohito visited the museum in person and reportedly congratulated Yoshichika on his accomplishment.[78] The museum also contributed objects to exhibitions at other museums around the country as well as overseas. The museum contributed a set of two scrolls by Maruyama Ōkyo to an exhibition of Japanese art held in Berlin in 1939[79] and the same year sent objects to an exhibition organized by the Society for the Study of Military History (Gunjishi gakkai) at an unnamed venue in Japan.[80]

No explicit connection between the founding of the Tokugawa Art Museum and the turbulent national politics of the 1930s is recorded in extant documents. But the timing of Yoshichika's creation of the Tokugawa Reimeikai Foundation in the same year as his donation of funds to the Cherry Blossom Society for the March Incident and of his establishment of the Tokugawa Art Museum a few months before his planned involvement in the February 26th Incident seems too exact to attribute to chance. In his autobiography, Yoshichika describes himself in the 1930s as a kind of bumbling professor, idly pursuing his research despite the momentous happenings in Japanese politics, but this self-portrait is disingenuous in light of his influence with nationalists and militarists. Perhaps Yoshichika knew that his hoped-for revolution would necessitate removal of the modern nobility, pitting the survival of his family against the survival of the nation.[81]

The Tokugawa Art Museum was an inspired solution, preserving the heritage of Yoshichika's lineage—with a major focus on objects associated with Ieyasu—while supporting a politically expedient view of Japanese history. Yoshichika's immediate goal of "preservation of the tools of the daimyo"[82] aligned perfectly with the goals of Pan-Asian nationalists, such as Yoshichika's friend, Ōkawa Shūmei, who wanted Japan to be the "champion of Asia" in the fight against the West. Celebrating a monolithic Japanese warrior culture, as the government's publication *Cardinal Principles of the National Body (Kokutai no Hongi)* did in 1937, allowed propagandists to pit Japanese aesthetics versus Western science, and the *private* culture of Japan's aristocratic elite versus the *public political* culture of Western democracies. Ōkawa was fond of a quotation from the Prophet Mohammad that distills these debates rather clearly and shows the connection between art and politics: "Heaven lies in the shadow of the sword." If the soul of the Empire of Japan was a sword, the Tokugawa Art Museum could serve as a scabbard.

Swords—such as the huge collection in the Tokugawa Art Museum, the majority of which came from Ieyasu—became markers of the philosophical and martial traditions that were supposed to carry Japan to victory in the Pacific War; they were seen, for example, in a sword clenched by Yoshichika in a photograph of him in military regalia in Singapore. Both as tools of the warrior and as signs of an imagined martial past, swords like this one were uniquely powerful symbols in wartime Japan. But in the postwar period, Japanese institutions needed to sanitize swords and other markers of imperial and warrior culture. They did this by aestheticizing these objects as symbols of philosophical "ways" or products of artistic traditions. Swords in the postwar catalogs of the Tokugawa Art Museum are no longer treated as weapons; they are art objects to be collected, categorized, and displayed.

As the former curator of the Tokugawa Art Museum (and the grandson of Yoshichika), Tokugawa Yoshinobu put it in a lecture to the Asiatic Society of Japan, "I hope I have made it clear that the fundamental governing policy of the Tokugawa shogunate was based on culture, and that the shogun and daimyos were not the barbarians depicted in the novel and TV drama 'Shogun.'"[83] In other words, in the political culture of postwar Japan, the Tokugawa Art Museum needed to cast aside the wartime association of the daimyo and reinvent the Tokugawa as cultured rulers. This goal was accomplished through a newly sanitized and pacified version of Tokugawa spectacular accumulation, seen in the art exhibitions, educational programs, and scholarship of the Tokugawa art museum.[84]

Epilogue

Museums and Japanese History

> Politics can take many forms: the politics of diversion and of display; the politics of authenticity and of authentication; the politics of knowledge and of ignorance; the politics of expertise and sumptuary control; the politics of connoisseurship and of deliberately mobilized demands.
>
> —Arjun Appadurai, *The Social Life of Things*

Objects from Ieyasu's material afterlife have traveled overseas on a number of occasions. One influential example was a major international exhibition organized by the Tokugawa Art Museum in the 1980s (not coincidentally, at the time of its fiftieth anniversary) that was mounted under the title "The Shogun Age Exhibition: From the Tokugawa Art Museum, Japan." The exhibition appeared at the Los Angeles County Museum of Art in 1983–1984, the Dallas Museum of Art in 1984, the Haus der Kunst in Munich in 1985, and the Espace Pierre Cardin in Paris in 1985, as well as at the Montreal Museum of Fine Arts in 1989 under the revised title "The Tokugawa Collection: The Japan of the Shoguns."[1] Like the seventeenth-century apotheosis of Ieyasu as Tōshō Daigongen and the rehabilitation of the Tokugawa in the founding of the Tokugawa Art Museum in Nagoya in 1935, these postwar exhibitions represent a continuation of the strategic deployment of Ieyasu's material culture in the service if politics. The context and the message of those politics, however, had shifted.

The 1989 catalog's Foreword by Tokugawa Yoshinobu is revealing. He writes that although some exhibitions may focus on a specific genre or the works of one artist, this exhibition "endeavors to re-create a whole culture," namely, the world of the warlords and "the family of shoguns who breathed new life into the country from the early seventeenth until the mid-nineteenth century—the Tokugawa." He goes on to explain that "all the objects in the exhibition . . . are true reflections of Japan's particular aesthetic sensibility, which was cultivated over the centuries and into which foreign elements were so harmoniously integrated."[2] Yoshinobu thus fairly explicitly substitutes the history of warlords (*daimyo*) and in particular the Tokugawa for the entire history and culture of Japan. This trend continues in Yoshinobu's historical essay, which covers Japanese history from Emperor Jimmu in 660 BC to the death of Hideyoshi in 1598 in little more than a page, whereas Ieyasu and the policies of the Tokugawa shogunate, and particularly Ieyasu's "respect for traditional aesthetics," receive four pages of attention. In both essays Yoshinobu makes the argument that the Tokugawa, and by extension Japan, can best be understood as an aesthetic power that absorbs foreign elements in a process of harmonious integration. This contention effectively answers the old worries about wartime Japan's association with expansionist violence as well as the new 1980s concern that Japan was seeking to conquer through economic dominance. The historical essay concludes by claiming that "the shogunate, headed by Tokugawa Ieyasu, created a new etiquette, suited to the new administrative order,"[3] articulating Japan's distinctiveness entirely in cultural terms, and preparing the exhibit visitor or catalog reader to encounter all that matters about Japan in the displayed objects. The exhibition and catalog thus imply that the material culture of Ieyasu and his descendants is both representative of the heritage of the nation and of the unique accomplishments of the Tokugawa as former rulers of Japan. The Tokugawa patrimony and Japanese traditional culture are posited to be equivalent, a convenient and problematic collapsing of Japan's long, diverse, and contentious political and cultural history into a sanitized and aesthetically pleasing selection from one period.

The Tokugawa Art Museum was not the only institution in postwar Japan to continue championing the central role of Tokugawa Ieyasu in Japanese history and culture. The major Tōshōgū at Nikkō also expanded beyond the traditional scope of shrine activities to become a museum, a publisher, and a sponsor of projects to gain international recognition, such as the shrine's involvement in the campaign to see Nikkō named a UNESCO World Heritage site. One recent example of the Nikkō Tōshōgū's continued production of historical knowledge about Ieyasu is its involvement in an exhibition mounted in 2005 at the Royal Armouries in Leeds, England, the national military history museum of the United Kingdom that has been "twinned" with the Nikkō Tōshōgū since 1991.[4] The comments of Hisao Inaba, head priest of the shrine, open the book: "Born in the strife-torn period of Japan's civil war, Lord Tokugawa Ieyasu, to whom our shrine is dedicated, was the great statesman who laid the foundations of modern Japan. Overcoming all sorts of adversity, he succeeded in unifying the country, and ushered in the Edo era, a 260-year period of peace unparalleled in world history. Here at Nikko Toshogu, we hope that this exhibition will be seen by large numbers of visitors from the UK and other countries, increasing public awareness of his extraordinary achievements."[5] This statement (and a similar one by the director of the Royal Armouries Museum) is bookended by images from hagiographic handscrolls that show Ieyasu's mother praying, receiving a visit from the Buddhist deity Yakushi Nyōrai, and then giving birth to the divine Ieyasu. The captions to these images do not note the context for their production, but instead draw uncritically on them as evidence—presumably reliable—of Ieyasu's actual life. The entire catalog, in other words, seems to accept the conflation of the historical subject with the divine avatar that lies at the heart of the Tōshōgū's approach to hagiographical scholarship. This presentation is another important example of the intertwining, not just during the Tokugawa period but in recent decades as well, of the Tokugawa Ieyasu biography and hagiography.[6] The exhibit itself employed colored lights and background sound effects of battle to create a mysterious and otherworldly atmosphere. This mystery was not just acknowledged but advertised in the promotional materials, which read "Treasures from Another World." The exhibits fetishized military exploits and battle, though these subjects are of course the bread and butter of the Royal Armouries Museum. Most surprising was the manner in which the divine status of Ieyasu was offered up as a fact rather than a historically contingent and socioculturally specific event to be contextualized.[7] The Royal Armouries, one could argue, became a kind of overseas extension of the Tōshōgū.

In addition to shrine collections, a number of important objects from Tokugawa Ieyasu's collection have ended up in national or regional museums in Japan because the Owari Tokugawa were able to preserve and to donate them. The Owari were the only branch Tokugawa family to successfully keep most of the heritage of Ieyasu intact in the transition into the Meiji period and then in the tumultuous years of Japanese empire and the Pacific War.[8] Most warlord houses, including the Tokugawa branch houses, sold off parts or all of their collections in the late nineteenth and early twentieth centuries after losing their income and most of their status, though some did receive new rankings as members of the modern nobility.[9] Many of these pieces, as well as items from the Tōshōgū shrines, the Tokugawa Art Museum, and the more recently founded Tokugawa Museum in Mito, were shown in a huge exhibition mounted in 2007 at the Tokyo National Museum. The exhibit was called "Dai Tokugawa Ten (Exhibition of the Great Tokugawa)" in Japanese, though in English, the title was "Legacy of the Tokugawa: The Glories and Treasures of the Last Samurai Dynasty" in the accompanying catalog and promotional materials.[10] This enormous exhibit at Japan's most important museum was a major accomplishment for the Tokugawa. The "neutral venue" meant that the various factions of the Tokugawa and Tōshōgū that might not normally cooperate could contribute objects and materials to the same event. As a result, the exhibition brought together a more complete assemblage of Tokugawa materials, including many pieces associated with Ieyasu, than had ever been attempted previously. The show also attracted major crowds and was widely praised for the objects on display and the high quality of the catalog.[11] This exhibit demonstrated that even 391 years after the death of Ieyasu, his legacy—the material remnants left to his descendants and protected in the Tōshōgū shrines—continued to serve as the central focus for the reproduction of historical knowledge about the Tokugawa founder and his age.

Much has been written on the complex origins of museums in the age of empire and colonial dominance, their attempts to adapt to decolonization and the rise of new social and political movements, and the changing role of museums in a period of globalization and digital revolution. Historians such as Tony Bennett have called attention to the role of the museum in shaping the bourgeois liberal subject "as a reformatory of manners in which a wide range of regulated social routines and performances take place."[12]

Surprisingly little attention has been paid, however, to the role of museums in the production of historical knowledge about Japan. Of particular concern is the ongoing, complex relationship between Japanese notions of heritage—facilitated by the Japanese government through strict laws that designate important cultural properties and national treasures—and the educational goals of museums that are, according to the International Council of Museums, "in the service of society and its development."[13] Although many museums have increasingly embraced the vital goal of "working against received images," as Barbara Kirshenblatt-Gimblett has put it, and some have even rejected the notion that original objects are still the primary reason for the existence of their institutions, on the whole exhibitions of Japanese art inside and outside of Japan continue to fetishize the quality and originality of works as art over their social, political, and cultural contexts, or their meaning as historical sources.[14] So-called blockbuster exhibitions in particular tend to borrow significant pieces from Japan, which necessitates the involvement of the Japanese Agency for Cultural Affairs in the planning of the exhibition and the writing of the catalog.

Why is this involvement a problem? As the example of Tokugawa Ieyasu's material heritage demonstrates, while objects such as swords and Chinese ceramics endure, their framing narratives are ephemeral. As Philip Fisher has argued, a sword begins its social life as an instrument of war but then is transformed into a ritual object, then an antique, and eventually ends up in a museum, as a metonym for the civilization itself. I would add that certain intense moments of ideological production—the mid-seventeenth-century hagiographic constructions of Iemitsu, for example, or the nationalist interpretations of 1930s Japan—result in discourses and representational conventions that are attached to both objects and the historical subjects with which they are identified. As a result, when works from the collection of Tokugawa Ieyasu or other luminaries from the sixteenth century are displayed in museums today, the tendency is to frame them in ways that perpetuate the mythohistory of the Momoyama period. This Momoyama narrative is historically inaccurate because it reads modern notions of value and accomplishment—the primacy of individualism and originality, for example—back onto the sixteenth century. It also devalues significant issues that deserve our attention: the intense internationalism of the age, the presence of Chinese and Korean laborers in Japan, socioeconomic conflict and class warfare played out in the fields of cultural production, and extreme acts of violence and destruction by the Three Unifiers and their armies, to name just a few topics that might profitably be explored.

For example, consider swords, perhaps the most easily identifiable symbol of the samurai and one of the most numerous object types collected by Ieyasu and preserved by his descendants. Swords tend to be displayed in museums and in catalogs as static, aestheticized objects, with the blades detached from the mounting and guard. Their arrangement in symmetrical display cases in exhibitions or photograph boxes in catalogs transforms them into objets d'art, with an emphasis on their clean lines, sharp edges, and exceptional craftsmanship. Catalog entries usually provide details about the place of production and the name of the maker, as well as a genealogy of elite warrior owners. However, such displays fail to acknowledge the instrumentality of swords, their changing role in Japanese society all the way up to the modern period. Swords were, of course, used in battle in medieval Japan, but by the sixteenth century they were less important in individual acts of combat than for the all-important ritual of removing the heads of defeated foes. Likewise, ears and noses of lower-ranking enemies, and of thousands of Koreans killed during the Imjin War in particular, were removed using swords of the sort that were later passed down by Tokugawa-period warrior houses. Perhaps this is too graphic a detail to merit inclusion in family-friendly exhibitions, but the alternative seems to sanitize and whitewash a history of violence in an unpardonable fashion. Swords were weapons and were often used for cutting human bodies and taking what Simon Harrison has called "dark trophies."[15] The collecting of body parts in military conflicts and particularly in colonial contexts, and the close associations between these acts and practices of hunting, resonates with the late medieval Japanese examples explored in this book. Even during the relatively peaceful early modern period, the sword was a symbol of masculine warrior power and social status, and always symbolized the right to engage in acts of violence against those with less power. To deny this legacy by substituting aesthetic and artisanal beauty for historical didactics is to present weapons to families in a far more problematic fashion. From Nobunaga's use of the lacquered skulls of his defeated enemies in a celebratory banquet to Ieyasu's determined salvaging of the treasures of the Toyotomi, the history of war and of the collection and display of valuable objects were inextricably linked in the late sixteenth century and beyond.

It is all too easy to dismiss historically and aesthetically significant things such as ceramics or swords as static objects, but in this book I have made the argument that things have a form of agency in the societies through which they travel, as well as in their deployments in instances of hagiography and historiography. In fact, in modern museums things become a synecdoche for an entire culture's history, in effect carrying a load far greater than they should possibly be expected to shoulder. Tokugawa Ieyasu and his material heritage illustrate that this burden is hardly a new problem, however, but an example of the manner in which we entrust things with the weighty responsibility of carrying on, of shaping the future by transmitting parts of ourselves forward even after we are gone. Bill Brown notes that "the story of objects asserting themselves as things . . . is the story of a changed relation to the human subject and thus the story of how the thing really names less an object than a particular subject-object relation."[16]

What are the relationships, then, named in the story of the life and afterlives of Ieyasu and his things? Or, more broadly, what relations are revealed by our treatment of the material culture of the samurai in general? Certainly the story of Ieyasu shows the need of historical subjects to control the past by shaping the inheritance passed on to future generations. This was true for Ieyasu, who wanted to root his rule in precedent; for the early modern Tokugawa, seeking to protect their authority through a strategic politics of mythmaking and ritual deployment of material culture; and for the modern representatives of the Tokugawa, reinventing their familial tradition within the context of twentieth-century nationalism, empire, and its aftermath. However, rather than accept the edited and naturalized heritage bequeathed to the present, it might be more profitable to acknowledge that beautiful and historic things are both shared and contested.[17] Authority, identity, and inheritance are not fixed but made, and museums and historians can contribute to conversations about their making and unmaking by recognizing the polyvocal character of all of our sources. Things can help us to rethink our relationship to the past and its problematic authority by recognizing that it endures into and indeed shapes the politics of culture in the present.

Notes

Prologue

Epigraph. Sahlins 1985, vii.

1. I examine this attack in detail in chapter 5.

2. See Ono, "Sunpuki," 203, entry for Keichō 20/intercalary 6/9 (1615; one month before the shift to Genna 1).

3. Tokugawa Bijutsukan, *Ieyasu no isan,* 234; Ono, "Sunpuki," 205, entry for 16/intercalary 6/Keichō 20.

4. See Seikadō Bunko Bijutsukan, *Seikadō chadōgu,* 2, 12.

5. It may be that this reconstitution of part of the Toyotomi collection is an example of what Gerald Schwedler and Eleni Tounta have called a "usurping ritual"; Schwedler and Tounta, "Usurping Rituals," 349–358.

6. A recent example of a biographical and cultural history of collecting in Song-dynasty China is Patricia Ebrey's marvelous study, *Accumulating Culture,* and its associated anthology, Ebrey and Bickford, *Emperor Huizong and Late Northern Song China.*

7. Schama, "Perishable Commodities," 485; Tsing, *Friction,* 72–77.

8. The widespread acceptance by historians of nationalist terminology that seems to presume that the Japanese nation is a timeless entity, or at the very least a useful analytical concept as far back as the sixteenth century, is deeply problematic. The hegemonic warlords of the period were certainly concerned with pacifying the realm and with carefully facilitating relations with representatives of other cultures (such as Iberian Jesuits and Chinese merchants), but their efforts did not constitute either a unification or a nation-building process.

9. Hanley, *Everyday Things in Premodern Japan;* Kornicki, *Book in Japan;* Sand, *House and Home.*

10. The works of many art historians influenced this project, particularly Louise Cort's prominent works on Japanese ceramics and Gregory Levine's interdisciplinary study of the Kyoto temple Daitokuji. See, e.g., Cort, *Shigaraki, Potter's Valley;* Levine, *Daitokuji.* I have reviewed some of the changing goals and methods of art history in the context of the study of Asian art in Pitelka, "Introduction: Wrapping and Unwrapping Art," 1–20.

11. For a helpful overview, see Hicks, "The Material-Cultural Turn," 25–98.

12. See Miller, *Material Culture and Mass Consumption;* Gell, *Art and Agency.*

13. See Adorno and Horkheimer, *Dialectic of Enlightenment,* particularly "The Culture Industry: Enlightenment as Mass Deception."

14. The list of books in Japanese on Ieyasu's biography and his historical impact is extensive. A few representative examples include the large number of works of Nakamura Kōya, who is discussed in this chapter; Kitajima, *Tokugawa Ieyasu;* Kuwata, *Tokugawa Ieyasu;* the works of Fujino, including *Tokugawa Ieyasu jiten;* and those of Tokugawa Yoshinobu.

15. Sadler, *Maker of Modern Japan,* 9–10.

16. Ibid., 21.

17. See, e.g., Whyman, *Sociability and Power;* Russell and Tuite, *Romantic Sociability;* Hoffman, *Politics of Sociability.*

18. Conlan, *From Sovereign to Symbol,* 14.

19. See Stavros, "Locational Pedigree and Warrior Status," 3–18.

20. See Futaki's *Chūsei buke girei no kenkyū* and *Buke girei kakushiki no kenkyū.*

21. Futaki, *Buke girei,* 218–304.

22. Ibid., 352–380.

23. Roberts, *Performing the Great Peace.*

24. See the writings of Watanabe Hiroshi, such as *Tō Ajia no ōken to shisō* and *A History of Japanese Political Thought.* Similar examples include Mary Elizabeth Berry's description of the Tokugawa state as a "flamboyant architecture of power," Philip C. Brown's similar use of the term "flamboyant" in reference to Tokugawa authority, and Constantine Nomikos Vaporis' use of the phrase "theaters of power" to describe processions and other political spectacles. See Berry, "Public Peace and Private Attachment," 270; Brown, *Central Authority and Local Autonomy in the Formation of Early Modern Japan,* 233; Vaporis, *Tour of Duty,* 71.

Chapter 1: Famous Objects

1. Ōta, *Shinchō kōki,* bk. 7, sec. 1, p. 165. In English, see Ōta, *Chronicle of Lord Nobunaga,* 204.

2. See Lamers, *Japonius Tyrannus,* 28–32, on the *umamawarishū* and their presence at this banquet.

3. See, e.g., Pitelka, *Handmade Culture;* Maske, *Potters and Patrons in Edo Period Japan.*

4. Many Japanese-language catalogs and object series (*zenshū*) record the extensive and diverse field of extant tea utensils (*denseihin*) in private and museum collections in Japan today. One example pertinent to this study is Tokugawa Bijutsukan, *Chanoyu dōgu.*

5. See Pitelka, *Japanese Tea Culture,* for more information on the relationship between art and tea in Japanese history.

6. Recently, advances in the study of the medical impact of drinking caffeinated beverages have revealed that tea has various health benefits in addition to its stimulatory properties. Green tea, in particular, is high in catechins, which seem to be "more powerful than vitamins C and E in halting oxidative damage to cells and appear to have other disease-fighting properties." See, e.g., "Time for tea." *Harvard Women's Health Watch* 12, no. 2 (October 2004): 7.

7. Lu, *Classic of Tea.*

8. See Furuta, *Eisai.* In English, see Welter, "Zen as the Ideology of the Japanese State," 65–112.

9. See, e.g., the account of attending a tea battle in "Isei teikin ōrai," in Sen, *Chadō koten zenshū,* 2:200–203.

10. Shiga, "Muromachi shōgunke no shihō o saguru," 158–169.

11. Yukio Lippit cautions against anachronistic thinking regarding the notion of an "Ashikaga collection," which he notes was perhaps not as tangible an assemblage of objects as the phrase, or indeed the more common Japanese appellation "Higashiyama gyomotsu" implies. His discussion of Ashikaga collecting practices is excellent; Lippit, *Painting of the Realm*, 113–119.

12. Takemoto, *Shokuhōki no chakai to seiji*, 6–7.

13. Reproduced in Tokyo Daigaku Shiryō Hensanjo, *Dai Nihon shiryō*, ser. 7, vol. 10, pp. 130–137, entry for Ōei 15/5/6. See also Tani S., "Gyomotsu on'e mokuroku," 439–447; Nakamura Tanio, "Gyomotsu." Although earlier scholars in Japan transcribed the first word in the title as "Gyomotsu," I have chosen to use the reading favored by Takeuchi J. in "Meibutsuki no seisei kōzō," 69.

14. Nezu Bijutsukan and Tokugawa Bijutsukan, *Higashiyama gyomotsu*, includes photographs, a transcription, and analysis of the document that records the decorative program for this visitation: "Muromachi dono gyōkō okazariki."

15. Manzai's diary is transcribed in Manzai, "Manzai Jugō nikki."

16. Morimoto Masahiro has charted many of these gift exchanges in his useful *Zōtō to enkai no chūsei*, 64–86. For another example, see the discussion of the gifts of the Asakura warlords to the shogunate in Satō Kei, "Asakura shi to Muromachi bakufu," 35–58.

17. See also Takemoto's discussion of these issues in *Shokuhōki no chakai to seiji*, 60–67, 124. Takemoto demonstrates that the Ashikaga's cultural advisers chose the best pieces from among the stream of Chinese things that were given to the shogunate as gifts, and these acquired the distinct quality of *gomotsu*, literally "honorable objects" or "his lordship's things," which generally is understood to mean objects from the collection of Ashikaga Yoshimasa, but which more broadly refers to the objects from the Ashikaga collection.

18. In English, see Lippit, *Painting of the Realm*, 119–125.

19. For a readable, introductory account, see Keene, *Yoshimasa and the Silver Pavilion*.

20. Yano, *Kundaikan sōchōki no sōgō kenkyū*, particularly pp. 6–11 of the research volume.

21. See, e.g., Murai, "The Development of *Chanoyu*," 3–32; Sen, *Japanese Way of Tea*, 117–158.

22. Yano, *Kundaikan sōchōki no sōgō kenkyū*, 53. Also, Mizuno, "Ichijōdani no bunka," 150.

23. See Fukui Kenritsu Ichijōdani Asakura-shi Iseki Shiryōkan, *Hana saku jōkamachi Ichijōdani*, 104–105, for a chronological overview.

24. For a broad summary with archaeological schematics, see Mizuno, "Ichijōdani Asakura-shi iseki shutsudo ibutsu," 253–370.

25. See the discussion of texts from this period such as *Ōgo dōgu nedan zuke*, *Noto meibutsuki* and *Chanoyu zu* in Yano, "Meibutsuki no seisei kōzō," pt. 2, 71–72.

26. Transcribed in Tsutsui, "Seigan meibutsuki," 373–402.

27. Takemoto, *Shokuhōki no chakai to seiji*, 93–95.

28. Ibid., 102–107.

29. Transcribed in Tsutsui, *Cha no koten*, 384, 388, 396.

30. This piece is listed as "Tsukumogami" (written in kana, rather than with kanji) in Ōta, *Shinchō kōki*, vol. 1, sec. 4, pp. 87–88, entry for Eiroku 11/10/2. The piece was also known as Matsunaga Nasu in some sources. See Tsutsui, *Shinpan chadō daijiten*, 791.

31. For a thorough exploration of Imai Sōkyū, the political valence of his gifts to Nobunaga, and Sōkyū's larger significance in the world of tea culture, see Watsky, "Commerce, Politics, and Tea." It is also worth noting that three extant tea caddies are known as Tsukumo Nasu, but the first of these—the one currently in the collection of the Seikadō Bunko Bijutsukan—is believed to be the version mentioned here. It will appear again in later chapters. See Tsutsui, *Shinpan chadō daijiten*, 570.

32. Ōta, *Shinchō kōki*, bk. 1, sec. 4, pp. 87–88. Both quotations are from Elisonas and Lamers' translation, Ōta, *Chronicle of Lord Nobunaga*, 123.

33. Ōta, *Shinchō kōki*, bk. 2, sec. 5, pp. 96–97. The quotation, slightly modified, is from Ōta, *Chronicle of Lord Nobunaga*, 132.

34. The phrase appears in poem 723 ("kurenai no / hatsuhana zome no / iro fukaku / omoishi kokoro / ware wasureme ya"), though "hatsuhana" is a common term that appears in many canonical pieces of Japanese literature and collections of poetry.

35. Hikita Sōkan (?–1572) was the founder of the Daimonjiya business. For references to him as a tea practitioner, see Gotō, *Yamanoue Sōjiki*. See also the record of the Daimonjiya house, "Senzoki," transcribed by Tani Akira in *Nomura Bijutsukan kiyō* 9 (2000).

36. *Yamanoue Sōjiki* has been transcribed in numerous volumes in Japanese. Most useful is the catalog by the Gotō Bijutsukan, *Yamanoue Sōjiki*, with the reference to "First Flower" appearing on pp. 29, 149.

37. Some historians interpret the documentary evidence to indicate that Imai Sōkyū rather than Tsuda Sōgyū gave the painting of sweets to Nobunaga. See Sōkyū's diary: Nagashima, *Imai Sōkyū chanoyu nikki nukigaki*, p. 21, entry for Eiroku 13 (1570)/4/1. Also, Watsky follows this interpretation in his "Commerce, Politics, and Tea."

38. Ōta, *Shinchō kōki*, bk. 2, sec. 3, p. 104. The quotation, slightly modified, is from Ōta, *Chronicle of Lord Nobunaga*, 140.

39. Morris, "The City of Sakai and Urban Autonomy," 23–54.

40. Toki-shi Mino Tōji Rekishikan, *Sakai-shū no yakimono*, 28–29.

41. Translated in Souryi, *World Turned Upside Down*, 200. See also Tani A., *Chakaiki no fūkei*, 3.

42. Morris, "Sakai," 156–158.

43. Toki-shi, *Sakai-shū no yakimono*, 19–26.

44. Eguchi, *Chajin Oda Nobunaga*, 63.

45. Ibid., 72–73.

46. This total does not include the additional fifty-three objects that extant sources (such as box inscriptions) claim were once in Nobunaga's collection. See Takemoto's exhaustive chart of the data in *Shokuhōki no chakai to seiji*, 129–165.

47. von Rohr, *Introduction to the Knowledge of Ceremony of Great Rulers*, cited in Koslofsky, *Evening's Empire: A History of the Night in Early Modern Europe*, 96.

48. Sōeki had previously served tea to Nobunaga on two documented occasions, in 1570 and 1573. See Watsky, "Commerce, Politics, and Tea," for a description of both those gatherings in English. See Nagashima, *Imai Sōkyū chanoyu nikki nukigaki*, 24–25, entry for Tenshō 1 (1573)/11/24 morning.

49. This painting may be *Misty Temple, Evening Bell*, attributed to Mu Qi in the collection of Hatakeyama Kinenkan, part of the Eight Views of Xiaoxiang series that became popular in Chinese visual culture and likewise held great authority among both collectors and painters in Korea and Japan. See Princeton University Art Museum, *Handbook of the Collections*, 22, for an early Chinese example.

50. Okuno, *Zōtei Oda Nobunaga monjo no kenkyū*, vol. 1, p. 588, item 349. See also n. 15 in the supplementary materials about the dating of this gift.

51. Ōta, *Shinchō kōki*, bk. 8, sec. 8, p. 187. In English, see Ōta, *Chronicle of Lord Nobunaga*, 243. See also the report in the diary of Tsuda Sōkyū, one of the participants: Nagashima, *Tennōjiya kaiki*, 245–246, entry for Tenshō 3/10/28.

52. Ludwig, "Chanoyu and Momoyama," 81. Takemoto convincingly argues that Nobunaga was not, strictly speaking, replicating the Ashikaga collection, but rather seeking to create his own version of that collection; to assemble, in other words, an Oda collection that would build on but ultimately rival that of the Ashikaga.

53. Tsuji, *Tamon'in nikki*, 2: 257.

54. Lamers, *Japonius Tyrannus*, 75–77. See also McMullin, *Buddhism and the State in Sixteenth-Century Japan*, 147–151.

55. Ōta, *Shinchō kōki*, bk. 4, sec. 5, pp. 126–127. In English, see Ōta, *Chronicle of Lord Nobunaga*, 165–166.

56. See Farris, *Japan's Medieval Population*, 192–198. Farris points out that casualty rates were not necessarily higher in this period, depending on the nature of the relationship between the contending forces, but the overall mortality rates were higher because more people were involved in, and impacted by, these conflicts. On the whole, Farris concludes that Japanese armies followed a global trend in becoming "increasingly lethal."

57. Ōta, *Shinchō kōki*, bk. 5, sec. 3, p. 134. In English, see Ōta, *Chronicle of Lord Nobunaga*, 171.

58. Ōta, *Shinchō kōki*, bk. 5, sec. 3, p. 135. In English, see Ōta, *Chronicle of Lord Nobunaga*, 173.

59. Igor Kopytoff reminds us that "the conceptual distinction between the universe of people and the universe of objects had become culturally axiomatic in the West by the mid-twentieth century," but the commoditization of people was relatively common in other parts of the world. Kopytoff, "Cultural biography," 84. This certainly seems to have been the case in Japan, as the work of Thomas Nelson and, more recently, Shimojū Kiyoshi demonstrates: Nelson, "Slavery in Medieval Japan," 463–392; Shimojū, *'Miuri' no Nihonshi*.

60. Umai, "Kinsei shōnin seido no rekishiteki zentei," 1–20. Many thanks to David Eason for this reference.

61. Kosto, *Hostages in the Middle Ages*, 1–8.

62. Miller, *Problem of Slavery as History*, 1.

63. See Constantine Vaporis' brief discussion of pre-Tokugawa hostage exchange, *Tour of Duty*, 12–13.

64. Ōta, *Shinchō kōki*, initial bk., sec. 12, 16, pp. 30, 35. In English, see Ōta, *Chronicle of Lord Nobunaga*, 66, 71.

65. Ōta, *Shinchō kōki*, initial bk., sec. 44, p. 80. In English, see Ōta, *Chronicle of Lord Nobunaga*, 114.

66. Ōta, *Shinchō kōki*, bk. 6, sec. 7, p. 150. In English, see Ōta, *Chronicle of Lord Nobunaga*, 187.

67. Ōta, *Shinchō kōki*, bk. 6, sec. 8, p. 151. In English, see Ōta, *Chronicle of Lord Nobunaga*, 189.

68. See Lamers' helpful summary of these events in *Japonius Tyrannus*, 156–162. Compare Nobunaga's extreme actions with the fairly rare instances of hostages who were executed in Europe over a period of almost one thousand years, compiled by Kosto in *Hostages in the Middle Ages*, 49–52.

69. Ōta, *Shinchō kōki*, bk. 13, sec. 1, p. 311. In English, see Ōta, *Chronicle of Lord Nobunaga*, 355.

70. Recorded in numerous documents, including Saiki, Hayashi, and Hashimoto, *Kan'ei shoka keizuden*, on Tenbun 11/12/26. Ieyasu's birth year has frequently been recorded as 1542 because most of Tenbun 11 corresponds to 1542. The twelfth month, however, overlaps with the beginning of 1543, so Ieyasu's birthday in the Western calendar is actually January 31, 1543. See Dos Santos, "Ieyasu (1542–1616) versus Ieyasu (1543–1616)," 9–26, for a detailed examination of this problem.

71. Ōkubo, *Mikawa monogatari*, 57–68.

72. Ibid., 73.

73. The document *Kinenroku* records the story that Imagawa Yoshimoto required Ieyasu to attend the domain's New Year's celebrations when he was nine years old. Several of Yoshimoto's vassals looked suspiciously at this proud boy, asking "Whose child is that?" Someone nearby answered, "The grandson of Matsudaira Kiyoyasu," but no one could believe it. So little known and insignificant was he in the halls of Sunpu Castle that its residents did not even recognize the inheritor of the Matsudaira line. Overhearing this discussion, Ieyasu said nothing but rose from his seat, walked determinedly to the veranda, and urinated over the edge, a kind of calculated but brazen display of warrior pride. See Nakamura, *Tokugawa Ieyasu kō den*, 74.

74. It may be, in fact, that the upbringing Ieyasu received in Sunpu Castle under the wealthy, culturally active, and powerful Imagawa Yoshimoto was more luxurious, at least in material terms, than growing up in Okazaki Castle would have been. As Kosto notes, "The possibilities for the good treatment of hostages had few limits." *Hostages in the Middle Ages,* 36.

75. See Sakata, *Hitojichi no rekishi,* for one of the few treatments of this issue in Japanese.

76. Ōkubo, *Mikawa monogatari,* 76. Also, Narushima, *Tōshōgū onjikki,* 29–30.

77. Narushima, *Tōshōgū onjikki,* 30.

78. The transcription of the commendation document, "Mikawa Daisenji ni ataeru jiryō kishinjō narabi ni kinsei," from Kōji 2 (1556) 6/24, can be found in Nakamura, *Tokugawa Ieyasu monjo no kenkyū,* 1:21–22. Such commendations have a long and complicated history in Japan. See Mass, "Of Hierarchy and Authority," 23–24, for a discussion of *kishinjō* up to the fourteenth century.

79. Matsudaira T., "Ietada nikki zōhō," n.p., entry for Kōji 3/1/15. MS collection, Waseda University Library. Sekiguchi may have been married to Yoshimoto's sister, making her Yoshimoto's niece.

80. Owada, "Saishō," 56.

81. See, e.g., Ōkubo, *Mikawa monogatari,* 76–77.

82. Kuwata, *Tokugawa Ieyasu,* 11.

83. Nakamura, *Tokugawa Ieyasu monjo no kenkyū,* 1:31–32.

84. Though the order of events seems to be askew, Ōkubo, *Mikawa monogatari,* records these movements and the subsequent battle, pp. 76, 78–79.

85. Ōta, *Shinchō kōki,* initial bk., pp. 52–58; see also Ōta, *Chronicle of Lord Nobunaga,* 88–89.

86. Ōta, *Shinchō kōki,* initial bk., p. 58; see also Ōta, *Chronicle of Lord Nobunaga,* 92. Nobunaga treasured this sword and reputedly had it engraved as follows: "The sword of Imagawa Yoshimoto, who was careless and killed by Nobunaga on 19/5/1560." Conlan, *Weapons and Fighting Techniques of the Samurai Warrior,* 116. See also Okuno, *Oda Nobunaga monjo no kenkyū,* 1:55–60.

87. Nakamura, *Tokugawa Ieyasu monjo no kenkyū,* 1:36.

88. Ibid., 1:37–44. Ieyasu also demonstrates his authority by allowing the use of the character "yasu" (from his name at the time, Motoyasu, as well as from previous generations of the Matsudaira family) in a "one character letter" (*ichi-ji jō*) from 1561. See Tokugawa Y., *Shinshū Tokugawa Ieyasu monjo no kenkyū,* 1:8.

89. Nakamura, *Tokugawa Ieyasu monjo no kenkyū,* 1:50–51.

90. Ōkubo, *Mikawa monogatari,* 132–133.

91. Matsudaira I., *Ietada nikki,* 1:50–51.

92. Owada, "Saishō," 58.

93. See Foucault, *Discipline and Punish,* 28–29, on the political investment of the body and the microphysics of power.

94. Berry, "Public Peace and Private Attachment," 263.

95. Narushima, *Tōshōgū onjikki,* 46.

96. On the history of swords as gifts, particularly during the Muromachi period, see Satō, "Muromachi jidai no zōtō tōken ni tsuite," 311–331. Also, Jeroen Lamers has convincingly made the case, through careful analysis of extant letters between Ieyasu and Nobunaga, that Ieyasu was not Nobunaga's vassal but was also not his equal. I therefore understand Ieyasu to be a junior partner in Nobunaga's endeavors, inferior to him but not feudally bound to him in a position of servitude. See Lamers, *Treatise on Epistolary Style,* 19–28.

Chapter 2: Grand Spectacle

1. The primary record of this event is reproduced in Hayashiya T., "Kitano ochanoyu no ki." For a comprehensive discussion of the event and the full range of primary sources

available to study it, Takeuchi et al., *Hideyoshi no chiryaku*. For a thorough overview in English, see Cort, "Grand Kitano Tea Gathering," 15–31. All translations from this primary source are taken from Cort's article, with one or two minor modifications.

2. Examples of this term, as well as "three hegemons" and "three heroes," include Elisonas, "Christianity and the Daimyo," 331; Elisonas, "Evangelic Furnace," 2:145; Hall, introduction to *Early Modern Japan*, 12.

3. McGirr, *Heroic Mode and Political Crisis*.

4. Jane Bennett makes the argument that there is a tangible "force of things," and relates this concept to Foucault's insight into the body and its social construction, particularly the point that "cultural forms are themselves powerful, material assemblages with *resistant force*," or what she also refers to as "the active role of nonhuman materials in public life." Bennett, *Vibrant Matter*, 1–2.

5. Witmore, *Culture of Accidents*.

6. Brucker, *Living on the Edge in Leonardo's Florence*, 67.

7. Shermer, *How We Believe*, 219.

8. Varley and Elison, "Culture of Tea," 212.

9. Berry explores this juxtaposition in *The Culture of Civil War in Kyoto*.

10. Watsky, "Commerce, Politics, and Tea," 24; Plutschow, *Rediscovering Rikyū and the Beginnings of the Japanese Tea Ceremony*, 80.

11. Morita, *Ashikaga Yoshimasa no kenkyū*, 208, describes the ritualized progression through the Southern Capital that Yoshimasa took in 1465, with the visit to Tōdaiji's Shōsōin as a key stop.

12. Ōta, *Shinchō kōki*, bk. 7, sec. 4, pp. 167–168; see also Ōta, *Chronicle of Lord Nobunaga*, 206–207.

13. Lamers and Elisonas translate the title of this painting as *Myriad Miles of Rivers and Mountains* in a previous entry in Ōta, *Chronicle of Lord Nobunaga*, 170, that records Nobunaga's receipt of the painting.

14. Sen, *Chadō koten zenshū*, 196–197. The Ranjatai wood fragment still exists as part of the Shosoin collection today. It is more than 5 feet in length and weighs approximately 25 pounds. The measurement for quantity of 1 *to* was not carefully fixed in the late sixteenth century, so it is difficult to know the actual volume of wood collected.

15. Takemoto, *Shokuhōki no chakai to seiji*, 35.

16. Ōta, *Shinchō kōki*, bk. 9, sec. 1, p. 207. Lamers and Elisonas translate *katajikenaki shidai* as "a happy event"; Ōta, *Chronicle of Lord Nobunaga*, 248.

17. Ōta, *Shinchō kōki*, bk. 9, sec. 4, p. 212; translation from Ōta, *Chronicle of Lord Nobunaga*, 252.

18. Ōta, *Shinchō kōki*, bk. 10, sec. 13, p. 234; see also Ōta, *Chronicle of Lord Nobunaga*, 276.

19. Ōta, *Shinchō kōki*, bk. 14, sec. 15, pp. 371–372; see also Ōta, *Chronicle of Lord Nobunaga*, 420.

20. Takemoto, *Shokuhōki no chakai to seiji*, 33.

21. Ōta, *Shinchō kōki*, bk. 8, sec. 14, p. 205; see also Ōta, *Chronicle of Lord Nobunaga*, 246–247.

22. Ōta, *Shinchō kōki*, bk. 10, sec. 14, pp. 234–235; see also Ōta, *Chronicle of Lord Nobunaga*, 277.

23. Ōta, *Shinchō kōki*, bk. 10, sec. 9–10, pp. 230–231; see also Ōta, *Chronicle of Lord Nobunaga*, 272–273.

24. Takemoto, *Shokuhōki no chakai to seiji*, 30.

25. Kuwata Tadachika highlights Hideyoshi's introduction to the politics of tea in the very first section devoted to *chanoyu*, titled "Tea License (Chanoyu menkyo)" in *Toyotomi Hideyoshi kenkyū*, 500. Takemoto provides the entire letter that Imai Sōkyū and Sōkun wrote on Nobunaga's behalf, as well as detailed analysis, in *Shokuhōki no chakai to seiji*, 30–31.

26. Nagashima, *Tennōjiya kaiki*, 355.

27. Werbner, *Holy Hustlers, Schism, and Prophecy*.

28. See Taniguchi, *Kenshō Honnōji no hen,* for a detailed analysis of the available primary sources for the study of this event. In English, see Lamers, *Japonius Tyrannus,* 215–216.

29. Ōkubo, *Mikawa monogatari,* 140–141. See also Nobunaga's letter commenting on Ieyasu's trip to Sakai in Okuno, *Oda Nobunaga monjo no kenkyū,* 2:657–658.

30. See Imai Sōkyū's comments in the extracts from his diary, published as Nagashima Fukutaro, ed., *Imai Sōkyū chanoyu nikki nukigaki,* 34; Tsuda Sōgyū's comments in Nagashima, *Tennōjiya kaiki,* 364. Both also note the assassination of Nobunaga the following day.

31. Ōta, *Shinchō kōki,* bk. 15, sec. 31, p. 415; translation from Ōta, *Chronicle of Lord Nobunaga,* 468.

32. Ōta, *Shinchō kōki,* bk. 15, sec. 32, pp. 416–417; translation from Ōta, *Chronicle of Lord Nobunaga,* 469.

33. Ōta, *Shinchō kōki,* bk. 15, sec. 32, p. 417; see also Ōta, *Chronicle of Lord Nobunaga,* 470.

34. Okamoto, "Hideyoshi no jidai," 234–235.

35. See Teruhiko, Hiroshi, and Hoan, *Taikōki,* 67.

36. Matsudaira I., *Ietada nikki,* 1:131.

37. Many sources record these events. See, e.g., "Taikō sama gunki no uchi," in Kuwata, *Taikō shiryō shū,* 177–178; "Kawazumi Taikōki," in the same volume, 237–250.

38. Kuwata, *Taikō shiryō shū,* 264.

39. This event, too, is reported in many sources. See, e.g., "Koretō muhōki" (also known as "Koretō taijiki"), in Kuwata, *Taikō shiryō shū,* 35–36.

40. Matsudaira I., *Ietada nikki,* 1:132.

41. Nakamura, *Tokugawa Ieyasu monjo no kenkyū,* 1:286.

42. See letters from Ieyasu to this effect in Nakamura, ibid., 1:290–296.

43. See Nakamura, ibid., 1:303–307, for samples, a chart of extant letters, and analysis.

44. Matsudaira I., *Ietada nikki,* 1:182; Ōkubo, *Mikawa monogatari,* 147.

45. See Ieyasu's letter in Nakamura, *Tokugawa Ieyasu monjo no kenkyu,* 1:519–520. The English translation is from Totman, *Tokugawa Ieyasu,* 46.

46. Oda, "Chaire," 214.

47. Matsudaira I., *Ietada nikki,* 1:160. Ietada mistakenly describes this tea caddy as *kotsubo,* or small jar.

48. Nakamura, *Tokugawa Ieyasu kō den,* 230.

49. Matsudaira I., *Ietada nikki,* 1:229.

50. Ibid., 1:230.

51. Takeuchi, *Tamon'in nikki,* entry for Tensho 14/1/18.

52. Matsudaira I., *Ietada nikki,* 2:25.

53. Ibid., 2:26.

54. Ibid., 2:27; also, Kuwata, *Tokugawa Ieyasu,* 102.

55. Berry, *Hideyoshi,* 80.

56. Takemoto, *Shokuhōki no chakai to seiji,* 352–357.

57. According to the tea diary of Tsuda Sōgyū, the participants included Matsui Yūkan (a merchant turned Oda retainer who had served as one of the collection agents in Nobunaga's Hunt for Famous Objects) and his nephew Yasuyuki, the warrior Hosokawa Yusai, Sen no Rikyū and his son Dōan and son-in-law Mozuya Sōan, the tea master Imai Sōkyū and his son Sōkun, Sōgyū himself and his son Sōbon, the tea master Yamanoue Sōji and his son Shichidō, the warrior Kodera Kyūmu, the warrior Ukita Tadaie, the Sakai merchant Yamaoka (also Sumiyoshiya) Sōmu, the Sakai merchant Mitsuda Muneharu, the tea master Jū no Sōhō, the warrior Tomita Tomonobu, the warrior Sakuma Moriharu, the warrior Takayama Ukon, the warrior Shibayama Munetsuna, the warrior Furuta Oribe, the warrior Nakagawa Hidemasa, the warrior Hosoi Shinsuke, the Noh actor Kanze Sōsatsu, the warrior Makimura Toshisada, the Buddhist priest Enjōbō Sōen, the warrior Higuchi Iwami, and Hideyoshi's doctor, Yakuin Zensō. Nagashima, *Tennōjiya kaiki,* 405.

58. The title is miswritten in Sōgyū's diary, but clearly refers to the well-known painting that was in Hideyoshi's collection and which he received from Nobunaga.

59. Nagashima, *Tennōjiya kaiki*, 409–411.

60. See Berry, *Hideyoshi*, 177–179, for a summary of these events in English; Ōmura, *Tenshō-ki*, 79–84, for the original Japanese record.

61. Records of the event are collated in Tokyo Daigaku, *Dai Nihon shiryō*, ser. 11, vol. 17, pp. 78–83, entry for Tenshō 13/10/7.

62. Varley, "Culture of Tea," 219.

63. Takeuchi, *Tamon'in nikki*, 5, entry for Tenshō 14/1/20. See also Hanawa, *Oyudono no ue no nikki*, 43–44, entry for Tenshō 14/1/16. See also Saiki and Someya, *Kanemi kyōki*, entry for Tenshō 14/1/20.

64. Ōtomo Sōrin's comments are reproduced in Kuwata, *Toyotomi Hideyoshi kenkyū*, 513–514. See also Varley and Elison, "Culture of Tea," 219.

65. See Bettina Klein, "Japanese Kinbyobu." On the role of ornament, including the use of gold, in the expression of Buddhist notions of the sacred, see Watsky, *Chikubushima*, 36.

66. Cort, "Grand Kitano Tea Gathering," 38.

67. Matsudaira I., *Ietada nikki*, 2:32–59. Also, Nakamura, *Tokugawa Ieyasu monjo*, 1:704–713.

68. See the series of letters in Nakamura, *Tokugawa Ieyasu monjo*, 1:716–720.

69. Matsudaira I., *Ietada nikki*, 2:66.

70. Ibid., 2:66–67.

71. See Berry's discussion of the imperial progression, *Hideyoshi*, 184–187.

72. Nakamura, *Tokugawa Ieyasu monjo*, 1:721.

73. Ibid., 1:724.

74. Ibid., 1:753–757.

75. Matsudaira I., *Ietada nikki*, 2:124–125.

76. Ibid., 2:129.

77. Ibid., 2:135; Zoku, *Tōdaiki*, 56–57; Ōkubo, *Mikawa monogatari*, 163.

78. Ōkubo, *Mikawa monogatari*, 164; Zoku, *Tōdaiki*, 56–57.

79. See Berry, "Public Peace and Private Attachments," 264.

80. Zoku, *Tōdaiki*, 57.

Chapter 3: The Politics of Sociability

1. On Hideyori's arrival, see Zoku, *Tōdaiki*, 172, entry for 16/3/28. On Toyokuni Shrine, see Watsky, *Chikubushima*, 204–208.

2. Zoku, *Tōdaiki*, 172–173, entry for Keichō 16/3/28.

3. Ibid., 173–174, entry for 16/3/28 (and the unmarked days after).

4. See Bell, *Ritual Theory, Ritual Practice*.

5. Ikegami, *Bonds of Civility*. For a helpful collection of essays on the topics of ritual, violence, and dominance, see Kitts, ed., *State, Power, and Violence*.

6. Berry's discussion of gifts in "Public Peace and Private Attachment" (263–268) was extremely helpful in conceptualizing this chapter.

7. Mauss, *The Gift*, 14.

8. Rupp, *Gift-Giving in Japan*, 197.

9. See Morimoto Masahiro, *Nihon chūsei no zōyo to futan*; chapter 2 discusses horses, chapter 3 discusses melons. On earlier practices of banqueting, see Selinger, *Authorizing the Shogunate*, 97–100.

10. Segal, *Coins, Trade, and the State*, 140–146.

11. Conlan, *State of War*, 156–157.

12. Auslander, *Cultural Revolutions,* 27.

13. Ōta, *Shinchō kōki,* bk. 13, sec. 1, p. 314. See also Ōta, *Chronicle of Lord Nobunaga,* 357–358; translators Elisonas and Lamers provide a brief but helpful analysis of the exchange, p. 357n5. For a discussion of such gifts, see also Lamers' translation of Rodrigues' text on letter writing: Lamers, *Treatise on Epistolary Style,* 83–84.

14. See Hitomi Tonomura's discussion of the role of gift giving among Honai merchants and various patrons ("an upward flow of gifts ensured the economically beneficial exchange between the patron authority and the client merchants") in *Community and Commerce in Late Medieval Japan,* 124.

15. Cooper, *João Rodrigues's Account of Sixteenth-Century Japan,* 206–207.

16. Ōta, *Shinchō kōki,* initial bk., sec. 24, p. 55; see also Ōta, *Chronicle of Lord Nobunaga,* 88.

17. Ōta, *Shinchō kōki,* initial bk., sec. 24, p. 58; see also Ōta, *Chronicle of Lord Nobunaga,* 91.

18. See Ōta, *Shinchō kōki,* initial bk., sec. 25, p. 60; also Ōta, *Chronicle of Lord Nobunaga,* 93, for the first reference; Ōta, *Shinchō kōki,* initial bk., sec. 40, p. 77; Ōta, *Chronicle of Lord Nobunaga,* 111, for the second.

19. Ōta, *Shinchō kōki,* bk. 1, sec. 3, p. 85; see also Ōta, *Chronicle of Lord Nobunaga,* 118.

20. Thoen, *Strategic Affection?,* 20.

21. Conlan, *State of War,* 151.

22. Ōta, *Shinchō kōki,* bk. 9, sec. 4, p. 213; see also Ōta, *Chronicle of Lord Nobunaga,* 252.

23. Matsudaira I., *Ietada nikki,* 2:27.

24. Accounts of Hideyoshi's relationship with the court are plentiful in English. See Berry, *Hideyoshi,* 176–190; Butler, *Emperor and Aristocracy,* 124–168; Lillehoj, *Art and Palace Politics in Early Modern Japan,* 25–63.

25. Nakamura, *Tokugawa Ieyasu monjo no kenkyū,* 1:175, 197–198.

26. Narushima, *Tōshōgū onjikki,* 46.

27. Tokugawa Bijutsukan, *Ieyasu no isan,* 78 and 234, entry 156. See also Takemoto, *Shokuhōki no chakai to seiji,* 164.

28. Tokugawa Yoshinobu, *Shinshū Tokugawa Ieyasu monjo no kenkyū,* 1:835–868.

29. Nakamura, *Tokugawa Ieyasu monjo no kenkyū,* 1:725–726.

30. Ibid., 2:177.

31. Elisonas, "Inseparable Trinity," 265–267.

32. Nakamura, *Tokugawa Ieyasu monjo no kenkyū,* 2:190.

33. Noted in Yamashina's diary: Yamashina Tokitsune, *Tokitsune kyōki,* vol. 11, no. 5, p. 28.

34. Haga, "Sōtan nikki," 266.

35. Matsudaira I., *Ietada nikki,* 2:188.

36. Elisonas, "Inseparable Trinity," 272.

37. Swope, *Dragon's Head and Serpent's Tail,* 89.

38. Translated in Hawley, *Imjin War,* 193.

39. Nakamura, *Tokugawa Ieyasu monjo no kenkyū,* 2:227.

40. Matsudaira I., *Ietada nikki,* 2:244; Nakamura, *Tokugawa Ieyasu monjo no kenkyū,* 2:238–241.

41. Nakamura, *Tokugawa Ieyasu kō den,* 651.

42. Elisonas, "Inseparable Trinity," 285–286.

43. For an exhaustive study of the earthquake, see geologist Iida Kumiji's *Tenshō daijishin shi.*

44. Kurokawa and Noda, "Fushimi jō to jōkamachi," 334–335.

45. Ibid., 335.

46. Zoku, *Tōdaiki,* 68–69. For useful summaries in English, see also Berry, *Hideyoshi,* 232–233; Elisonas, "Inseparable Trinity," 284–285.

47. Yamashina, *Tokitsune kyōki,* vol. 11, no. 7, p. 287.

48. See, e.g., entries in Yamashina, *Tokitsune kyōki,* vol. 11, no. 7, pp. 369, 377, and no. 8, p. 15.

49. Zoku, *Rokuon nichiroku,* 2:370, entry for Keichō 2/10/1.

50. On the Hosokawa exchange, see Nakamura, *Tokugawa Ieyasu kō den,* 294. Also, on the gift to Shōkokuji, see Zoku, *Rokuon nichiroku,* 2:375, entry for Keichō 2/11/12.

51. Zoku, *Rokuon nichiroku,* 2:375, entry for Keichō 2/11/13 entry.

52. The meaning of the two lines of omitted text is unclear, but they translate to something like the following: "The next five curtains are progressing, I will tell you the details later." See Nakamura, *Tokugawa Ieyasu monjo no kenkyū,* 2:283.

53. Ibid., 2:290–293.

54. For a narrative of this process, including translations of the relevant documents, see Berry, *Hideyoshi,* 234–235.

55. For a useful chart of the documents as well as full transcriptions, see Nakamura, *Tokugawa Ieyasu monjo no kenkyū,* 2:301–302, 304–314.

56. Fujii, *Sekigahara kassen shiryōshū,* 492–493; Nakamura, *Tokugawa Ieyasu monjo no kenkyū,* 2:757.

57. See, e.g., Fujii, *Sekigahara kassen shiryōshū,* 503.

58. Ibid., 504–505.

59. Nakamura, *Tokugawa Ieyasu monjo no kenkyū,* 2:777–782.

60. Ibid., 2:754–755.

61. Hanawa, *Oyudono no ue no nikki,* 9:15, entry for Keichō 5/10/7, and 9:177, entry for Keichō 5/10/24.

62. Hanawa, *Oyudono no ue no nikki,* 9:179, entry for Keichō 5/11/9.

63. Yamashina, *Tokitsune kyōki,* vol. 11, pt. 11, p. 15, somewhat oddly located in the entry for Keichō 6/1/13.

64. Futaki, *Buke girei kakushiki no kenkyū,* 219–224.

65. Tokugawa Bijutsukan, *Ieyasu no isan,* 222–223.

66. Nakamura, *Tokugawa Ieyasu monjo no kenkyū,* 3:4–5.

67. Fujii Joji, *Edo kaibaku,* 26–29, provides maps and a useful summary.

68. See Hotta, *Kansei chōshū shokafu,* 3:204, entry for Kuroda Yoshitaka.

69. Gien, *Gien Jugō nikki,* 2:288. See also Edo Tokyo Hakubutsukan, *Nijōjō ten.*

70. Nakamura, *Tokugawa Ieyasu monjo no kenkyū,* 3:56.

71. Hanawa, *Oyudono no ue no nikki,* 9:213, entry for Keichō 6/7/4.

72. Ibid., 9:219, entry for 6/8/18.

73. Ibid., 9:220, entry for 6/8/27.

74. Nakamura, *Tokugawa Ieyasu kō den,* 340, 559–565.

75. See, e.g., the regulations issued to the temples on Mount Kōya in Kii Province in Nakamura, *Tokugawa Ieyasu monjo no kenkyū,* 3:64–70.

76. For Ieyasu's regulations for the village of Azai in Mikawa, see Nakamura, *Tokugawa Ieyasu monjo no kenkyū,* 3:59–60.

77. See, e.g., Hanawa, *Oyudono no ue no nikki,* 9:227, entry for Keichō 6/11/1, and 9:245, entry for Keichō 8/1/14.

78. Yamashina, *Tokitsune kyōki,* vol. 11, pt. 11, p. 238, entry for Keichō 7/2/14.

79. Yamashina, *Tokitsune kyōki* is Yamashina's diary and records many examples. See, e.g., Yamashina, *Tokitsune kyōki,* vol. 11, pt. 11, p. 241, entry for Keichō 7/2/20. See also Butler, *Emperor and Aristocracy in Japan,* 114–123.

80. Yamashina, *Tokitsune kyōki,* vol. 11, pt. 11, p. 260, entry for Keichō 7/3/28. On Kōwakamai, see Miner, Morrell, and Odagiri, *Princeton Companion to Classical Japanese Literature,* 322–323; Oyler, *Swords, Oaths, and Prophetic Visions,* 146–148.

81. Harold Bolitho, *Treasures among Men,* 11.

82. Zoku, *Tōdaiki,* 78 for the latter instruction.

83. Ibid., 79–80.

84. Kimura, *Butoku hennen shūsei,* 2:48, entry for Keichō 6/12/5.

85. Hanawa, *Oyudono no ue no nikki,* 9:246, entry for Keichō 8/1/21; Funahashi, *Keichō nikken roku,* 22, entry for Keichō 8/1/21.

86. Hanawa, *Oyudono no ue no nikki,* 9:248, entry for Keichō 8/2/11.

87. Nakamura, *Tokugawa Ieyasu monjo no kenkyū,* 3:305–306.

88. Hanawa, *Oyudono no ue no nikki,* 9:254–256, entry for Keichō 8/3/25.

89. Yamashina, *Tokitsune kyōki,* vol. 11, pt. 12, p. 114, entry for Keichō 8/7/7.

90. Zoku, *Tōdaiki,* 81.

91. Butler, "Tokugawa Ieyasu's Regulations for the Court," 509–551.

92. Matsudaira T., "Ietada nikki zōhō," entry for Keichō 8/10/3.

93. Hanawa, *Oyudono no ue no nikki,* 9:280, entry for Keichō 8/11/8.

94. Zoku, *Tōdaiki,* 82.

95. Tokyo Daigaku, *Tokitsune kyōki,* 12:263, entry for Keichō 9/4/5.

96. Ibid., 12:300–302, entries for Keichō 9/6/22–24.

97. Hanawa, *Oyudono no ue no nikki,* 9:314, entry for Keichō 9/6/26.

98. Zoku, *Tōdaiki,* 84.

99. Tokyo Daigaku, *Dai Nihon shiryō,* ser. 12, vol. 2, p. 588, entry for Keichō 9/intercalary 8/10.

100. Zoku, *Shunkyūki,* 2:135–136, entries for Keichō 9/8/14–18. Watsky summarizes Boshun's detailed descriptions of the festival in *Chikubushima,* 209, and of the folding-screen paintings that the Toyotomi commissioned to depict the festival, 211–216.

101. In all, out of twenty-six months as shogun, Ieyasu spent only eight in Edo, or about 31 percent of his time in this post.

102. Brownlee, *Political Thought in Japanese Historical Writing,* 54.

103. Tokyo Daigaku, *Dai Nihon shiryō,* ser. 12, vol. 2, p. 974, entry for Keichō 10/2/24.

104. Tokyo Daigaku, *Tokitsune kyōki,* 13:155–156, entry for Keichō 10/4/1.

105. Kimura, *Butoku hennen shūsei,* 2:41, entry for Keichō 10/4/7. Also, Matsudaira T., "Ietada nikki zōhō," entry for Keichō 10/4/7.

106. Tokyo Daigaku, *Tokitsune kyōki,* 13:159, entry for Keichō 10/4/8.

107. Ibid., 13:166, entry for Keichō 10/4/16.

108. There are many examples, but perhaps the most notable is the otherwise reliable essay by Hall, "*Bakuhan* System," 146.

109. Tokyo Daigaku, *Dai Nihon shiryō,* ser. 12, vol. 3, p. 193, entry for Keichō 10/5/10.

110. Zoku, *Rokuon nichiroku,* entry for Keichō 10/6/16.

111. Tokyo Daigaku, *Tokitsune kyōki,* 13:206, entry for Keichō 10/7/7.

112. See, e.g., ibid., 13:219, entry for Keichō 10/8/6.

Chapter 4: Lordly Sport

1. Ono, "Sunpuki," 224, entry for Keichō 20/9/10.

2. Yamana, "Tokugawa Ieyasu to takagari," 62–63.

3. For a useful survey of premodern representations of sports in Japan, see Tokugawa Bijutsukan, *Bijutsu ni miru Nihon no supo-tsu.*

4. On Japanese raptors in English, see Ferguson-Lees and Christie, *Raptors of the World;* Ornithological Society of Japan, *Japanese Journal of Ornithology;* Tingay and Katzner, *Eagle Watchers.*

5. On falconry in Japan, see Nesaki, *Shogun no takagari;* Okazaki, *Taka to shōgun.* In English, for a brief overview of falconry in Japan with emphasis on early modern visual materials, see Saunders, "Pursuits of Power." Falcons and falconry are also mentioned briefly in Pflugfelder and Walker, *JAPANimals.*

6. See Morimoto, "Sengoku ki no taka kenjō to zōtō girei," for more on this phenomenon.

7. Yamana, "Tokugawa Ieyasu to takagari," 65–66.

8. See also the many letters from this period that mention falcons and falconry, including Tokugawa, *Shinshū Tokugawa Ieyasu monjo no kenkyū,* 1:482, 536, 556; 2:529, 538, 539, 557; Nakamura, *Tokugawa Ieyasu monjo no kenkyū,* 3:776, 781.

9. Cooper, *João Rodrigues's Account of Sixteenth-Century Japan,* 110.

10. See Pitelka, "The Empire of Things."

11. See, e.g., the references to falcons (or *hayabusa*) in *Kojiki* and *Nihon shoki;* to falconers (or *taka kaibe*) in *Nihon shoki;* and to raptors (or *taka*) in *Man'yōshū.* Nesaki summarizes these and other early references to falcons and falconry, *Shōgun no takagari,* 9–11.

12. Nesaki, *Shōgun no takagari,* 12–13.

13. Murasaki, *Tale of Genji,* 18.

14. Ibid., 326.

15. Ibid., 535.

16. Ibid., 467–468.

17. Most famous is Minamoto Yoritomo's grand hunt in the Fuji-Nasuno region in the fifth month of 1193, detailed in *Azuma kagami.*

18. See Nihonmatsu, *Chusei takasho no bunka densho,* particularly chaps. 1–4.

19. Nesaki, *Shōgun no takagari,* 16. See also Morimoto, "Sengoku ki no taka kenjō to zōtō girei," 12.

20. A monk recorded some details of the success of the Asakura in the text *Record of Cultivating Falcons (Yōyōki),* which is transcribed in Hanawa, *Gunsho ruijū,* 12:476–478.

21. Horton, *Journal of Sōchō,* 45.

22. Morimoto, "Sengoku ki no taka kenjō," 3.

23. Ibid., 5.

24. Morimoto, *Nihon chūsei no zōyo to futan,* 287–297.

25. Norton, "Going to the Birds," 53–83.

26. Morimoto, *Nihon chūsei no zōyo to futan,* 315–321.

27. Ōta, *Shinchō kōki,* initial bk., sec. 7, p. 22; see also Ōta, *Chronicle of Lord Nobunaga,* 59.

28. Ōta, *Shinchō kōki,* initial bk., sec. 22, p. 50; see also Ōta, *Chronicle of Lord Nobunaga,* 84–85.

29. Ōta, *Shinchō kōki,* bk. 1, sec. 5, p. 90; see also Ōta, *Chronicle of Lord Nobunaga,* 125.

30. Ōta, *Shinchō kōki,* bk. 8, sec. 7, pp. 198, 200; see also Ōta, *Chronicle of Lord Nobunaga,* 240–241.

31. Ōta, *Shinchō kōki,* bk. 10, sec. 11, p. 233; see also Ōta, *Chronicle of Lord Nobunaga,* 274–275.

32. Ōta, *Shinchō kōki,* bk. 11, sec. 2, p. 239; see also Ōta, *Chronicle of Lord Nobunaga,* 280.

33. Morimoto, *Nihon chūsei no zōyo to futan,* 298–307.

34. Ōta, *Shinchō kōki,* bk. 14, sec. 1, p. 337; see also Ōta, *Chronicle of Lord Nobunaga,* 383. See also, Morimoto, "Sengoku ki no taka kenjō," 11–14.

35. See Futaki, *Chūsei buke no sahō,* 25–40, on rituals related to horses, horse paraphernalia, and their exchange. In English, see Bay, "Swift Horses of Nukanobu," 91–124.

36. Yamana, *Sengoku daimyō to takagari no kenkyū,* 2–3. See also Kuwata, *Toyotomi Hideyoshi kenkyū,* 560–561.

37. See Ota, *Taikōsama gunki no uchi,* 38–39.

38. See Hideyoshi's "red-seal letter" to Shimazu Yoshihiro in *Shimazu-ke monjo,* Tenshō 15/9/25, cited in Yamana, *Sengoku daimyō to takagari no kenkyū,* 5–6. On the terms of the Shimazu surrender to Hideyoshi, see Berry, *Hideyoshi,* 90.

39. Yamana, *Sengoku daimyō to takagari no kenkyū,* 19–20.

40. Ibid., 21.

41. Ibid., 21.

42. Berry, *Hideyoshi,* 220.

43. See Ōkubo, *Mikawa monogatari,* 73.
44. Nakamura, *Tokugawa Ieyasu monjo no kenkyū,* 1:168–169.
45. Tokugawa, *Shinshū Tokugawa Ieyasu monjo no kenkyū,* 1:59, 63.
46. Matsudaira I., *Ietada nikki,* 1:6–7.
47. Ibid., 1:2–5, 59, 61–67. Mentioned in Morimoto, *Nihon chūsei no zōyo to futan,* 128–129.
48. Morimoto, *Nihon chūsei no zōyo to futan,* 129–130.
49. Nakamura, *Tokugawa Ieyasu monjo no kenkyū,* 1:251.
50. Tokugawa, *Shinshū Tokugawa Ieyasu monjo no kenkyū,* 2:571.
51. Nakamura, *Tokugawa Ieyasu monjo no kenkyū,* 1:673–174.
52. Matsudaira I., *Ietada nikki,* 2:27.
53. See the series of letters in Nakamura, *Tokugawa Ieyasu monjo,* 1:716–720.
54. Matsudaira I., *Ietada nikki,* 2:66. Also see Hideyoshi's letter to Ieyasu from 1588 or Tenshō 16/12/4 that mentions Ieyasu's falconry, in Tokugawa, *Shinshū Tokugawa Ieyasu monjo no kenkyū,* 2:119. Likewise, falconry with Hideyoshi is mentioned in Ieyasu's letter to Tōdō Takatora from 1589 or Tenshō 17/11/14, Nakamura, *Tokugawa Ieyasu monjo,* 1:749.
55. Nakamura, *Tokugawa Ieyasu monjo,* 1:720, 761, 768.
56. Ibid., 1:726.
57. Kuwata, *Tokugawa Ieyasu,* 123.
58. Nakamura, *Tokugawa Ieyasu monjo no kenkyū,* 2:44–46.
59. Ibid., 2:82–88.
60. Fujii Joji, *Edo kaibaku,* 18.
61. On the hawking trip, see Zoku, *Shunkyūki,* 1:209, entry for Keichō 5/1/9. On the aborted visit to the court, see Yamashina, *Tokitsune kyōki,* pp. 108–109, entry for Keichō 5/1/17.
62. Nakamura, *Tokugawa Ieyasu monjo no kenkyū,* 2:466.
63. Kuwata, *Tokugawa Ieyasu,* 179–180.
64. Nakamura, *Tokugawa Ieyasu monjo no kenkyū,* 2:482.
65. Ibid., 2:494, 496.
66. Ibid., 2:496.
67. Kasaya, *Sekigahara: Ieyasu no senryaku,* 58–59.
68. Yamashina, *Tokitsune kyōki,* entry for Keichō 5/6/17. Kuwata, *Tokugawa Ieyasu,* 181. See also, Nakamura, *Tokugawa Ieyasu monjo no kenkyū,* 2:497–498.
69. See Nakamura, *Tokugawa Ieyasu monjo no kenkyū,* 3:7, for a 1601 letter to Mogami Yoshiakira thanking him for falcons; see also two 1602 letters to Sō Yoshitoshi regarding negotiations with Korea that mention hawk exchanges, pp. 180, 231.
70. Nakamura, *Tokugawa Ieyasu monjo no kenkyū,* 3:393. See Walker, *Conquest of Ainu Lands,* 102, on falcons in the larger trade between Ezo and the Tokugawa and their representatives.
71. Tokugawa, *Shinshū Tokugawa Ieyasu monjo no kenkyū,* presents three nearly identical letters: 2:538, 539, 591.
72. Ibid., 2:529.
73. Ibid., 2:557.
74. Okazaki, *Taka to shōgun;* Nesaki, *Shōgun no takagari* and *Edo bakufu hōyō seido no kenkyū.*
75. See, e.g., the regulations issued to the temples on Mount Kōya in Kii Province; Nakamura, *Tokugawa Ieyasu monjo no kenkyū,* 3:64–70.
76. See Ieyasu's regulations for the village of Azai in Mikawa; Nakamura, *Tokugawa Ieyasu monjo no kenkyū,* 3:59–60.
77. See summary in Nakamura, *Tokugawa Ieyasu monjo no kenkyū,* 3:58. See also, Kornicki, "Books in the Service of Politics," 74–75.
78. Nakamura, *Tokugawa Ieyasu monjo no kenkyū,* 3:60. See also Nesaki, *Edo bakufu hōyō seido no kenkyū,* 207.
79. See Akutagawa Tatsuo, "Sengoku bushō to taka," 543–562.
80. Butler, "Tokugawa Ieyasu's Regulations for the Court," 521–522.

81. Nakamura, *Tokugawa Ieyasu monjo no kenkyū,* 3:776.
82. Ibid., 3:780.
83. Nesaki, *Edo bakufu hōyō seido no kenkyū,* 28–52.
84. Ono, "Sunpuki," 140.
85. Nesaki, *Edo bakufu hōyō seido no kenkyū,* 62–68.
86. Ibid., 69.
87. Ibid., 72.
88. Ibid., 76.
89. Ibid., 209–210.
90. Totman, *Green Archipelago,* 60–63.
91. Ono, "Sunpuki," 223–224.
92. Tokugawa, *Shinshū Tokugawa Ieyasu monjo no kenkyū,* 2:564.
93. Ibid., 2:483–84, 520–24. See also Tokugawa Bijutsukan, *Ieyasu no isan,* 224–225, 249.
94. Tokugawa, *Shinshū Tokugawa Ieyasu monjo no kenkyū,* 2:527–528. 576–578. See also Tokugawa Bijutsukan, *Ieyasu no isan,* 79–80.
95. Tokugawa, *Shinshū Tokugawa Ieyasu monjo no kenkyū,* 2:538–568.
96. Ibid., 2:556–562.
97. Zoku, *Shintei Honkō Kokushi nikki,* 3:331, entry for Genna 2/1/21.
98. Ibid., 3:341, entry for Genna 2/2/21.
99. Tokyo Daigaku, *Dai Nihon shiryō,* ser. 12, vol. 24, p. 91, entry for Genna 2/2/9.
100. Tokyo Daigaku, *Dai Nihon shiryō,* ser. 12, vol. 24, p. 154, entry for Genna 2/3/27.
101. Tokyo Daigaku, *Dai Nihon shiryō,* ser. 12, vol. 24, p. 325, entry for Genna 2/4/17.
102. Ōta, *Shinchō kōki,* bk. 13, sec. 1, pp. 313–314; Lamers and Elisonis render Randori as "Catch as Catch Can," but "plunder" is a better translation in this context because the term was often used in descriptions of sixteenth-century warfare to explain the ravishing of a defeated enemy's land. Ōta, *Chronicle of Lord Nobunaga,* 356–359. Thanks to David Eason for bringing this reference to my attention.
103. See Poliquin, *Breathless Zoo,* on the culture and spectacle of stuffing animals, including raptors. See also Skabelund's *Empire of Dogs,* which uses modern taxidermy as one form of historical evidence.
104. See Pitelka, *Handmade Culture,* 111–131 on this process.
105. See Bodart-Bailey, *The Dog Shogun,* 147–150.
106. Tokugawa Bijutsukan, *Ieyasu no isan,* 132, object no. 288.
107. I have referred elsewhere to the assumed "monolithic sincerity" of things, particular objects that lack text or other obviously complex inscriptions of discourse. I argue against the assumption that things are unchanging or can be anachronistically linked to modern notions of aesthetics or affect in Pitelka, "A Raku Wastewater Container and the Problem of Monolithic Sincerity." For a haunting account of the extinction of wolves in Japan and the silence of that extinction in the historiography, see Walker's *Lost Wolves of Japan.*

Chapter 5: Severed Heads and Salvaged Swords

1. Conlan, *From Sovereign to Symbol.*
2. See Futaki, *Buke girei kakushiki no kenkyū.*
3. Bell, *Ritual Theory, Ritual Practice,* 173.
4. Tyler, *The Tale of the Heike,* 388.
5. Ibid., 565.
6. Ibid., 475.
7. Ibid., 522.
8. Palmer, *The Severed Head,* 17.
9. Tyler, *Heike,* 522.

10. See Botsman, *Punishment and Power,* 72, on the privilege reserved for samurai, "the customary right of warriors to strike down on the spot any commoner who behaved disrespectfully toward them." He also discusses the exhibition of heads as examples of "fearful displays of power," 20–26.

11. Kasaya, *Sekigahara kassen to Ōsaka no jin,* 11.

12. Nakamura, *Tokugawa Ieyasu monjo no kenkyū,* 2:446–47.

13. Ibid., 2:501–503.

14. Ibid., 2:503–512. Ieyasu wrote eight letters on 7/7 alone, in addition to the aforementioned military code. He also continued to bombard his vassals and allies with missives while on the road.

15. The document reads as follows:

List of Charges against the Inner Minister [Ieyasu]

- He has repeatedly ostracized two of the Magistrates [Ishida Mitsunari and Asano Nagamasa], despite signing a pledge of cooperation between the Elders and the Magistrates.
- He informed Maeda Toshinaga that he was being subjugated [after the death of his father, Maeda Toshiie] and took hostages to encage him.
- He is assaulting Uesugi Kagekatsu, who has done nothing wrong, which is in clear violation of the regulations left by the Lord of the Realm (Hideyoshi).
- He issues enfeoffments only to those under his command, beggaring belief. He made promises to forestall such commissions [until Hideyoshi's heir Hideyori was of age], yet grants lands to those who, like him, lack loyalty.
- He drove out the Keeper of Osaka Castle installed by the Lord of the Realm [Hideyoshi] and installed his own lackeys.
- Although it is forbidden for Elders or Magistrates to form new alliances, he has broken this promise and signed pledges with numerous outsiders.
- He is occupying the residence [the Nishinomaru Palace in Osaka Castle] of Kita no Mandokoro [Hideyoshi's wife].
- He constructed a tower [in the Nishinomaru Palace in Osaka Castle] as if it were his own inner citadel.
- He has taken all of the warriors' wives and children as hostages, but sent those who are his favorites back to their homes.
- As for marriage arrangements, he has turned his back on the proscription [left by Hideyoshi] and registered more than anyone knows.
- He has instigated and agitated the youth, creating his own band of conspirators.
- He arbitrarily sees to state affairs that the Elders need to dispose of jointly.
- He permitted a land survey to occur at Iwashimizu Hachiman at the suggestion of his wife.

In a brief postscript, the Magistrates enjoined recipients to come quickly to Hideyori's aid. Also included was a separate letter from the Elders Mōri Terumoto and Ukita Hideie, similarly arguing that Ieyasu had turned his back on Hideyoshi's wishes, and that all warlords must stand with Hideyori against Ieyasu. See Fujii Jizaemon, *Sekigahara kassen shiryōshū,* 162–164; see also Nakamura, *Tokugawa Ieyasu monjo no kenkyū,* 2:514–517. The translation is my own.

16. Fujii Jizaemon, *Sekigahara kassen shiryōshū,* 173–182; also, Kasaya, *Sekigahara: Ieyasu no senryaku,* 44–45.

17. Kasaya, *Sekigahara to Osaka no jin,* 95–98. Fujii Jizaemon, *Sekigahara kassen shiryōshū,* 257–260.

18. See the documents related to Ieyasu's launch of the army from Edo in Fujii Jizaemon, *Sekigahara kassen shiryōshū,* 316–319. In particular, as Kasaya notes in *Sekigahara: Ieyasu no sen-*

ryaku, 103–105, the document *Keichō nenchū boku saiki* includes a passage that comments on the extraordinary conditions of Ieyasu's army's departure.

19. Kasaya, *Sekigahara kassen: Ieyasu no senryaku* has one of the more useful maps of the placement of troops, 130–131. The maps in his *Sekigahara to Osaka no jin* are inexplicably unclear and difficult to decipher.

20. Fujii Jizaemon, *Sekigahara kassen shiryōshū*, excerpt from *Keichō nenchū boku saiki*, 394.

21. Ibid., 396.

22. Ibid., 123.

23. Primary sources claim that as many as thirty men were killed immediately, but Kasaya and others think this figure is likely exaggerated because of the nature of the weapons. See Fujii Jizaemon, *Sekigahara kassen shiryōshū*, 397; Kasaya, *Sekigahara to Osaka no jin*, 123.

24. See Nakamura, *Tokugawa Ieyasu monjo no kenkyū*, 2:696.

25. Kitagawa, "An Independent Wife during the Warring States," 154–155.

26. Nakamura, *Tokugawa Ieyasu monjo no kenkyū*, 2:693–694. See also Kodama and Sasaki, *Shinpan shiryō ni yoru Nihon no ayumi*, 34–35.

27. See also Futaki, *Sekigahara kassen*, 125–140.

28. Kasaya, *Sekigahara kassen: Ieyasu no senryaku*, 152.

29. Ibid., 153.

30. Fujii Jizaemon, *Sekigahara kassen shiryōshū*, 401–402, 407.

31. Ibid., 414.

32. Ibid., 413–414.

33. Ibid., 473–478.

34. On the display of heads in public spaces, see Ikushima Terumi, "Chūsei kōki ni okeru 'kirareta kubi' no toriatsukai."

35. Fujii Jizaemon, *Sekigahara kassen shiryōshū*, 501–502.

36. For an illustration of a head examination, see Conlan, *State of War*, fig. 11. In Japanese, see Futaki, *Chūsei buke no sahō*, 58–63.

37. Futaki, *Sekigahara kassen*, 178–180.

38. For a thorough discussion of head examination practices in the late medieval period, see Ikushima, "Kirareta kubi." See also Karl Friday's discussion of this practice and its origins, in *Samurai, Warfare and the State*, 155 and throughout the volume.

39. Conlan, *State of War*, 21.

40. There are numerous examples in *The Chronicle of Lord Nobunaga*, such as his inspection of 3,000 heads after the battle of Okehazama. See Ōta, *Shinchō kōki*, initial bk., sec. 24, p. 58; see also Ōta, *Chronicle of Lord Nobunaga*, 91.

41. Thanks to David Eason for reminding me of this lexical connection.

42. Fujii Jizaemon, *Sekigahara kassen shiryōshū*, 415–417.

43. Shirane, *Early Modern Japanese Literature*, 40.

44. Oka et al., *Kan'ei bunka no nettowaaku*; Kumakura Isao, *Kan'ei bunka no kenkyū* and *Gomizuno'o in*; Yamamoto Hirofumi, *Kan'ei jidai*. See also Butler, "Tokugawa Ieyasu's Regulations for the Court," 521–522.

45. Butler, "Tokugawa Ieyasu's Regulations for the Court," 525.

46. See, e.g., Ieyasu's correspondence for the fourth through sixth months of Keichō 18: Nakamura, *Tokugawa Ieyasu monjo no kenkyū*, 3:761–778.

47. Ibid., 3:821–822.

48. See Watsky's analysis of Hōkōji and its precedents; *Chikubushima*, 76–83.

49. See Kasaya's useful summary of the buildup to the battle in *Sekigahara kassen to Ōsaka no jin*, 204–215.

50. See, e.g., Ono, "Sunpuki," 120–121. See also Tokyo Daigaku, *Dai Nihon shiryō*, ser. 12, vol. 14, p. 294. "Sunpuki" is also reproduced in Zoku, *Tōdaiki, Sunpuki*.

51. See the Mōri example in Nakamura, *Tokugawa Ieyasu monjo no kenkyū*, 3:840.

52. Many of the letters around these incidents are reproduced in Nakamura, *Tokugawa Ieyasu monjo no kenkyū*, 3:848–853.

53. Ono, "Sunpuki," 136–137. Also see Konchi'in Sūden's account of these events in Zoku, *Shintei Honkō Kokushi nikki*, 3:26–27.

54. Ono, "Sunpuki," 138–139.

55. Major figures are listed in Kasaya, *Sekigahara kassen to Ōsaka no jin*, 217.

56. Ōsaka-jō, *Toyotomi-ki Ōsaka zu byōbu*.

57. Ono, "Sunpuki," 155.

58. Ibid., 157–158.

59. Kasuya, *Sekigahara kassen to Ōsaka no jin*, 230–235; Ono, "Sunpuki," 160–161. Kasuya says the assault on Sanada-maru began on 12/2, but Ono, "Sunpuki," lists 12/4.

60. Hora Tomio, *Teppō*, 241–248. See also Lidin, *Tanegashima*, esp. a translation of the 1634 text *Kunitomo teppōki* that mentions this use of firearms, 137; Kokuritsu Rekishi Minzoku Hakubutsukan, *Rekishi no naka no teppō denrai*, illustrates a 500 *monme* [a unit of weight] cannon used by the Satake clan during the Osaka campaigns (47). Thanks to Daniele Lauro for his help in compiling these references.

61. Ono, "Sunpuki," 163–165. David Eason pointed out in private correspondence that similar descriptions can be found in accounts of other battles from the long sixteenth century, meaning that this strategy may have been common, or it may have been a narrative trope for talking about warfare.

62. Shirane, *Early Modern Japanese Literature*, 40.

63. Ono, "Sunpuki," 167.

64. Ibid., 171–172. Kasuya, *Sekigahara kassen to Ōsaka no jin*, 238–239.

65. Zoku, *Tōdaiki*, 212–213; Ono, "Sunpuki," 173.

66. Ono, "Sunpuki," 174.

67. Kasaya, *Sekigahara kassen to Ōsaka no jin*, 239–242.

68. Ono, "Sunpuki," 181.

69. See, e.g., references to secret meetings and conferences on Genna 1/2/8 and 3/1 in Ono, "Sunpuki," 182–186.

70. Tokyo Daigaku Shiryō Hensanjo, *Dai Nihon shiryō*, ser. 12, vol. 17, p. 826, entry for Genna 1/2/14.

71. Tokyo Daigaku Shiryō Hensanjo, *Dai Nihon shiryō*, ser. 12, vol. 17, p. 1033, entry for Genna 1/3/28.

72. Ono, "Sunpuki," 184–185, entry 3/15 for Hideyori's messengers, entry 3/17 for Date Masamune's arrival, bearing gifts, from Kyoto.

73. Kasaya, *Sekigahara kassen to Ōsaka no jin*, 242–243.

74. Ono, "Sunpuki,"186–187, entry for 4/5.

75. Tokyo Daigaku, *Dai Nihon shiryō*, ser. 12, vol. 18, p. 20, entry for Genna 1/4/4; Ono, "Sunpuki," 187, entry for Genna 1/4/6.

76. Ono, "Sunpuki," 189–191.

77. Kasaya, *Sekigahara kassen to Ōsaka no jin*, 264.

78. Ōsaka-jō, *Ikusa-ba no kōkei*, 118–119.

79. Tokyo Daigaku, *Dai Nihon shiryō*, ser. 12, vol. 19, p. 980, entry for Genna 1/5/7.

80. Kasaya, *Sekigahara kassen to Ōsaka no jin*, 264–279. Tokyo Daigaku Shiryō Hensanjo, *Dai Nihon shiryō*, collects a huge assortment of sources (424 pages of material) that comment on Hideyori's and Yododono's deaths; ser., 12, vol. 19, pp. 980–1014, and ser. 12, vol. 20, pp. 1–290.

81. Cooper, *They Came to Japan*, 28.

82. Watanabe T., *Toyotomi Hideyoshi o saihakkutu suru*, 151–195.

83. Watanabe T., " 'Ōsaka natsu no jin Echizen hei kubitori jō' ni tsuite."

84. See Watanabe Daimon's discussion of head taking in *Ōsaka rakujō*, 175–177.

85. *Keichō kenmon sho* in Tokyo Daigaku Shiryō Hensanjo, *Dai Nihon shiryō*, ser. 12, vol. 20, p. 293, entry for Genna 1/5/8.

86. Tokyo Daigaku, *Dai Nihon shiryō*, ser. 12, vol. 20, p. 299.

87. Ono, "Sunpuki," 196; entry for Genna 1/5/10, *Dai Nihon shiryō*, ser., 12, vol. 20, p. 327.

88. Tokyo Daigaku, *Dai Nihon shiryō*, ser. 12, vol. 20, p. 414, entries for Genna 1/5/15.

89. Ibid., 491, entries for Genna 1/5/18.

90. Ibid., 497, entries for Genna 1/5/21.

91. Ono, "Sunpuki," 198, entry for Keichō 20/5/23.

92. Ibid., 203, entry for Keichō 20/intercalary 6/9 (1615; one month before the shift to Genna 1).

93. Tokugawa Bijutsukan, *Ieyasu no isan*, 234.

94. Ono, "Sunpuki," 205, entry for Keichō 20/intercalary 6/16.

95. These documents are translated in De Bary, Gluck, and Tiedemann, *Sources of Japanese Tradition*, 2:12–18.

96. Tokugawa Bijutsukan, *Ieyasu no isan*, fig. 151.

97. Gotō Bijutsukan, *Yamanoue Sōjiki*, 78, includes images of the piece and its bags as well as relevant passages from *Yamanoue Sōjiki* and other texts.

98. Quoted in Cooper, "Early Europeans and Tea," 116.

99. The Noh play "Kokaji" is translated in Sadler, *Japanese Plays;* Parker, "Kokaji."

100. Oyler, *Swords, Oaths, and Prophetic Visions*, 116–117.

101. Botsman, *Punishment and Power*, 20.

102. This anecdote is helpfully translated by Willem Boot in De Bary, Gluck, and Tiedemann, *Sources of Japanese Tradition*, 2:25.

103. An essential resource for the study of Ieyasu's huge collection of swords is Tokugawa Bijutsukan, *Sunpu owakemono tōken to sengoku bushō gazō*. More recently, a helpful resource that situates this collection in the broader history of swords in Japan is Sano Bijutsukan, *Meibutsu tōken*.

104. Oyler, *Swords*, 134–135.

105. Tokyo Daigaku Shiryō Hensanjo, *Dai Nihon shiryō*, ser. 12, vol. 21, p. 329.

106. Ono, "Sunpuki," 212–213.

107. Bolitho, "The *Han*," 4:193.

108. See Butler's translation in "Tokugawa Ieyasu's Regulations for the Court," 532–536.

109. Kornicki, "Books in the Service of Politics," 78; Butler, "Tokugawa Ieyasu's Regulations for the Court," 525–532.

110. The actual event at Nijō Castle is recorded in Ono, "Sunpuki," 216–217, entry for Keichō 20/7/17. Butler's discussion of the code in "Tokugawa Ieyasu's Regulations for the Court," 536–551, is essential.

Chapter 6: Apotheosis

1. See, e.g., Pitelka, "Review of *Art of the Samurai: Japanese Arms and Armor*"; Pitelka, "Should Museums Welcome Parody? Review of *Lords of the Samurai;* Sand, "Monumentalizing the Everyday."

2. Gerhart, *Eyes of Power*, 75.

3. Or as Willem Boot put it, "Ask any Japanese, and he is likely to tell you that deifying humans is just one of those Japanese customs. Perhaps he will even add, that foreigners do not understand. In fact, however, the number of clearly identifiable historical figures who have been deified is not all that great." Boot, "Death of a Shogun," 144. Boot questions whether the famous examples of Hachiman and Sugawara no Michizane—the two most often-cited examples of pre-sixteenth-century deification—can even be considered instances of the worship of deceased human subjects.

4. See Watsky, *Chikubushima,* 204–208. For an account of the deification, see Boot, "Death of a Shogun," 156–157.

5. See Sonehara, *Shinkun Ieyasu no tanjō,* 19–26, on the Toyotomi precedent.

6. Boot, "Death of a Shogun," 148. See also Sonehara, *Tokugawa Ieyasu shinkakuka e no michi;* see also Boot, "Tokugawa Ieyasu no shinkakuka o megutte."

7. See Boot's useful description of the ceremony, based on Bonshun's diary; "Death of a Shogun," 149–150.

8. Some key documents related to the founding and ongoing maintenance of the Tōshōgū on Mount Kunō, including photographs of originals as well as details on objects in the shrine's collection, can be found in Tottori-shi Rekishi Hakubutsukan, *Tōshōgū ten,* 4–16. Also see the document "Kunōzan odōgū no oboe," in Mitsui Kinen Bijutsukan, *Tokugawa Ieyasu no iaihin,* 141–144.

9. Boot, "Death of a Shogun," 150.

10. Gerhart notes that there is no mention of cremation in any of the remaining texts, and that her assumption is that it was the actual body of Ieyasu that was moved; *Eyes of Power,* 169n11.

11. Boot, "Death of a Shogun," 155.

12. Sonehara, *Shinkun Ieyasu no tanjō,* 66.

13. See Tokugawa Kinen Zaidan, *Nikkō Tōshōgū to shōgun shasan* (Tokyo: Tokugawa Kinen Zaidan, 2011) for a thorough overview of the pilgrimages of Ieyasu's successors. It is worth noting that even those shoguns who were unable to visit the shrine-temple complex still sent representatives, annually, to attend anniversary rituals (8).

14. In this area of interpretation, I disagree with the conclusions of Boot, whose work I otherwise rely on here. Boot sees the worship of Ieyasu as being primarily a religious development, rather than a cultural or political matter. In "Death of a Shogun" (162), he writes, "Within this religious context, I think it is fair to say that the driving force behind the worship of Ieyasu was in the first instance a personal relation to Ieyasu, and a deeply felt, personal belief." These strike me as unsubstantiated and indeed unknowable claims. What qualified as "a personal relation" in the cultural logic of the seventeenth century cannot be assumed to correspond to twentieth- and twenty-first-century notions of friendship and family; likewise, making assumptions about "belief" when much of the documentary record in this regard focuses on ritual, strikes me as an egregious act of anachronistic thinking. Religious ritual and the emplacement of ritual sites and structures on a geographical and political map of power was clearly one of the primary means by which premodern rulers in Japan established and maintained their authority, as has been demonstrated in the work of countless scholars working in Japanese, and also recently in English in the work of Herman Ooms, Thomas Conlan, Matthew Stavros, Andrew Watsky, Gregory Levine, Karen Gerhart, Mary Elizabeth Berry, Beatrice Bodart-Bailey, Laura Nenzi, and others.

15. Nakano Mitsuhiro, *Shokoku Tōshōgū no shiteki kenkyū,* 9–10.

16. On Iemitsu, I have relied heavily on Fujii Joji, *Tokugawa Iemitsu,* and Nikkō Tōshōgū Shamusho, *Tokugawa Iemitsu kō den.* In English, on Iemitsu's impact on the Tokugawa bureaucracy, see Totman, *Politics in the Tokugawa Bakufu,* 207–208. For a recent treatment of Iemitsu's suppression of the Shimabara Rebellion and the so-called Sakoku edicts, see Laver, *Sakoku Edicts and the Politics of Tokugawa Hegemony.*

17. Gerhart, *Eyes of Power,* 5.

18. Coaldrake, *Architecture and Authority in Japan,* 138–162.

19. Coaldrake, "Building a New Establishment," 155. See also Coaldrake, *Architecture and Authority in Japan,* 164–80.

20. Coaldrake, "Building a New Establishment," 159.

21. Nikkō Tōshōgū Shamusho, *Tokugawa Iemitsu kō den,* 213–215. Iemitsu may have been the richest of all Tokugawa shoguns. In addition to the massive wealth inherited from Ieyasu

and Hidetada, the gold and silver mines that Ieyasu took over in the first decade of the seventeenth century would continue to be productive for another decade or so, and levies on the warlords proved to be a remarkably effective method of fund-raising. See Totman, *Politics in the Tokugawa Bakufu,* 77, for more details. See also Bodart-Bailey, *Dog Shogun,* 184–192, on the consequences of Iemitsu's financial policies.

22. Sonehara, *Shinkun Ieyasu no tanjō,* 66.

23. UNESCO, *WHC Nomination Documentation,* File 913.pdf, p. 1.

24. Takafuji Harutoshi, "Nikkō Tōshōgū no chōkoku ni tsuite," in *Nikkō Tōshōgū no sōshoku mon'yō,* ed. Graphic-sha (Tokyo: Graphic-sha, 1994), 114–127.

25. Okawa, *Edo Architecture,* and Gerhart, *Eyes of Power,* are the two most important examples.

26. The letter is reproduced and transcribed in Kobori, *Kobori Enshū no shojō,* 44.

27. Quoted in Toby, *State and Diplomacy,* 203.

28. Ibid., 204.

29. Ibid.

30. On the money Ieyasu left to his descendants, see Totman, *Politics in the Tokugawa Bakufu,* 77.

31. The original *Sunpu owakemono odōgū chō* is in the collection of the Tokugawa Art Museum in Nagoya. It is also transcribed in two separate sections in Tokyo Daigaku, *Dai Nihon shiryō.* The first section (registers 1–5) is, somewhat confusingly, reproduced in ser., 12, vol. 24, pp. 756–865, while the second section (registers 6–11) is reproduced before this, in ser., 12, vol. 24, pp. 652–739. The final register, Money, is technically dealt with in a separate document, *Kunō okura kingin uketori chō,* which appears in Tokyo Daigaku Shiryō Hensanjo, *Dai Nihon shiryō,* ser. 12, vol. 24, pp. 746–756.

32. The most comprehensive source for the study of extant objects from the former collection of Ieyasu is Tokugawa Bijutsukan, *Ieyasu no isan,* 1992.

33. Pitelka, "The Empire of Things," 19–32.

34. This theme is similar to another Hu Zhifu painting of Budai, from the Fukuoka Art Museum, that appeared in Levine and Lippit, *Awakenings,* 94–95.

35. Other warrior families also categorized their heirloom treasures, passing them down from one generation to the next, including objects received from the Tokugawa. The Hosokawa, for example, maintained a ledger known as *Summary of the Famous Objects of [This] Honorable House (On'ie meibutsu no taigai).* The first two items listed are swords received from Tokugawa Hidetada and Ieyasu, respectively. See the transcription of this document, as well as many extant objects named within, in Yamanashi Kenritsu Bijutsukan, *Daimyō Hosokawa-ke no shihō,* 175.

36. Fisher, *Making and Effacing Art.*

37. Wakayama Kenritsu Hakubutsukan, *Kishū Tōshōgū no meihō,* 8–9.

38. Gerhart, *Eyes of Power,* 111.

39. Ōta, *Chronicle of Lord Nobunaga,* 20.

40. Fujii Joji weaves Iemitsu's illness into the main fabric of his biography of the shogun. See in particular chapter 5, "The Development of the Shogunal Administration and Iemitsu's Illness," and chapter 8, "The Death of Iemitsu," on his deterioration over the period 1639–1651. Also see Gerhart, *Eyes of Power,* 138, and "Visions of the Dead." For a comprehensive overview of extant portraits of Tōshō Daigongen/Ieyasu, see Tokugawa Kinen Zaidan, *Tokugawa Ieyasu shōzō.*

41. On warrior portraits, see Miyajima, "Buke no shōzō."

42. Gerhart, "Visions of the Dead," discusses evidence that Iemitsu may have considered himself to be a reincarnation of Ieyasu, even though he was born while the Tokugawa founder was still alive, and certainly wanted to model his reign on that of his ancestor (10–11).

43. Even doctors and construction contractors, who had a kind of in-between status, were included in the compilation. See Fujii Joji, *Tokugawa Iemitsu*, 145–146. See also Saiki, Hayashi, and Hashimoto, *Kan'ei shoka keizuden.*

44. Berry, *Japan in Print*, 113–114.

45. See also Ng, "Redefining Legitimacy in Tokugawa Historiography," on the marshaling of Chinese concepts of legitimacy and sovereignty in the service of Tokugawa ideology, including attempts to reinvent Ieyasu as a Chinese-style sage ruler who had received the mandate of heaven.

46. Zaidan Hōjin Shintō Taikei Hensankai, *Tōshōgū*, a volume in *Zoku Shintō taikei* (Tokyo: Zaidan Hōjin Shintō Taikei Hensankai, 2004) contains the sources.

47. Ishii, *Shōgun no seikatsu*, 71.

48. See Leor Halevi's study *Muhammad's Grave* for comparison.

49. See the prescriptions for visits to Nikkō, aimed at warriors but illustrative for all visitors, in Ishii, *Tokugawa kinrei kō*, 1:1243–1248.

50. See Sugawara, *Nihonjin no kami to hotoke*, on this topic.

51. Boot, "Religious Background of the Deification of Tokugawa Ieyasu," 2:332–333.

52. Kaibara, *Azumaji no ki, Kishi kiko, Seiyuki*, 72–76.

53. Nenzi, *Excursions in Identity*, 34–35.

54. Ibid., 56.

55. See also the account of a group of women travelers who visited the Tōshōgū at Nikkō despite the fact that they lacked the necessary travel permits, requiring them to hike overland through rough terrain. Shiba, *Literary Creations on the Road*, 74.

56. Takafuji Harutoshi, *Ieyasu-kō to zenkoku no Tōshōgū*, charts this development.

57. See Kano et al., *Kinsei sairei getsuji fūzoku emaki.*

58. Okazaki, for example, holds an Ieyasu procession (*Ieyasu gyōretsu*) as part of its Cherry Blossom Festival each spring, which involves more than one thousand participants dressed as samurai or other historical figures. It is unlikely, however, that this festival was organized in the same fashion during the Tokugawa period.

59. See, e.g., the writings of Fukuzawa Yukichi, Fujita Mokichi, and other scholars of the "civilization and enlightenment" (*bunmei kaika*) persuasion.

60. Bird, *Unbeaten Tracks in Japan*, letter 6, entry for June 13.

61. Karlin, "Tricentennial Celebration of Tokyo," 223.

62. Ibid., 221.

63. Ibid., 221.

64. Ōtsuki, *Tōkyō kaishi sanbyaku-nen sai*, particularly the section that begins "Koki tenrankai" (unnumbered p. 70).

65. Tokugawa Yoshichika, *Saigo no tonosama.*

66. Otabe, *Tokugawa Yoshichika no jūgonen sensō*, 62–66.

67. Tokugawa Yoshichika, *Saigo no tonosama*, 125. See also Scalapino, *Democracy and the Party Movement in Prewar Japan*, 365n27.

68. Tokugawa Yoshichika, *Saigo no tonosama*, 151–167; Otabe, *Tokugawa Yoshichika no jūgonen sensō*, 81–88.

69. On Yoshichika's regular interactions with Iwane Matsui and Ōkawa Shūmei, see Tokugawa Yoshichika, "Excerpts of the Diary of Tokugawa Yoshichika."

70. Tokugawa Yoshichika, *Saigo no tonosama*, 68–70. Moriyama, "Lord Hunting Tiger and Malay Learning in Japan," 61.

71. Moriyama, "Lord Hunting Tiger and Malay Learning in Japan," 57.

72. Tokugawa Yoshichika, *Saigo no tonosama*, 179–93.

73. Corner, *The Marquis*, 106. Also Tokugawa Yoshichika, *Saigo no tonosama*, 182.

74. As a colonial administrator, however, Yoshichika's focus was not just on culture. He was, for example, the author of a proposal for the administration of ethnic minorities in Southeast Asia, in which native minorities and foreign minorities would be separately cat-

egorized, and all would look to the Japanese for leadership and guidance. See Touwen-Bouwsma, "Japanese Policy towards the Chinese on Java," 55. He also supported a policy, despite his previous interactions with the sultan of Johore, of removing traditional political leaders throughout Southeast Asia. In the case of the sultans, this was rationalized by the claim that the Malayan people were now "subjects of the Japanese Emperor." Yoshichika's unpublished diary of his time in Malaya makes clear that he was a proponent of the hard-line approach toward "the Chinese, the sultan, and the Japanisation of the indigenous people through *Nippon-go* education." See Yoji, "Annotated Bibliographical Study of the Japanese Occupation of Malaya/Singapore," 266–267. Also, on Yoshichika's political involvements in Malaya, see Kratoska, *Japanese Occupation of Malaya,* 68; Bayly and Harper, *Forgotten Armies,* 220; Yoji, "Colonel Watanabe Wataru," 43–44.

75. Otabe, *Tokugawa Yoshichika no jūgonen sensō,* 46–49.

76. See Tokugawa Reimeikai, *Zaidan Hōjin Owari Tokugawa Reimeikai dai yon kai hōkokusho* (1935), for details on the construction of the museum, as well as information on exhibitions.

77. *Tokugawa Reimeikai, Zaidan Hōjin Owari Tokugawa Reimeikai dai go kai hōkokusho* (1936).

78. Otabe, *Tokugawa Yoshichika no jūgonen sensō,* 49.

79. Staatliche Museen zu Berlin, *Gedächtniskatalog der Ausstellung altjapanischer Kunst,* 1:23; images appear on 2:389, 391. Thanks to Magdalena Kolodziej for informing me of this source.

80. Tokugawa Reimeikai, *Zaidan Hōjin Owari* (1939), 4.

81. It is also possible that Yoshichika was simply a bundle of intellectual contradictions, as his financial support of the Socialist Party in the years after the war imply. (See Otabe, *Tokugawa Yoshichika no jūgonen sensō,* 195–200.) He was clearly a preservationist, dedicated in equal measure to protecting the forests of Kiso, the treasures of the Tokugawa, and the palaces of the sultans. He also may have been a kind of revolutionary pan-Asianist, as suggested by Saaler and Szpilman in the introduction to their edited volume, *Pan-Asianism,* 30. Though less well known than the activities described in this chapter, Yoshichika was also a widely recognized expert on etiquette and manners, which can perhaps be understood as a form of preservation. His textbook *Nichijō reihō no kokoro* (1939) is seen as a classic of its era, and has been reprinted in the following collection: Sue and Watanuki, *Bunken senshū kindai nihon no reigi sahō, Shōwa hen.*

82. Tokugawa Yoshichika, *Saigo no tonosama,* 117.

83. Yoshinobu Tokugawa, "The Tokugawa Art Collection: An Illustrated Lecture," lecture given on 2002/1/21 at the 130th anniversary of the Asiatic Society of Japan, http://www.asjapan.org/web.php/lectures/2002/01.

84. For more on the national project of sanitizing the Japanese past in the world of museums, see Noriko Aso, *Public Properties: Museums in Imperial Japan* (Durham, NC: Duke University Press, 2014), 203–222.

Epilogue: Museums and Japanese History

Epigraph. Appadurai 1986, 57.

1. Each venue seems to have produced its own catalog, though I refer here primarily to the catalog from the final exhibition, which includes essays by Tokugawa Yoshinobu as well as a number of American scholars of Japanese art and history; Montreal Museum of Fine Arts, *Tokugawa Collection.*

2. Montreal Museum of Fine Arts, *Tokugawa Collection,* 13.

3. Yoshinobu Tokugawa, "Shogun and Daimyo," 24.

4. Royal Armouries Museum, *Shogun,* 8.

5. Ibid.

6. The Nikkō Tōshōgū also sponsored some of the early publications and document collections on Ieyasu's life, such as the prolific Tokugawa scholar Nakamura Kōya's first book on Ieyasu, rather explicitly titled *Biography of the Light of the East (Tōshōden)* in 1915.

7. I visited the exhibition on August 2, 2005.

8. See Otabe's account of the fate of the Kii Tokugawa in *Tokugawa Yoshichika no jūgonen sensō*, 55–58.

9. See, e.g., Tōkyū Bijutsu Kurabu, *Bishū Tokugawa ke gozōhin irefuda* (1921) for a sample of a sale of Owari Tokugawa items, or Tōkyū Bijutsu Kurabu, *Kishū Tokugawa ke gozōhin irefuda mokuroku* (1933) for a large sale of Kii Tokugawa items.

10. Tokyo Kokuritsu Hakubutsukan, *Dai Tokugawa ten*.

11. A press release on the website of the Tokyo National Museum from November 22, 2007, explained that the 30,000th visitor had arrived that day, ten days before the exhibition would close. Tokyo Kokuritsu Hakubutsukan, "Tokubetsuten 'Dai Tokugawa Ten' nyūjōsha sanjūmannin tassei."

12. Bennett, *Birth of the Museum*, i.

13. International Council of Museums, "Museum Definition."

14. Kirshenblatt-Gimblett, "Exhibitionary Complexes," 42.

15. Harrison, *Dark Trophies*.

16. Brown, "Thing Theory," 4.

17. Compare the role of material culture in Japan's modernity (seen, for example, in the predicament of making sense of late nineteenth-century concerns about Western dominance, followed by the challenge of silencing its own early twentieth-century history of aggression, violence, and war) with Mexico's concern with constructing a narrative of postcolonial sovereignty with a national center. On the former, see Tanaka, *New Times in Modern Japan*, 168–169; on the latter, see Lomnitz, "Elusive Property," 119–138.

Bibliography

Adorno, Theodor W., and Max Horkheimer. *Dialectic of Enlightenment.* New York: Verso, 2010.

Akutagawa Tatsuo. "Sengoku bushō to taka: Taikō Hideyoshi no Hyūga taka no sū bugyō setchi o megutte." In *Nihon chūsei no seiji to bunka,* edited by Toyoda Takeshi Sensei Koki Kinenkai, 543–562. Tokyo: Yoshikawa Kobunkan, 1980.

Allen, John. *Lost Geographies of Power.* Oxford: Wiley-Blackwell, 2003.

Althusser, Louis. *Philosophy of the Encounter: Later Writings, 1978–1987.* New York: Verso, 2006.

Appadurai, Arjun, ed. *The Social Life of Things: Commodities in Cultural Perspective.* New York: Cambridge University Press, 1986.

Asao Naohiro. "The Sixteenth-Century Unification." In *Early Modern Japan,* edited by John Whitney Hall. Vol. 4, *The Cambridge History of Japan.* New York: Cambridge University Press, 1991.

Aso, Noriko. *Public Properties: Museums in Imperial Japan.* Durham, NC: Duke University Press, 2014.

Auslander, Leora. *Cultural Revolutions: Everyday Life and Politics in Britain, North America, and France.* Berkeley: University of California Press, 2009.

Bay, Alexander. "The Swift Horses of Nukanobu: Bridging the Frontiers of Medieval Japan." In *JAPANimals: History and Culture in Japan's Animal Life,* edited by Gregory Pflugfelder and Brett Walker. Ann Arbor: Center for Japanese Studies, University of Michigan Press, 2005.

Bayly, Christopher Alan, and Timothy Norman Harper, eds. *Forgotten Armies: The Fall of British Asia, 1941–1945.* Cambridge, MA: Harvard University Press, 2005.

Bell, Catherine. *Ritual Theory, Ritual Practice.* New York: Oxford University Press, 1992.

Bennett, Jane. *Vibrant Matter: A Political Ecology of Things.* Durham, NC: Duke University Press, 2010.

Bennett, Tony. *The Birth of the Museum: History, Theory, Politics.* New York: Routledge, 1995.

Berry, Mary Elizabeth. *The Culture of Civil War in Kyoto.* Berkeley: University of California Press, 1994.

———. *Hideyoshi*. Harvard East Asian Monographs. Cambridge, MA: Harvard University Asia Center, 1982.

———. *Japan in Print: Information and Nation in the Early Modern Period*. Berkeley: University of California Press, 2006.

———. "Public Peace and Private Attachments: The Goals and Conduct of Power in Early Modern Japan." *Journal of Japanese Studies* 12, no. 2 (Summer 1986): 237–271.

Bird, Isabella. *Unbeaten Tracks in Japan*. London: John Murray, 1911.

Bisson, Thomas N. *The Crisis of the Twelfth Century*. Princeton, NJ: Princeton University Press, 2008.

Bodart-Bailey, Beatrice. *The Dog Shogun: The Personality and Policies of Tokugawa Tsunayoshi*. Honolulu: University of Hawai'i Press, 2006.

Bolitho, Harold. "The *Han*." In *Early Modern Japan*, edited by Marius Jansen. Vol. 4 of *The Cambridge History of Japan*. New York: Cambridge University Press, 1995.

———. *Treasures among Men: The Fudai Daimyo in Tokugawa Japan*. New Haven, CT: Yale University Press, 1974.

Boot, Willem Jan. "The Death of a Shogun: Deification in Early Modern Japan." In *Shinto in History: Ways of the Kami*, edited by John Breen and Mark Teeuwen. London: Curzon Press, 2000.

———. "The Deification of Tokugawa Ieyasu." *Japan Foundation Newsletter*. February 1987.

———. "The Religious Background of the Deification of Tokugawa Ieyasu." In *Rethinking Japan: Social Sciences, Ideology, and Thought*, edited by Adriana Boscaro, Franco Gatti, and Massimo Raveri, vol. 2. New York: St. Martin's Press, 1990.

———. "Tokugawa Ieyasu no shinkakuka o megutte." In *Nihon kyoikushi ronso: Motoyama Yukihiko Kyoju taikan kinen ronbunshu*, edited by Motoyama Yukihiko Kyoju Taikan Kinen Ronbunshu Iinkai, 417–435. Kyoto: Shibunkaku Shuppan, 1988.

Botsman, Daniel V. *Punishment and Power in the Making of Modern Japan*. Princeton, NJ: Princeton University Press, 2007.

Boxer, C. R. *The Affair of the "Madre de Deus": A Chapter in the History of the Portuguese in Japan*. London: Kegan Paul, Trench, Trubner, 1929.

———. *The Christian Century in Japan: 1549–1650*. Berkeley: University of California Press, 1951.

Brown, Bill. "Thing Theory." In *Things*, edited by Bill Brown. Chicago: University of Chicago Press, 2004.

Brown, Phillip C. *Central Authority and Local Autonomy in the Formation of Early Modern Japan: The Case of Kaga Domain*. Stanford, CA: Stanford University Press, 1993.

Brownlee, John S. *Political Thought in Japanese Historical Writing: From Kojiki (712) to Tokushi Yoron (1712)*. Waterloo, ON: Wilfrid Laurier University Press, 1991.

Brucker, Gene. *Living on the Edge in Leonardo's Florence*. Berkeley: University of California Press, 2005.

Brushke-Johnson, Lee. *Dismissed as Elegant Fossils: Konoe Nobutada and the Role of Aristocrats in Early Modern Japan*. Leiden: Hotei, 2004.

Butler, Lee. *Emperor and Aristocracy in Japan, 1467–1680*. Cambridge, MA: Harvard University Asia Center, 2002.

———. "Tokugawa Ieyasu's Regulations for the Court: A Reappraisal." *Harvard Journal of Asiatic Studies* 54, no. 2 (December 1994): 509–551.

Clulow, Adam. "From Global Entrepōt to Early Modern Domain: Hirado, 1609–1641." *Monumenta Nipponica* 65, no. 1 (2010): 1–35.

Clunas, Craig. *Pictures and Visuality in Early Modern China*. Princeton, NJ: Princeton University Press, 1997.

———. *Superfluous Things: Material Culture and Social Status in Early Modern China.* Champaign: University of Illinois Press, 1991.
Coaldrake, William H. *Architecture and Authority in Japan.* New York: Routledge, 1996.
———. "Building a New Establishment: Tokugawa Iemitsu's Consolidation of Power and the Taitokuin Mausoleum." In *Edo and Paris: Urban Life and the State in the Early Modern Era,* edited by James L. McClain, John M. Merriman, and Ugawa Kaoru, 153–172. Ithaca, NY: Cornell University Press, 1994.
Conlan, Thomas. *From Sovereign to Symbol: An Age of Ritual Determinism in Fourteenth Century Japan.* New York: Oxford University Press, 2011.
———. *State of War: The Violent Order of Fourteenth-Century Japan.* Ann Arbor: Center for Japanese Studies, University of Michigan, 2003.
———. *Weapons and Fighting Techniques of the Samurai Warrior, 1200–1877.* London: Amber Books, 2008.
Cooper, Michael. "The Early Europeans and Tea." In *Tea in Japan: Essays on the History of Chanoyu,* edited by Paul Varley and Kumakura Isao, 101–134. Honolulu: University of Hawai'i Press, 1989.
———, ed. *João Rodrigues's Account of Sixteenth-Century Japan.* London: Hakluyt Society, 2001.
———, ed. *Rodrigues the Interpreter: An Early Jesuit in Japan and China.* New York: Weatherhill, 1974.
———, ed. *They Came to Japan: An Anthology of European Reports on Japan, 1543–1640.* Ann Arbor: Center for Japanese Studies, University of Michigan, 1995.
Corner, E. J. H. *The Marquis: A Tale of Syonan-to.* Singapore: Heinemann Asia, 1981.
Cort, Louise Allison. "The Grand Kitano Tea Gathering." *Chanoyu Quarterly* 31 (1982): 15–31.
———. *Shigaraki, Potter's Valley.* Reprint, Bangkok: Orchid Press, 2006.
de Bary, William Theodore, Carol Gluck, and Arthur E. Tiedemann, comps. *Sources of Japanese Tradition, 1600–2000.* 2nd ed. Vol. 2. New York: Columbia University Press, 2006.
Dobbins, James C. *Jōdo Shinshū: Shin Buddhism in Medieval Japan.* Honolulu: University of Hawai'i Press, 2002.
Dos Santos, José Miguel Pinto. "Ieyasu (1542–1616) versus Ieyasu (1543–1616): Calendrical Coversion Tables for the 16th and 17th Centuries." *Bulletin of Portuguese/Japanese Studies* 5 (December 2003): 9–26.
Ebrey, Patricia Buckley. *Accumulating Culture: The Collections of Emperor Huizong.* Seattle: University of Washington Press, 2008.
Ebrey, Patricia Buckley, and Maggie Bickford, eds. *Emperor Huizong and Late Northern Song China: The Politics of Culture and the Culture of Politics.* Cambridge, MA: Harvard University Asia Center, 2006.
Edo Tokyo Hakubutsukan. *Nijōjō ten.* Tokyo: Edo Tokyo Hakubutsukan, 2012.
Eguchi Kōzō. *Chajin Oda Nobunaga: Chanoyu no rekishi o kaeta Sengoku bushō.* Tokyo: PHP Kenkyūjo, 2010.
Elison, George, and Smith, Bardwell L., eds. *Warlords, Artists, and Commoners: Japan in the Sixteenth Century.* Honolulu: University of Hawai'i, 1981.
Elisonas, J. S. A. "The Evangelic Furnace: Japan's First Encounter with the West." In de Bary, Gluck, and Tiedemann.
Elisonas, Jurgis. "Christianity and the Daimyo." In *Early Modern Japan,* edited by John Whitney Hall. Vol. 4 of *The Cambridge History of Japan,* 301–372. New York: Cambridge University Press, 1991.

———. "The Inseparable Trinity: Japan's Relations with China and Korea." In *Early Modern Japan,* edited by John Whitney Hall. Vol. 4 of *The Cambridge History of Japan,* 235–300. New York: Cambridge University Press, 1991.

Farris, William Wayne. *Japan's Medieval Population: Famine, Fertility, and Warfare in a Transformative Age.* Honolulu: University of Hawai'i Press, 2006.

Ferguson-Lees, James, and David A. Christie. *Raptors of the World.* London: A&C Black, 2001.

Fisher, Philip. *Making and Effacing Art: Modern American Art in a Culture of Museums.* New York: Oxford University Press, 1991.

Foucault, Michel. *Archaeology of Knowledge and the Discourse on Language.* New York: Routledge, 2005.

———. *Discipline and Punish: The Birth of the Prison.* New York: Vintage Books, 1979.

Friday, Karl F. *Samurai, Warfare and the State in Early Medieval Japan.* New York: Routledge, 2004.

Fujii Jizaemon. *Sekigahara kassen shiryōshū.* Tokyo: Shinjinbutsu Ōraisha, 1979.

Fujii Joji. *Edo kaibaku.* Tokyo: Shūeisha, 1992.

———. *Tokugawa Iemitsu.* Tokyo: Yoshikawa Kōbunkan, 1997.

Fujino Tamotsu. *Tokugawa Ieyasu jiten.*Tokyo: Shinjinbutsu Ōraisha, 1990.

Fukui Kenritsu Ichijōdani Asakura-shi Iseki Shiryōkan. *Hana saku jōkamachi Ichijōdani.* Fukui: Fukui Kenritsu Ichijōdani Asakura-shi Iseki Shiryōkan, 2005.

Funahashi Hidekata. *Keichō nikken roku.* Nihon Koten Zenshū Kankō Kai, 1939.

Furuta Shōkin. *Eisai: Kōzen gokokuron, Kissa yōjōki.* Vol. 1 of *Nihon no Zen goroku.* Tokyo: Kōdansha, 1994.

Futaki Ken'ichi. *Buke girei kakushiki no kenkyū.* Tokyo: Yoshikawa Kōbunkan, 2003.

———. *Chūsei buke girei no kenkyū.* Tokyo: Yoshikawa Kōbunkan, 1985.

———. *Chūsei buke no sahō.* Tokyo: Yoshikawa Kōbunkan, 1999.

———. *Sekigahara kassen: Sengoku no ichiban nagai hi.* Tokyo: Chūō Kōronsha, 1982.

Gallie, Duncan. *Social Precarity and Social Integration.* Luxembourg: Office for Official Publications of the European Communities, 2003.

Gell, Alfred. *Art and Agency: A New Anthropological Theory.* New York: Oxford University Press, 1998.

Gerhart, Karen M. *The Eyes of Power: Art and Early Tokugawa Authority.* Honolulu: University of Hawai'i Press, 1999.

———. "Visions of the Dead: Kano Tan'yū's Paintings of Tokugawa Iemitsu's Dreams." *Monumenta Nipponica* 59, no. 1 (2004): 1–34.

Gien Jugō. *Gien Jugō nikki.* 4 vols. Kyoto: Daigoji, 1984.

Gonoi Takashi. *Tokugawa shoki Kirishitanshi kenkyu.* Tokyo: Yoshikawa Kōbunkan, 1993.

Gotō Bijutsukan. *Yamanoue Sōjiki: Tenshō 14-nen no me.* Tokyo: Gotō Bijutsukan, 1995.

Haga Kōshirō, ed. "Sōtan nikki." In *Chadō koten zenshū,* edited by Sen Sōshitsu, 133–382. Vol. 6. Tokyo: Tankō Shinsha, 1958.

Halevi, Leor. *Muhammad's Grave: Death Rites and the Making of Islamic Society.* New York: Columbia University Press, 2007.

Hall, John Whitney. "The *Bakuhan* System." In *Early Modern Japan,* edited by John Whitney Hall. Vol. 4 of *The Cambridge History of Japan,* 128–182. New York: Cambridge University Press, 1991.

———. Introduction to *Early Modern Japan,* edited by John Whitney Hall. Vol. 4 of *The Cambridge History of Japan,* 1–39. New York: Cambridge University Press, 1991.

———. "Japan's Sixteenth-Century Revolution." In *Warlords, Artists, and Commoners: Japan in the Sixteenth Century,* edited by George Elison and Bardwell L. Smith, 7–21. Honolulu: University of Hawai'i Press, 1981.
Hanawa Hokinoichi, ed. *Gunsho ruijū.* Vol. 12. Tokyo: Keizai zashisha, 1905.
———, ed. *Oyudono no ue no nikki, Zoku gunsho ruiju.* Supp. Vols. 8–9. Kyoto: Taiyō Shinsha, 1943.
Hanley, Susan B. *Everyday Things in Premodern Japan: The Hidden Legacy of Material Culture.* Berkeley: University of California Press, 1997.
Harrison, Simon. *Dark Trophies: Hunting and the Enemy Body in Modern War.* New York: Berghahn Books, 2012.
Hawley, Samuel. *The Imjin War: Japan's Sixteenth-Century Invasion of Korea and Attempt to Conquer China.* Seoul: Royal Asiatic Society, 2005.
Hayashiya Seizō. "Tea Ceramics of the Momoyama Period." In *Raku: A Dynasty of Japanese Ceramists,* edited by Hayashiya Seizō, Raku Kichizaemon, and Akanuma Taka, 19–21. Paris: Maison de la culture du Japon à Paris, 1997.
Hayashiya Tatsusaburo. "Kitano ochanoyu no ki." In *Chadō koten zenshū,* edited by Sen Sōshitsu, 3–48. Vol. 6. Kyoto: Tankōsha, 1956.
Hendrickx, Katrien. *Origins of Banana-fibre Cloth in the Ryukyus, Japan.* Brussels: Leuven University Press, 2007.
Hickman, Money L. *Japan's Golden Age: Momoyama.* Dallas Museum of Art, 1996.
Hicks, Dan. "The Material-Cultural Turn: Event and Effect." In *The Oxford Handbook of Material Culture Studies,* edited by Dan Hicks and Mary C. Beaudry, 25–98. New York: Oxford University Press, 2010.
Hoffman, Stefan-Ludwig. *The Politics of Sociability: Freemasonry and German Civil Society, 1840–1918.* Translated by Tom Lampert. Ann Arbor: University of Michigan Press, 2007.
Hora Tomio. *Teppō: Denrai to sono eikyō.* Kyoto: Shibunkaku, 1991.
Horton, H. Mack. *The Journal of Sōchō.* Stanford, CA: Stanford University Press, 2002.
Hotta Masaatsu, ed. *Kansei chōshū shokafu.* 9 vols. Tokyo : Eishinsha Shuppanbu, 1917–1918.
Iida Kumiji. *Tenshō daijishin shi.* Nagoya: Nagoya Daigaku Shuppankai, 1987.
Ikegami, Eiko. *Bonds of Civility: Aesthetic Networks and the Political Origins of Japanese Culture.* New York: Cambridge University Press, 2005.
Ikegami Hiroko. *Shokuhō seiken to Edo bakufu.* Tokyo: Kōdansha, 2002.
Ikeuchi Shōichi. "Komaki, Nagakute no tatakai." In *Tokugawa Ieyasu jiten,* edited by Fujino Tamotsu, Murakami Tadashi, and Tokoro Rikio, 214–217. Tokyo: Shinjinbutsu Ōraisha, 1990.
Ikushima Terumi. "Chūsei kōki ni okeru 'kirareta kubi' no toriatsukai: kubi jikken to kyōshu no sozai." *Bunka shigaku* 50 (November 1994): 130–151.
Insatsushi Kenkyūkai, ed. *Hon to katsuji no rekishi jiten.* Tokyo: Kashiwashobo, 2000.
International Council of Museums (ICOM). "Museum Definition." ICOM Statutes. Twenty-first General Conference, Vienna, Austria, 2007. http://icom.museum/who-we-are/the-vision/museum-definition.html.
Ishii Ryōsuke. *Shōgun no seikatsu.* Tokyo: Akashi Shoten, 1990.
———, ed. *Tokugawa kinrei kō.* Tokyo: Sōbunsha, 1959.
Kaibara Ekiken. *Azumaji no ki, Kishi kiko, Seiyuki.* Vol. 98 of *Nihon koten bungaku taikei.* Tokyo: Iwanami Shoten, 1991.
Kaneko Hiraku. *Kioku no rekishigaku: Shiryō ni miru sengoku.* Tokyo: Kōdansha, 2011.

Kang, Etsuko Hae-Jin. *Diplomacy and Ideology in Japanese-Korean Relations.* New York: St. Martin's Press, 1997.

Kano Hiroyuki et al., eds. *Kinsei sairei getsuji fūzoku emaki.* Osaka: Tōhō shuppan, 2005.

Karlin, Jason G. "The Tricentennial Celebration of Tokyo: Inventing the Modem Memory of Edo." In *Image and Identity: Rethinking Japanese Cultural History,* edited by Yamaji Hidetoshi and Jeffrey E. Hanes. Kobe: Research Institute for Economics and Business Administration, Kobe University, 2004.

Kasaya Kazuhiko. *Sekigahara kassen: Ieyasu no senryaku to bakuhan taisei.* Tokyo: Kōdansha, 1994.

———. *Sekigahara kassen to Ōsaka no jin.* Tokyo: Yoshikawa Kōbunkan, 2007.

Kasaya Kazuhiko and Futaki Ken'ichi. *Sekigahara kassen: Sengoku no ichiban nagai hi.* Tokyo: Chūō Kōronsha, 1982.

Keene, Donald. *Yoshimasa and the Silver Pavilion: The Creation of the Soul of Japan.* New York: Columbia University Press, 2003.

Kimura Takaatsu, ed. *Butoku hennen shūsei.* 2 vols. Tokyo: Meichō Shuppan, 1976.

Kirshenblatt-Gimblett, Barbara. "Exhibitionary Complexes." In *Museum Frictions: Public Cultures / Global Transformations,* edited by Ivan Karp et al., 35–45. Durham, NC: Duke University Press, 2006.

Kitagawa, Tomoko. "An Independent Wife during the Warring States: The Life of Kitamandokoro Nei (1548–1624) in Letters." PhD diss., Princeton University, 2009.

Kitajima Masamoto. *Tokugawa Ieyasu.* Tokyo: Chūō Kōronsha, 1963.

———. *Tokugawa Ieyasu no subete.* Tokyo: Shinjinbutsu Ōraisha, 1983.

Kitts, Margo, ed. *State, Power, and Violence.* Vol. 3 of *Ritual Dynamics and the Science of Ritual.* Wiesbaden: Harrassowitz Verlag, 2010.

Klein, Bettina. "Japanese Kinbyobu: The Gold-leafed Folding Screens of the Muromachi Period (1333–1573)." Adapted and expanded by Carolyn Wheelwright. *Artibus Asiae* 45, no. 1 (1984): 5–33, and nos. 2–3 (1984): 101–173.

Kobori Sōkei. *Kobori Enshū no shojō.* Tokyo: Tōkyōdō Shuppan, 2002.

Kodama Kōta and Sasaki Junnosuke, eds. *Shinpan shiryō ni yoru Nihon no ayumi.* Tokyo: Yoshikawa Kōbunkan, 1996.

Kokuritsu Rekishi Minzoku Hakubutsukan. *Rekishi no naka no teppō denrai: Tanegashima kara Boshin Sensō made.* Sakura, Japan: Kokuritsu Rekishi Minzoku Hakubutsukan, 2006.

Kopytoff, Igor. "The Cultural Biography of Things: Commoditization as Process." In *The Social Life of Things: Commodities in Cultural Perspective,* edited by Arjun Appadurai, 64–91. NY: Cambridge University Press, 1986.

Kornicki, Peter. *The Book in Japan: A Cultural History from the Beginnings to the Nineteenth Century.* Boston: Brill, 1998.

———. "Books in the Service of Politics: Tokugawa Ieyasu as Custodian of the Books of Japan." *Journal of the Royal Asiatic Society,* ser. 3, vol. 18, no. 1 (2008): 71–82.

Koslofsky, Craig. *Evening's Empire: A History of the Night in Early Modern Europe.* New York: Cambridge University Press, 2011.

Kosto, Adam J. *Hostages in the Middle Ages.* Oxford: Oxford University Press, 2012.

Kratoska, Paul H. *The Japanese Occupation of Malaya, 1941–1945.* Honolulu: University of Hawai'i Press, 1997.

Kumakura Isao. *Gomizuno'o in.* Tokyo: Asahi Shinbunsha, 1982.

———. *Kan'ei bunka no kenkyū.* Tokyo: Yoshikawa Kōbunkan, 1988.

"Kundaikan Sōchōki." In *Chadō koten zenshū,* edited by Sen Sōshitsu, Vol. 2. Kyoto: Tankōsha, 1982.

Kurokawa Naonori and Noda Tadao. "Fushimi jō to jōkamachi." In *Momoyama no kaika,* edited by Hayashiya Tatsusaburō, Vol. 4 of *Kyoto no rekishi.* Kyoto: Kyotoshi, 1971.
Kuwata Tadachika, ed. *Taikō shiryō shū.* Tokyo: Jinbutsu Ōraisha, 1965.
———. *Tokugawa Ieyasu: Sono tegami to ningen.* Tokyo: Ōbunsha, 1987.
———. *Toyotomi Hideyoshi kenkyū.* Tokyo: Kadokawa Shoten, 1975.
Lake, Rodrigo Rivero. *Namban: Art in Viceregal Mexico.* Madrid: Turner Libros, 2005.
Lamers, Jeroen Pieter. *Japonius Tyrannus: The Japanese Warlord Oda Nobunaga Reconsidered.* Leiden: Hotei, 2000.
———. *Treatise on Epistolary Style: João Rodriguez on the Noble Art of Writing Japanese Letters.* Ann Arbor: Center for Japanese Studies, University of Michigan, 2002.
Latour, Bruno. *Reassembling the Social: An Introduction to Actor-Network-Theory.* New York: Oxford University Press, 2005.
Laver, Michael S. *The Sakoku Edicts and the Politics of Tokugawa Hegemony.* Amherst, NY: Cambria Press, 2011.
Levine, Gregory, and Yukio Lippit. *Awakenings: Zen Figure Painting in Medieval Japan.* New Haven, CT: Yale University Press, 2007.
Levine, Gregory P. A. *Daitokuji: The Visual Cultures of a Zen Monastery.* Seattle: University of Washington Press, 2005.
Lewis, James B. *Frontier Contact between Choson Korea and Tokugawa Japan.* New York: RoutledgeCurzon, 2003.
Lidin, Olof G. *Tanegashima: The Arrival of Europe in Japan.* Copenhagen: NIAS Press, 2002.
Lillehoj, Elizabeth. *Art and Palace Politics in Early Modern Japan, 1580s–1680s.* Boston: Brill, 2011.
Lippit, Yukio. *Painting of the Realm: The Kano House of Painters in 17th-Century Japan.* Seattle: University of Washington Press, 2012.
Lomnitz, Claudio. "Elusive Property: The Personification of Mexican National Sovereignty." In *The Empire of Things: Regimes of Value and Material Culture,* edited by Fred R. Myers, 119–138. Santa Fe, NM: School of American Research Press, 2001.
Ludwig, Theodore W. "Chanoyu and Momoyama: Conflict and Transformation in Rikyū's Art." *Tea in Japan: Essays on the History of Chanoyu,* edited by Paul Varley and Kumakura Isao, 71–100. Honolulu: University of Hawai'i Press, 1989.
Lüdtke, Alf. "War as Work: Aspects of Soldiering in Twentieth-Century Wars." In *No Man's Land of Violence: Extreme Wars in the 20th Century,* edited by Alf Lüdtke and Bernd Weisbrod, 127–151. Göttingen: Wallstein Verlag, 2006.
Lu Yu. *The Classic of Tea: Origins and Rituals.* Translated by Francis Ross Carpenter. New York: Ecco Press, 1974.
Manzai Jugō. "Manzai Jugō nikki." *Zoku gunsho ruijū.* Supp. 1. Tokyo: Zoku Gunsho Ruijū Kanseikai, 1958.
Marx, Karl. *The Eighteenth Brumaire of Louis Bonaparte.* Chicago: Charles H. Kerr, 1907.
Maske, Andrew L. *Potters and Patrons in Edo Period Japan: Takatori Ware and the Kuroda Domain.* Burlington, VT: Ashgate, 2011.
Mass, Jeffrey P. "Of Hierarchy and Authority at the End of Kamakura." In *The Origins of Japan's Medieval World: Courtiers, Clerics, Warriors, and Peasants in the Fourteenth Century,* edited by Jeffrey P. Mass, 17–38. Stanford, CA: Stanford University Press, 1997.
Mateo, José Eugenio Borao. "The Arrival of the Spanish Galleons in Manila from the Pacific Ocean and Their Departure along the Kuroshio Stream (16th and 17th Centuries)." *Journal of Geographical Research* 47 (November 2007): 17–37.
Matsudaira Ietada. *Ietada nikki.* 2 vols. Kyoto: Rinsen Shoten, 1968.

Matsudaira Tadafuku. "Ietada nikki zōhō." Manuscript Collection. Waseda University Library.

Mauss, Marcel. *The Gift: Forms and Functions of Exchange in Archaic Societies.* London: Cohen and West, 1966.

McGirr, Elaine M. *Heroic Mode and Political Crisis, 1660–1745.* Newark: University of Delaware Press, 2009.

McMullin, Neil. *Buddhism and the State in Sixteenth-Century Japan.* Princeton, NJ: Princeton University Press, 1994.

Miller, Daniel. *Material Culture and Mass Consumption.* Oxford, UK: Blackwell, 1987.

Miller, Joseph C. *The Problem of Slavery as History.* New Haven, CT: Yale University Press, 2012.

Miner, Earl Roy, Hiroko Odagiri, and Robert E. Morrell, eds. *Princeton Companion to Classical Japanese Literature.* Princeton, NJ: Princeton University Press, 1988.

Mitsui Kinen Bijutsukan. *Tokugawa Ieyasu no iaihin: Denseihin de miru Ieyasu no bunkamen.* Tokyo: Mitsui Kinen Bijutsukan, 2010.

Miyajima Shin'ichi, ed. "Buke no shōzō." *Nihon no bijutsu,* no. 385 (June 15, 1998).

Miyamoto Yoshimi. "Nagashino no tatakai." In *Tokugawa Ieyasu jiten,* edited by Fujino Tamotsu, Murakami Tadashi, and Tokoro Rikio, 207–211. Tokyo: Shinjinbutsu Ōraisha, 1990.

Mizuno Kazuno. "Ichijōdani Asakura-shi iseki shutsudo ibutsu." In *Sengoku daimyō Asakura-shi to Ichijōdani,* edited by Mizuno Kazuno and Satō Kei. Tokyo: Kōshi Shoin, 2002.

———. "Ichijōdani no bunka." In *Sengoku daimyō Asakura-shi to Ichijōdani,* edited by Mizuno Kazuno and Satō Kei. Tokyo: Kōshi Shoin, 2002.

Montreal Museum of Fine Arts. *The Tokugawa Collection: The Japan of the Shoguns.* Montreal: Montreal Museum of Fine Arts, 1989.

Morimoto Masahiro. *Nihon chūsei no zōyo to futan.* Tokyo: Azekura Shobō, 1997.

———. "Sengoku ki no taka kenjō to zōtō girei." *Rekishigaku kenkyū* 662 (1994/9): 1–15.

———. *Zōtō to enkai no chūsei.* Tokyo: Yoshikawa Kōbunkan, 2008.

Morita Kōji. "Mikatagahara no tatakai." In *Tokugawa Ieyasu jiten,* edited by Fujino Tamotsu, Murakami Tadashi, and Tokoro Rikio, 200–207. Tokyo: Shinjinbutsu Ōraisha, 1990.

Morita Kyōji. *Ashikaga Yoshimasa no kenkyū.* Osaka: Izumi Shoin, 1993.

Moriyama, Mikihiro. "Lord Hunting Tiger and Malay Learning in Japan." In *Lost Times and Untold Tales from the Malay World,* edited by Jan van der Putten and Mary Kilcline Cody, 54–65. Singapore: National University of Singapore Press, 2009.

Morris, V. Dixon. "The City of Sakai and Urban Autonomy." In *Warlords, Artists, and Commoners: Japan in the Sixteenth Century,* edited by George Elison and Bardwell L. Smith, 23–54. Honolulu: University of Hawai'i Press, 1987.

———. "Sakai: From Shōen to Port City." In *Japan in the Muromachi Age,* edited by John Whitney Hall and Toyoda Takeshi, 89–105. Berkeley: University of California Press, 1977.

Murai Yasuhiko. "The Development of *Chanoyu:* Before Rikyū." Translated Paul Varley. In *Tea in Japan: Essays on the History of Chanoyu,* edited by Paul Varley and Kumakura Isao, 3–32. Honolulu: University of Hawai'i Press, 1989.

Murasaki Shikibu. *The Tale of Genji.* Translated by Edward G. Seidensticker. New York: Knopf, 1976.

Nagashima Fukutaro, ed. *Imai Sōkyū chanoyu nikki nukigaki.* Vol. 10 of *Chadō koten zenshū,* edited by Sen Soshitsu. Kyoto: Tankosha, 1961. Reprint, 1977.

———, ed. *Tennōjiya kaiki*. Vol. 7 of *Chadō koten zenshū*, edited by Sen Soshitsu. Kyoto: Tankosha, 1957–62. Reprint, 1977.
NAi Publishers. "A Precarious Existence: Vulnerability in the Public Domain." *Open*, no. 17 (2009): 4–5.
Nakamura Kōya. *Tokugawa Ieyasu kō den*. Tokyo: Kōdansha, 1965.
———. *Tokugawa Ieyasu monjo no kenkyū*. 4 vols. Tokyo: Nihon Gakujutsu Shinkōkai, 1958–1962.
———. *Tōshōkōden*. Tokyo: Shōbidō Shoten, 1915.
Nakamura Tadashi, ed. *Eiinbon ikoku nikki: Konchiin Suden gaikō monjo shūsei*. Tokyo: Tokyo Bijutsu, 1989.
Nakamura Tanio. "Gyomotsu on'e mokuroku no senja Nōami ni kansuru ikkōsatsu." *Tōkyo Kokuritsu Hakubutsukan kiyō* 7 (1971): 157–250.
Nakano Mitsuhiro. *Shokoku Tōshōgū no shiteki kenkyū*. Tokyo: Meichō Kankōkai, 2008.
Naomi Okawa. *Edo Architecture: Katsura and Nikko*. Translated by Alan Woodhull and Akito Miyamoto. New York: Weatherhill, 1964. Reprint, 1975.
Narushima Motonau, ed. *Tōshōgū onjikki*. Vol. 38 of *Tokugawa jikki*, edited by Kuroita Katsumi. Tokyo: Yoshikawa Kōbunkan, 1964.
Nelson, Thomas. "Slavery in Medieval Japan." *Monumenta Nipponica* 59, no. 4 (Winter 2004): 463–392.
Nenzi, Laura. *Excursions in Identity: Travel and the Intersection of Place, Gender, and Status in Edo Japan*. Honolulu: University of Hawai'i Press, 2008.
Nesaki Mitsuo. *Edo Bakufu hōyō seido no kenkyū*. Tokyo : Yoshikawa Kobunkan, 2008.
———. *Shogun no takagari*. Tokyo: Dōseisha, 1999.
Nezu Bijutsukan and Tokugawa Bijutsukan. *Higashiyama gyomotsu: "Zakka hoin" ni kansuru shinshiryō o chūshin ni*. Tokyo: Nezu Bijutsukan and Tokugawa Bijutsukan, 1976.
Ng, Wai-ming. "Redefining Legitimacy in Tokugawa Historiography." *Sino-Japanese Studies* 18 (2011): 1–20.
Nihonmatsu Yasuko. *Chusei takasho no bunka densho*. Tokyo: Miyai Shoten, 2011.
Nikkō Tōshōgū Shamusho. *Tokugawa Iemitsu kō den*. Nikkō: Nikkō Tōshōgū Shamusho, 1961.
Norton, Marcy. "Going to the Birds: Animals as Things and Beings in Early Modernity." In *Early Modern Things: Objects and Their Histories, 1500–1800*, edited by Paula Findlen. New York: Routledge, 2013.
Nukii Masayuki. *Toyotomi-Tokugawa jidai to Chōsen: Sensō soshite tsūshin no jidai e*. Tokyo: Akashi Shoten, 2010.
Oda Ei'ichi. "Chaire." In *Chadō bijutsu kanshō jiten*, edited by Ikeda Iwao. Kyoto: Tankosha, 1980.
Oka Yoshiko et al. *Kan'ei bunka no nettowaaku: "Kakumeiki" no sekai*. Kyoto: Shibunkaku Shuppan, 1998.
Okamoto Ryoichi. "Hideyoshi no jidai." In *Momoyama no kaika*. Vol. 4 of *Kyoto no rekishi*, edited by Hayashiya Tatsusaburo. Kyoto: Kyotoshi, 1971.
Okazaki Hironori. *Taka to shōgun: Tokugawa shakai no zōto shisutemu*. Tokyo: Kōdansha, 2009.
Ōkubo Hikozaemon. *Mikawa monogatari*. Vol. 26 of *Nihon Shisō Taikei*. Tokyo: Iwanami Shoten, 1974.
Okuno Takahiro. *Oda Nobunaga monjo no kenkyū*. 3 vols. 1969. Reprint, Tokyo: Yoshikawa Kōbunkan, 1988.
———. *Zōtei Oda Nobunaga monjo no kenkyū*. Vol. 1. Tokyo: Yoshikawa Kōbunkan, 1988.

Ōmura Yūkō. *Tenshō-ki*. In *Taikō shiryōshū*, edited by Kuwata Tadachika. Tokyo: Shinjinbutsu Ōraisha, 1971.

Ono Shinji, "Sunpuki." In *Ieyasu shiryo shu*, edited by Ono Shinji. Tokyo: Jinbutsu Ōraisha, 1965.

Ooms, Herman. *Tokugawa Ideology: Early Constructs, 1570–1680*. Princeton, NJ: Princeton University Press, 1989.

Ornithological Society of Japan. *Japanese Journal of Ornithology*. 1972–.

Ōsaka-jō Tenshukaku. *Ikusa-ba no kōkei*. Osaka: Ōsaka-jō tenshukaku, 2009.

———, ed. *Toyotomi-ki Ōsaka zu byōbu*. Osaka: Ōsaka-jō tenshukaku, 2009.

Ōta Gyūichi. *The Chronicle of Lord Nobunaga*. Translated by J. S. A. Elisonas and J. P. Lamers. Boston: Brill, 2011.

———. *Shinchō kōki*. Edited by Okuno Takahiro and Iwasawa Yoshihiko. Tokyo: Kadokawa Shoten, 1991.

———. *Taikōsama gunki no uchi*. Tokyo: Kyūko Shoin, 1975.

Otabe Yūji. *Tokugawa Yoshichika no jūgonen sensō*. Tokyo: Aoki Shoten, 1988.

Ōtsuki Shūji. *Tōkyō kaishi sanbyaku-nen sai*. Tokyo: Ōtsuki Shūji, 1890.

Owada Michiko. "Saishō." In *Tokugawa Ieyasu jiten*, edited by Fujino Tamotsu, Murakami Tadashi, and Tokoro Rikio , 56–65. Tokyo: Shinjinbutsu Ōraisha, 1990.

Oyler, Elizabeth. *Swords, Oaths, and Prophetic Visions: Authoring Warrior Rule in Medieval Japan*. Honolulu: University of Hawai'i Press, 2006.

Palmer, Patricia. *The Severed Head and the Grafted Tongue: Literature, Translation and Violence in Early Modern Ireland*. New York: Cambridge University Press, 2014.

Paramore, Kiri. *Ideology and Christianity in Japan*. New York: Routledge, 2009.

Parker, C. K. "Kokaji: A Nō Play in Two Acts." *Monumenta Nipponica* 3, no. 2 (July 1940): 619–629.

Petrucci, Grazia. "Pirates, Gunpowder, and Christianity in Late Sixteenth-Century Japan." In *Elusive Pirates, Pervasive Smugglers: Violence and Clandestine Trade in the Greater China Seas*, edited by Robert J. Antony, 59–72. Hong Kong: Hong Kong University Press, 2010.

Pflugfelder, Gregory M., and Brett L. Walker, eds. *JAPANimals: History and Culture in Japan's Animal Life*. Ann Arbor: Center for Japanese Studies, University of Michigan, 2005.

Pitelka, Morgan. "Art, Agency, and Networks in the Career of Tokugawa Ieyasu." In *Blackwell Companion to Asian Art*, edited by Deborah Hutton and Rebecca Brown, 447–470. New York: Wiley-Blackwell, 2011.

———. "The Empire of Things: Tokugawa Ieyasu's Material Legacy and Cultural Profile." *Japanese Studies* 29, no. 1 (May 2009): 19–32.

———. *Handmade Culture: Raku Potters, Patrons, and Tea Practitioners in Japan*. Honolulu: University of Hawai'i Press, 2005.

———. "Introduction: Wrapping and Unwrapping Art." In *What's the Use of Art? Asian Visual and Material Culture in Context*, edited by Jan Mrazek and Morgan Pitelka, 1–20. Honolulu: University of Hawai'i Press, 2007.

———, ed. *Japanese Tea Culture: Art, History, and Practice*. New York: Routledge, 2003.

———. "A Raku Wastewater Container and the Problem of Monolithic Sincerity." *Impressions* 30 (2008): 67–72.

———. "Review of *Art of the Samurai: Japanese Arms and Armor, 1156–1868*, edited by Morhihiro Ogawa." *Japanese Studies* 30, no. 3 (December 2010): 466–469.

———. "Should Museums Welcome Parody? Review of *Lords of the Samurai: The Legacy of a Daimyo Family*." *Early Modern Japan* 19 (2011): 58–61.

Plutschow, Herbert. *Rediscovering Rikyū and the Beginnings of the Japanese Tea Ceremony.* Folkstone, UK: Global Oriental, 2003.
Poliquin, Rachel. *The Breathless Zoo: Taxidermy and the Cultures of Longing.* University Park: Pennsylvania State University Press, 2012.
Princeton University Art Museum. *Handbook of the Collections.* Princeton, NJ: Princeton University Art Museum, 2007.
Rambelli, Fabio. *Buddhist Materiality: A Cultural History of Objects in Japanese Buddhism.* Stanford, CA: Stanford University Press, 2007.
Roberts, Luke S. *Performing the Great Peace: Political Space and Open Secrets in Tokugawa Japan.* Honolulu: University of Hawai'i Press, 2012.
Roessingh, M. P. H. *English Summary of the Inventory of the Archives of the Dutch Factory in Japan, 1609–1860.* The Hague: Nationaal Archief, n.d.
Rosenberg, Charles E., and Janet Golden, eds. *Framing Disease: Studies in Cultural History.* Piscataway, NJ: Rutgers University Press, 1991.
Royal Armouries Museum. *Shogun: The Life of Lord Tokugawa Ieyasu.* Leeds, UK: Royal Armouries Museum, 2005.
Rupp, Katharine. *Gift-Giving in Japan: Cash, Connections, Cosmologies.* Stanford, CA: Stanford University Press, 2003.
Russell, Gillian, and Clara Tuite, eds. *Romantic Sociability: Social Networks and Literary Culture in Britain, 1770–1840.* New York: Cambridge University Press, 2002.
Saaler, Sven, and Christopher W. A. Szpilman, eds. *Pan-Asianism: A Documentary History: 1850–1920.* Lanham, MD: Rowman and Littlefield, 2011.
Sadler, A. L. *Japanese Plays: Noh, Kyogen, Kabuki.* Singapore: Periplus Editions, 2010.
———. *The Maker of Modern Japan: The Life of Shogun Tokugawa Ieyasu.* Rutland, VT: Charles E. Tuttle, 1937.
Sahlins, Marshall. *Islands of History.* Chicago: University of Chicago Press, 1985.
Saiki Kazuma, Hayashi Ryōshō, and Hashimoto Masanobu, eds. *Kan'ei shoka keizuden.* 17 vols. Tokyo: Zoku Gunsho Ruiju Kanseikai, 1980–1997.
Saiki Kazuma and Someya Mitsuhiro, eds. *Kanemi kyōki.* Tokyo: Zoku Gunsho Ruijū Kanseikai, 1971.
Sakata Fumiko. *Hitojichi no rekishi: Kage no Nihonshi.* Tokyo: Nihon Shoseki, 1979.
Sand, Jordan. *House and Home: Architecture, Domestic Space, and Bourgeois Culture, 1880–1930.* Cambridge, MA: Harvard University Asia Center, 2005.
———. "Monumentalizing the Everyday: The Edo-Tokyo Museum." *Critical Asian Studies* 33, no.3 (2001): 351–378.
Sano Bijutsukan et al., eds. *Meibutsu tōken: Hōmotsu no Nihon tō.* Mishima: Sano Bijutsukan, 2011.
Sato Kei. "Asakura shi to Muromachi bakufu: Orei shinjō o chūshin to shite." In *Sengoku daimyō Asakura-shi to Ichijōdani,* edited by Mizuno Kazuno and Satō Kei, 35–58. Tokyo: Kōshi Shoin, 2002.
Satō Toyozō. "Muromachi jidai no zōtō tōken nit suite." *Kinko sōsho* 15 (March 1988): 311–331.
Saunders, Rachel. "Pursuits of Power: Falconry in Edo Period Japan." *Orientations* 36, no. 2 (March 2005): 82–92.
Scalapino, Robert A. *Democracy and the Party Movement in Prewar Japan: The Failure of the First Attempt.* Berkeley: University of California Press, 1975.
Schama, Simon. "Perishable Commodities: Dutch Still-Life Paintings and the 'Empire of Things.'" In *Consumption and the World of Goods,* edited by John Brewer, 478–488. London: Routledge, 1993.

Schwedler, Gerald, and Eleni Tounta. "Usurping Rituals: The Correlation between Formalised Repetitive Behaviour and Legitimacy." In *State, Power, and Violence*, edited by Axel Michaels. Vol. 3 of *Ritual Dynamics and the Science of Ritual*, 349–358. Wiesbaden: Harrassowitz Verlag, 2010).

Segal, Ethan Isaac. *Coins, Trade, and the State: Economic Growth in Early Medieval Japan*. Cambridge, MA: Harvard University Asia Center, 2011.

Seikadō Bunko Bijutsukan. *Seikadō chadōgu: Kanshō no tebiki* Tokyo: Seikadō Bunko Bijutsukan, 2010.

Selinger, Vijayanthi R. *Authorizing the Shogunate: Ritual and Material Symbolism in the Literary Construction of Warrior Order*. Boston: Brill, 2013.

Shapinsky, Peter D. *Lords of the Sea: Pirates, Violence, and Commerce in Late Medieval Japan*. Ann Arbor: Center for Japanese Studies, University of Michigan, 2014.

———. "Predators, Protectors, and Purveyors Pirates and Commerce in Late Medieval Japan." *Monumenta Nipponica* 64, no. 2 (Autumn 2009): 273–313.

Shermer, Michael. *How We Believe: The Search for God in an Age of Science*. New York: Owl Books, 2000.

Shiba, Keiko. *Literary Creations on the Road: Women's Travel Diaries in Early Modern Japan*. Translated by Motoko Ezaki. Lanham, MD: University Press of America, 2012.

Shiga Tarō. "Muromachi shōgunke no shihō o saguru." In *Muromachi shōgunke no shihō o saguru*, edited by Tokugawa Bijutsukan, 158–169. Nagoya: Tokugawa Bijutsukan, 2008.

Shimojū Kiyoshi. *'Miuri' no Nihonshi: Jinshin baibai kara nenki bōkō e*. Tokyo: Yoshikawa Kōbunkan, 2012.

Shirane, Haruo, ed. *Early Modern Japanese Literature*. New York: Columbia University Press, 2002.

Shiseki Kenkyūkai, ed. *Keichō kenbunroku anshi, Keichō nikki, Keichō nenroku, Genna nenroku*. Tokyo: Kyūko Shoin, 1986.

Skabelund, Aaron Herald. *Empire of Dogs: Canines, Japan, and the Making of the Modern Imperial World*. Ithaca, NY: Cornell University Press, 2011.

Slusser, Dale. "The Transformation of Tea Practice in Sixteenth-Century Japan." In *Japanese Tea Culture: Art, History, and Practice*, edited by Morgan Pitelka, 39–60. New York: Routledge, 2003.

Smits, Gregory. "Examining the Myth of Ryukyuan Pacifism." *Asia-Pacific Journal*, 37/3/10 (September 13, 2010). http://japanfocus.org/-gregory-smits/3409/article.html.

———. *Visions of Ryukyu: Identity and Ideology in Early-Modern Thought and Politics*. Honolulu: University of Hawai'i Press, 1999.

Sonehara Satoshi. *Shinkun Ieyasu no tanjo: Tōshōgū to Gongensama*. Tokyo: Yoshikawa Kōbunkan, 2008.

———. *Tokugawa Ieyasu: Shinkakuka e no michi*. Tokyo: Yoshikawa Kōbunkan, 1996.

Sōshitsu Sen, ed. *Chadō koten zenshū*. Vol. 2, 200–203. Kyoto: Tankōsha, 1982.

———. *The Japanese Way of Tea: From Its Origins in China to Sen Rikyū*. Honolulu: University of Hawai'i Press, 1998.

Souryi, Pierre. *The World Turned Upside Down: Medieval Japanese Society*. New York: Columbia University Press, 2001.

Staatliche Museen zu Berlin. *Gedächtniskatalog der Ausstellung altjapanischer Kunst*. Berlin: Japanischen Ausschuss für die Berliner Ausstellung Altjapanischer Kunst, 1939.

Stavros, Matthew. "Locational Pedigree and Warrior Status in Medieval Kyoto: The Residences of Ashikaga Yoshimitsu." *Japanese Studies* 29, no.1 (May 2009): 3–18.

Sue Tomoko and Watanuki Toyoaki, eds. *Bunken senshū kindai nihon no reigi sahō, Shōwa hen*. Tokyo: Nihon Tosho Sentaa, 2008.
Sugawara Shinkai. *Nihonjin no kami to hotoke: Nikkōzan no shinkō to rekishi*. Kyoto: Hōzōkan, 2001.
Suzuki Masao. *Edo to jōkamachi: Tenshō kara Meireki made*. Tokyo: Shinjinbutsu Ōraisha, 1976.
Swope, Kenneth. *A Dragon's Head and a Serpent's Tail: Ming China and the First Great East Asian War, 1592–1598*. Norman: University of Oklahoma Press, 2009.
Takafuji Harutoshi. *Ieyasu kō to zenkoku no Tōshōgū*. Tokyo: Tokyo Bijutsu, 1992.
———. "Nikkō Tōshōgū no chōkoku ni tsuite." In *Nikkō Tōshōgū no sōshoku mon'yō*, edited by Graphic-sha, 114–127. Tokyo: Graphic-sha Pub. Co., 1994.
Takemoto Chizu. *Shokuhōki no chakai to seiji*. Kyoto: Shibunkaku Shuppan, 2006.
Takeuchi Jun'ichi et al., eds. *Hideyoshi no chiryaku: "Kitano ōchanoyu" daikenshō*. Tokyo: Tankōsha, 2009.
———. "Meibutsuki no seisei kōzō: migaku to henshū no hazama." *Cha no koten*, edited by Tsutsui Hiroichi, 45–62. Vol. 10, *Chadō gaku taikei*. Tokyo: Tankōsha, 2001.
Takeuchi Rizo, ed. *Tamon'in nikki*. Vol. 4, *Zoho zoku shiryō taisei*. Kyoto: Rinsen Shoten, 1978.
Tana'ami Hiroshi. *Kodai no kōtsū*. Tokyo: Yoshikawa Kōbunkan, 1995.
Tanaka, Stefan. *New Times in Modern Japan*. Princeton, NJ: Princeton University Press, 2006.
Tani Akira. *Chakaiki no fūkei*. Kyoto: Kawara Shoten, 1995.
———, transcriber. "Senzoki." *Nomura Bijutsukan kiyō* 9 (2000): 101–120.
Taniguchi Katsuhiro. *Kenshō Honnōji no hen*. Tokyo: Yoshikawa Kōbunkan, 2007.
Tani Shin'ichi. "Gyomotsu on'e mokuroku." *Bijutsu kenkyū* 58 (October 1936): 439–447.
Teruhiko Hinotani, Hiroshi Emoto, and Hoan Oze. *Taikōki*. Tokyo: Iwanami Shoten, 1996.
Thoen, Irma. *Strategic Affection? Gift Exchange in Seventeenth-Century Holland*. Amsterdam: Amsterdam University Press, 2007.
Tingay, Ruth E., and Todd E. Katzner, eds. *The Eagle Watchers: Observing and Conserving Raptors around the World*. Ithaca, NY: Cornell University Press, 2010.
Toby, Ronald. *State and Diplomacy in Early Modern Japan: Asia in the Development of the Tokugawa Bakufu*. Stanford, CA: Stanford University Press, 1984.
Toki-shi Mino Tōji Rekishikan. *Sakai-shū no yakimono*. Toki: Toki-shi Mino Tōji Rekishikan, 1996.
Tokugawa Bijutsukan. *Bijutsu ni miru Nihon no supo-tsu*. Nagoya: Tokugawa Bijutsukan, 1994.
———. *Chanoyu dōgu*. Nagoya: Tokugawa Bijutsukan, 2000.
———. *Ieyasu no isan: Sunpu owakemono*. Nagoya: Tokugawa Bijutsukan, 1992.
———. *Sunpu owakemono tōken to sengoku bushō gazō*. Nagoya: Tokugawa Bijutsukan, 1974.
Tokugawa Kinen Zaidan. *Tokugawa Ieyasu shōzō: Edo jidai no hitobito no Ieyasu kan*. Tokyo: Tokugawa Kinen Zaidan, 2012.
———. *Nikkō Tōshōgū to shōgun shasan: kikakuten*. Tokyo: Edo-Tokyo Hakubutsukan, 2011.
Tokugawa Reimeikai. *Zaidan Hōjin Owari Tokugawa Reimeikai dai yon kai hōkokusho*. Nagoya: Tokugawa Reimeikai, 1935.
———. *Zaidan Hōjin Owari Tokugawa Reimeikai dai go kai hōkokusho*. Nagoya: Tokugawa Reimeikai, 1936.

———. *Zaidan Hōjin Owari Tokugawa Reimeikai dai hakkai hōkokusho.* Nagoya: Tokugawa Reimeikai, 1939.

Tokugawa Yoshichika. *Saigo no tonosama: Tokugawa Yoshichika jiden.* Tokyo: Kōdansha, 1973.

———. "Excerpts of the Diary of Tokugawa Yoshichika, Translated into English." *Tokyo War Crimes Trial: A Digital Exhibition.* University of Virginia Law Library Special Collections. http://lib.law.virginia.edu/imtfe/. 1946/6/7, box 3, folder 1, MSS 78–3, item 27—doc. no. 19469-A.

Tokugawa Yoshinobu. "Hatsuhana katatsuki no denrai ni tsuite." *Kinko sōsho* 18 (March 1991): 289–339.

———. "Ichiren no Tokugawa Ieyasu no gihitsu to nikka nenbutsu." *Kinko sōsho* 8 (March 1981): 627–797.

———. *Shinshū Tokugawa Ieyasu monjo no kenkyū.* 2 vols. Tokyo: Yoshikawa Kōbunkan, 1983–2006.

———. "Shogun and Daimyo." In *The Tokugawa Collection: The Japan of the Shoguns.* Montreal: Montreal Museum of Fine Arts, 1989.

Tokyo Daigaku Shiryō Hensanjo, ed. *Dai Nihon shiryō.* Tokyo: Tokyo Daigaku Shuppankai, 1964–.

———, ed. *Tokitsune kyōki.* In the series *Dai Nihon kokiroku.* Tokyo: Tōkyō Daigaku Shiryō Hensanjo, 1992.

Tokyo Kokuritsu Hakubutsukan. *Dai Tokugawa ten.* Tokyo: Tokyo Kokuritsu Hakubutsukan, 2007.

———. "Tokubetsuten 'Dai Tokugawa Ten' nyūjōsha sanjūmannin tassei." http://www.tnm.jp/jp/exhibition/special/200710daitokugawa_30man_20071122.html. Accessed January 8, 2008.

Tōkyū Bijutsu Kurabu. *Bishū Tokugawa ke gozōhin irefuda.* Tokyo: Tōkyū Bijutsu Kurabu, 1921.

———. *Kishū Tokugawa ke gozōhin irefuda mokuroku.* Tokyo: Tōkyū Bijutsu Kurabu, 1933.

Tonomura, Hitomi. *Community and Commerce in Late Medieval Japan.* Stanford, CA: Stanford University Press, 1992.

Totman, Conrad D. *The Green Archipelago: Forestry in Preindustrial Japan.* Berkeley: University of California Press, 1989.

———. *Politics in the Tokugawa Bakufu, 1600–1843.* Cambridge, MA: Harvard University Press, 1967.

———. *Tokugawa Ieyasu, Shogun: A Biography.* San Francisco: Heian, 1983.

Tottori-shi Rekishi Hakubutsukan. *Tōshōgū ten: Tōshōgū no meihō, shodaimyō to Tōshōgū.* Tottori: Tottori-shi Rekishi Hakubutsukan, 2003.

Touwen-Bouwsma, Elly. "Japanese Policy towards the Chinese on Java, 1942–1945." In *Southeast Asian Minorities in the Wartime Japanese Empire,* edited by Paul H. Kratoska. New York: RoutledgeCurzon, 2002.

Traganou, Jilly. *The Tōkaidō Road: Traveling and Representation in Edo and Meiji Japan.* New York: RoutledgeCurzon, 2004.

"Travels in Japan." *Asiatic Journal and Monthly Register for British and Foreign India, China, and Australia.* New Ser. Vol. 2 (May–August 1830): 193–200.

Tsang, Carol Richmond. *War and Faith: Ikkō Ikki in Late Muromachi Japan.* Cambridge, MA: Harvard University Asia Center, 2007.

Tsing, Anna Lowenhaupt. *Friction: An Ethnography of Global Connection.* Princeton, NJ: Princeton University Press, 2004.

Tsuji Zennosuke, ed. *Tamon'in nikki.* Tokyo: Kadokawa shoten, 1967.

Tsutsui Hiroichi, ed. *Cha no koten*. Vol. 10 of *Chadō gaku taikei*. Tokyo: Tankōsha, 2001.
———. "Seigan meibutsuki." In *Cha no koten*, edited by Tsutsui Hiroichi. Vol. 10 of *Chadō gaku taikei*, 373–402. Tokyo: Tankōsha, 2001.
———, *Shinpan chadō daijiten*. Kyoto: Tankōsha, 2010.
Tyler, Royall trans. *The Tale of the Heike*. New York: Penguin, 2012.
Uehara Kenzen. *Shimazu shi no Ryūkyū shinryaku: Mō hitotsu no Keichō no eki*. Ginowan, Okinawa: Gajumaru Shorin, 2009.
Umai Yūkiko. "Kinsei shōnin seido no rekishiteki zentei." *Kokushi danwakai zasshi* 40 (1999): 1–20.
United Nations Educational, Scientific and Cultural Organization (UNESCO). *WHC Nomination Documentation: Shrines and Temples of Nikko*. Paris: UNESCO, 1999.
Vaporis, Constantine Nomikos. *Tour of Duty: Samurai, Military Service in Edo, and the Culture of Early Modern Japan*. Honolulu: University of Hawai'i Press, 2008.
Varley, H. Paul, and George Elison. "The Culture of Tea: From Its Origins to Sen no Rikyū." In *Warlords, Artists, and Commoners: Japan in the Sixteenth Century*, edited by George Elison and Bardwell L. Smith, 187–222. Honolulu: University of Hawai'i Press, 1982.
Velazco, Rodrigo de Vivero y. "Relación del Japón (1609)." *Anales del Museo Nacional de México*. Vol. 1. Period 5ª (1934): 67–111.
Wakayama Kenritsu Hakubutsukan. *Kishū Tōshōgū no meihō*. Wakayama: Wakayama kenritsu hakubutsukan, 1989.
Wakita Haruko. *Women in Medieval Japan: Motherhood, Household Management and Sexuality*. Translated by Alison Takita. Clayton, Australia: Monash Asia Institute, 2006.
Walker, Brett L. *The Conquest of Ainu Lands: Ecology and Culture in Japanese Expansion, 1590–1800*. Berkeley: University of California Press, 2001.
———. *The Lost Wolves of Japan*. Seattle: University of Washington Press, 2005.
Walthall, Anne. "Do Guns have Gender? Technology and Status in Early Modern Japan." In *Recreating Japanese Men*, edited by Anne Walthall and Sabine Fruhstuck, 25–47. Berkeley: University of California Press, 2011.
Watanabe Daimon. *Ōsaka raku-jō: Sengoku shūen butai*. Tokyo: Kadokawa Gakugei Shuppan, 2012.
Watanabe Hiroshi. *A History of Japanese Political Thought, 1600–1901*. Translated by David Noble. Tokyo: International House of Japan, 2012.
———. *Tō Ajia no ōken to shisō*. Tokyo: Tokyo Daigaku Shuppankai, 1997.
Watanabe Takeru. " 'Ōsaka natsu no jin Echizen hei kubitori jō' ni tsuite." *Ōsaka-jō Tenshukaku kiyō* 1 (1965).
———. *Toyotomi Hideyoshi o saihakkutu suru*. Tokyo: Shinjinbutsu Ōraisha, 1996.
Watsky, Andrew M. *Chikubushima: Deploying the Sacred Arts in Momoyama Japan*. Seattle: University of Washington Press, 2005.
———. "Commerce, Politics, and Tea: The Career of Imai Sōkyū (1520–1593)." In *Japanese Tea Culture: Art, History, and Practice*, edited by Morgan Pitelka, 18–38. New York: Routledge, 2003.
Welter, Albert. "Zen as the Ideology of the Japanese State: Eisai and the Kōzen gokokuron." In *Zen Classics: Formative Texts in the History of Zen Buddhism*, edited by Steven Heine and Dale S. Wright, 65–112. New York: Oxford University Press, 2006.
Werbner, Richard P. *Holy Hustlers, Schism, and Prophecy: Apostolic Reformation in Botswana*. Berkeley: University of California Press, 2011.
Whyman, Susan E. *Sociability and Power in Late-Stuart England*. New York: Oxford University Press, 1999.

Witmore, Michael. *Culture of Accidents: Unexpected Knowledges in Early Modern England.* Stanford, CA: Stanford University Press, 2001.

Yamada Kuniaki. *Sengoku no komyunike-shon: Jijō to tsūshin.* Tokyo: Yoshikawa Kōbunkan, 2002.

Yamamoto Hirofumi. *Kan'ei jidai.* Yoshikawa Kōbunkan, 1989.

Yamana Takahiro. *Sengoku daimyō to takagari no kenkyū.* Iwaki-shi: Sanshūdō, 2006.

———. "Tokugawa Ieyasu to takagari." *Kokugakuin zasshi* 82, no. 4 (1991): 54–67.

Yamanashi Kenritsu Bijutsukan. *Daimyō Hosokawa-ke no shihō: Bunbu no rekishi to miyabi no bunka.* Kōfu: Yamanashi Kenritsu Bijutsukan, 2001.

Yamashina Tokitsune. *Tokitsune kyōki.* In *Dai Nihon kokiroku,* 14 vols. Tokyo: Iwanami Shoten, 1959–1991.

Yano Tamaki. *Kundaikan sōchōki no sōgō kenkyū.* Tokyo: Bensei Shuppan, 1999.

———. "Meibutsuki no seisei kōzō: Jikken to henshū no hazama," pt. 2. In *Cha no koten,* edited by Tsutsui Hiroichi. Vol. 10 of *Chadō gaku taikei.* Tokyo: Tankōsha, 2001.

Yoji, Akashi. "An Annotated Bibliographical Study of the Japanese Occupation of Malaya/Singapore, 1941–45." In *New Perspectives on the Japanese Occupation in Malaya and Singapore, 1941–1945,* edited by Akashi Yoji and Yoshimura Mako, 250–284. Singapore: National University of Singapore Press, 2008.

———. "Colonel Watanabe Wataru: The Architect of the Malayan Military Administration, December 1941–March 1943." In *New Perspectives on the Japanese Occupation in Malaya and Singapore, 1941–1945,* edited by Akashi Yoji and Yoshimura Mako, 33–64. Singapore: National University of Singapore Press, 2008.

Zaidan Hōjin Shintō Taikei Hensankai, ed. *Tōshōgū.* Tokyo: Zaidan Hōjin Shintō Taikei Hensankai, 2004.

Zoku Gunsho Ruijū Kanseikai, ed. *Rokuon nichiroku.* 1934; Reprint, Tokyo: Zoku Gunsho Ruiju Kanseikai, 1991.

———, ed. *Shintei Honkō Kokushi nikki.* Tokyo: Zoku Gunsho Ruijū Kanseikai, 1966–1971.

———, ed. *Shunkyūki.* 5 vols. Tokyo: Zoku Gunsho Ruijū Kanseikai, 1970–1983.

———, ed. *Tōdaiki, Sunpuki.* Tokyo: Heibonsha, 1995.

Index

Page numbers in boldface type refer to illustrations.

agency: of objects, 7, 11, 16, 44, 114, 156, 176; of human subjects, 34, 36, 43
Akechi Mitsuhide, 47, 51–53
Asakura, 17–18, 24–26, 32, 48–49, 100–101
Asano Nagayoshi, 75, 78, 107, 192n15
Ashikaga collection, 20–27, 31, 74, 179n11, 180n52
Ashikaga shoguns, 13–14, 45, 50, 59–60, 80–81, 99; as collectors, 2, 8, 20–27, 74, 140, 153
Ashikaga Yoshiaki, 17, 33, 70, 74, 101
Azai family, 17–18, 32
Azuchi, **xvi,** 39, 47, 52, 70–71, 102

Battle of Mikatagahara, **12,** 158
Battle of Sekigahara, **xv, xvi,** 120–127, **123;** and falconry, 108–112; in historiography, 9, 11, 43; and rituals of war, 14, 16; and sociability, 67, 80–85, 89
Battles of Komaki and Nagakute, 55
biography, 8–11, 47, 85, 140, 145–146, 157, 160, 173
Bonshun (1553–1632), 146

calligraphy, 1, 20, **58, 115,** 153, 157, 166, 168
cash (exchanged as gifts), 27–28, 65–72, 87, 91, 114, 148, 151
Catalog of Lordly Paintings (*Gomotsu on'e mokuroku*), 22
chakaiki. *See* tea diaries
Chinese things, 20, 25, 27, 31, 179n17
civil war, 6–7, 9, 11, 89, 92, 124, 172
clothing (exchanged as gifts), 66, 69, 71, 74–75, 87, 127, 142
contingency, 8, 16, 43–44, 52
cultural advisers (*dōbōshū*), 20

Daitokuji, **xvii,** 57, 59
Date Masamune, 61, 74–75, 80, 94, 107, 111
Date Terumune, 100, 106
dividuation, 50

early modern system: establishment of, 6–8, 43, 77, 85, 88, 112, 137; and objectification, 109; and sociability, 66, 116; and Tōshō Daigongen, 148, 153
Ebina Kokaji, 138, **139**
Edo, **xiv, xv;** before and during Sieges of Osaka Castle, 129–133; Ieyasu's absence from while shogun, 77–78, 83–93; Ieyasu's apotheosis and, 147–148, 161; as a late medieval castle town, 63–64; as location of the shogunate, 8–9, 15, 108–109, 120–121; as Tokyo, 164
Eggplant Tsukumo (Tsukumo Nasu), 2, **4,** 5, 25, 57
Eighth Month (*hassaku*), 22
Emperor Go-Hanazono, 22

Emperor Go-Mizunoo, 65, 157, 168
Emperor Go-Yōzei, 62, 65, 87–88
Emperor Hirohito, 168
Emperor Ōgimachi, 58
Enryakuji, 31–32, 106
Essentials of Good Government (Ch: *Zhenguan zhengyao;* J: *Jōgan Seiyō*), 77, 108, 142
examination of heads (*kubi jikken*), 32, 47, 52, 69, 119, 126–127, 135, **136**
exhibitions, 16, 59, 125, 166, 168, 171–175

falcon handlers, 94, **97,** 102–104, 112, 114
falconry grounds (*takaba*), 99, 104, 106, 111–112
First Flower (Hatsuhana), 27, 45, **46,** 49, 54–56, 138
fish (exchanged as gifts), 68, 74, 80, 85, 87
fowl (exchanged as gifts), 68, 75, 80, 87, 97–98, 100–102, 113
Fujiwara Seika, 77, 108, 142
Fushimi, **xvii,** 77–79, 83–93, 108, 110, 112, 133, 141

Gamō Ujisato, 74–75, 104, 107
gaze, 22, 27, 153
Gifu, **xvi,** 17, 30, 49, 121
Great Avatar Who Illuminates the East (Tōshō Daigongen or Gongen-sama), 143, 147–151, 157–163, **160,** 164, 171

hagiography, 9–11, 34, 44, 105, 126, 140, 145, 157–160, 173–176
Hamamatsu, **xiv–xv,** 39, 53, 106
Hatsuhana. *See* First Flower
Hayashi Razan, 160
heroic mode, 8–9, 43–44, 118
historiography, 8–9, 15, 30, 145, 176
Hōjō, 53–54, 62–63, 68, 100, 111
Hōkōji, 65, 91, 129, 145
Honnōji, **xvii,** 51–53, 68
horses (exchanged as gifts), 39–40, 65–67, 70–74, 98, 100–102
Hosokawa, 25, 78, 89
hostages (*hitojichi*): exchange of, 5, 15–16, 18, 31–34, 42, 96, 102–103, 119, 121; and Ieyasu, 8, 34, 36–41, 55–56, 105
Hunt for Famous Objects (*meibutsu gari*), 26–28

Imagawa Yoshimoto, 43, 34–41, 53, 69, 92, 154
Imai Sōkyū, 26–31, 45, 51
Imjin War, 75, 124, 175
Imperial Court, **xvii,** 45; falconry and, 98–102; gift giving and, 67, 70–72, 75–91; Ieyasu and, 75, 78–81, 84–85, 87, 91, 108, 110, 114; Kyoto culture and, 14, 27, 52; Tokugawa shogunate and, 9, 148, 157; Toyotomi and, 1, 57–59, 71–72
Invasions of Korea. *See* Imjin War
Isabella Bird, 164
Ishida Mitsunari, 76, 84, 109, 120–125, 127, 136
Ishikawa Kazumasa, 54–56
Itakura Katsushige, 93, 128, 133

Jesuits, 28, 131, 138
João Rodrigues, 69, 115, 117
Jurakutei, 62, 64, 103

Kaibara Ekiken, 161, 163
Kamiya Sōtan, 75
Kano Tan'yū, 157–160
karamono. See Chinese things
Katagiri Katsumoto, 81, 130
Katō Kiyomasa, 78, 80, 84, 89
Kikkawa Hiroie, 98, 124–125
Kita no Mandokoro (Kōdai'in), 93, 103, 124
Kitano Shrine, **xvii,** 42, 57–60
Kobayakawa Hideaki, 123–127
Kobori Enshū (Masakazu), 149
Konchiin Sūden, 141–142, 146–147
Kōwakamai, 86
Kundaikan sōchōki. See *Manual of the Attendant of the Shogunal Collection*

land surveys, 85, 110–111, 121

Maeda, 62, 77–79, 89, 92, 104, 192n15
Manual of the Attendant of the Shogunal Collection (*Kundaikan sōchōki*), 23–24
Manzai, 22
Matsudaira Hirotada, 34
Matsudaira Ietada, 39, 61, 105–106, 111
Matsudaira Nobuyasu, 36, 38–39
Matsui Yūkan, 27–28
Matsunaga Hisahide, 25–27, 30, 31, 50
memo (*oboegaki*), 113–114
Mikawa, 10, 34, 51, 54, 56, 63, 105, 108, 145
Minamoto, 26, 56, 119, 141

Ming Dynasty, 74, 76–78, 114
Miyoshi, 25–26, 31, 138
Mogami, 61–62, 94, 107
Mōri, 50, 52, 70; Mōri Hidemoto, 80, 123–125; Mōri Terumoto, 80, 120, 124–125, 192n15
Mount Hiei, 32, 61, 106
Mount Kunō, 145–146, 151
Mu Qi, 20, 25, 29
Murata Jukō, 24, 27, 47, 138

Nagoya Castle (Kyushu), **xiv,** 75–76, 104
Nagoya Castle (Owari), 16, 75, 96, 147, **162,** 166, 171
national unification, 6, 43, 53, 66, 118, 177n8
New Year's, 17, 74, 81, 85, 87, 89, 92, 106–107
Nijō Castle, **xvii,** 33, 65–66, 84–87, 89, 92, 132–137, 142, 148
Nikkō, **xiv, 31;** Tōshōgū, 11, 145–151, 156–157, 160, 172; as a park and UNESCO World Heritage Site, 143, 164; as a pilgrimage site, 161–163
Nitta, 138
Niwa Gorōzaemon (Nagahide), 27–28, 47, 52
Nōami, 22–23
Noh theater, 140; and Hideyoshi, 1–2, 58; and Ieyasu, 80, 86–87, 89, 93, 108, 114, 141; and Nobunaga, 102

objectification: and alienation, 7; of human bodies, 11, 16, 34–35, 39–41, 56, 69, 88; of people and things, 18, 66
Oda Nobuhide, 25, 34, 105
Oda Nobukatsu, 52, 62–64, 78
Oda Nobunaga: alliance with Ieyasu, 38–40, 105–106; as a collector, 5, 8, 16, 25–31, 44–50, 57; assassination of, 50–53; and the Battle of Okehazama, 36–37; and falconry, 100–102; and gift exchange, 68–73; and warrior power, 16–18, 31–33
Oda Nobutada, 49–50, 52, 54–55
Oda Uraku, 137
Odawara, **xv,** 62–63, 107, 122
Okazaki, **xiv, xv,** 34–37, 52, 55–56, 106
Okehazama, Battle of, 36, **37,** 69
Ōnin War, 23–24, 26, 74
Osaka Castle, **xiv, xvi,** 51–51; as Hideyori's home, 65–66, 88, 93, 107, 120–121; as Hideyoshi's headquarters, 55–57, 59, 62, 71, 76–78, 103, 106; as Ieyasu's headquarters, 80–84, 108; retrieval of famous objects from, 137–141; Sieges of, 1–2, **3,** 16, 111, 118, 128–135
Ōtani Yoshitsugu, 80, 125
Ōta Sukemune, 160
Otogoze, 31
Ōtomo Sōrin, 59, 138

pilgrimage, 16, 151, 161, 163

Ranjatai, 45–46
Record of Praiseworthy Famous Objects (*Seigan meibutsuki*), 24
Record of Utensils Inherited from Sunpu Castle (*Sunpu owakemono odōgū chō*), 151, **152**
Regulations for the Palace and Nobility, 142
Richard Cocks, 135
rōnin, 1, 83, 131–132
rookeries, 103, 112; Hyūga Rookery, 103; Higo Rookery, 110

Sakai, **xiv, xvi;** and merchant tea practitioners, 24–30, 44–47, 50–51, 53, 57, 138; as source of artillery, 132
Sarugaku, 86
Senhime, 87, 135
Sen no Rikyū (Sōeki), 29–31, 45–46, 57–59, 61, 84
Shibata Katsuie, 53–55, 70
Shimazu, 103–104, 130, 137
Shōka or "pine blossom," **60**
Shōsōin, 22, 45
Sōami, 22–24
Song Dynasty: calligraphy, **58,** 153; ceramics, 2, **4, 21,** 30, **46,** 54, **60,** 114, 138; paintings, 22, 29, **154**
Southeast Asia, 28, 45, 166
Sumiyoshi, 28, **29**
Sunpu, **xiv, xv;** as headquarters of the Imagawa, 34–36, 41; rebuilding of, 61; Ieyasu's home as Retired Shogun, 92–96, 106, 111, 113–114, 131, 133, 146, 151, **152;** as retirement home of Tokugawa Yoshinobu, the last shogun, 164
Swords: collecting, 2, 5–6, 16, 37; exchanged as gifts, 22, 36, 40, 49, 65–71, 73–75, 81, **82,** 100–101; as durable forms of material culture, 113, 116
system of alternate attendance, 7, 15, 88, 148

Takeda, 25, 40, 50, 53, 68, 85, 103, 110, 158; Katsuyori, 39, 70, 73, 100; Shingen, 17, 70, 73, 92, 105
Takeno Jōō, 5, 24, 26, 57
Tale of Genji, 116
Tale of Mikawa, 105
Tales of the Heike, 137
Tang Dynasty, 20, 77
tea bowls (*chawan*), 18–22; celadon, 47; Korean, 48; Mishima, 28, **49;** *tenmoku*, **21,** 25, 30–31, 57, 79; Yasui, 45
tea caddies (*chaire*); 2, **4,** 5, 25–27, 31, 45–46, 49, 54–57, 61, 74; with shoulders (*katatsuki*), 30, 48; salvaged from Osaka Castle, 137–140
tea diaries (*chakaiki*), 25, 27, 30, 140; *Gathering Records of Matsuya* (*Matsuya kaiki*), 25; *Gathering Records of Tennōjiya* (*Tennōjiya kaiki*), 25, 29, 45–46; *Record of Yamanoue Sōji* (*Yamanoue Sōjiki*), 138
tea gatherings (*chakai*), 2, 19–21, 25, 140; as a political privilege, 50; attended by Ieyasu, 51, 53, 75, 77, 80; sponsored by Hideyoshi, 42, 56–61, 76; sponsored by Nobunaga, 30–31, 45–46
tea jar (*chatsubo*), 26–27, 29, 31, **60,** 71, 78, 113
Tenkai, 146–147, 157–158, **159**
Tenshō Earthquake, 77
Three Unifiers, 7–8, 11, 13, 34, 44, 69, 175, 183n2
Tōdaiji, 45–46, 129
Tōkaidō, **xv,** 111, 121, 161
Tokugawa Art Museum, 16, 114, 145, 166–170, 171–173
Tokugawa branch domains: Owari Tokugawa, 61, 74, 81, 89, 143, 147, 151–156, 166–168, 173; Kii Tokugawa, 147, 156–157, 163; and Mito Tokugawa, 89, 147, 156, 173
Tokugawa Hidetada: and the Battle of Sekigahara, 120–121; and deification of Ieyasu, 146–148; as father of Senhime, 87–88, 135; as shogun, 92–93; and Sieges of Osaka, 130–135, 137, 141; as son of Ieyasu, 39, 89, 91
Tokugawa Iemitsu, 148–149, 157–161, 175
Tokugawa Reimeikai Foundation, 166–167, 169
Tokugawa Yorinobu, 89, 111, 156
Tokugawa Yoshichika, 143, 166–170
Tokugawa Yoshinao, 153
Tokugawa Yoshinobu (Keiki, the last shogun), 164, 168
Tokugawa Yoshinobu (scholar), 113, 170–172
Tokuhime (daughter of Ieyasu), 54
Tokuhime (daughter of Nobunaga), 38–39
Torigai Kunitoshi, 81, **82**
Tōshō Daigongen. *See* Great Avatar Who Illuminates the East
Tōshōgū, **144, 150, 181;** and hagiography, 160–163, 172–174; as mausoleum complex, 143, 146–149; as publisher, 10, 172–174; and spectacular accumulation, 5, 151, 156–157, 164
Toyokuni Shrine, 65, 129, 145
Toyotomi Hidenaga, 58
Toyotomi Hidetsugu, 105
Toyotomi Hideyori: and gift exchange, 65–66, 96; and the Sieges of Osaka Castle, 1–2, 111, 129–136; and Toyotomi power, 79, 81, 88, 91, 93, 107–108, 120
Toyotomi Hideyoshi: as a collector, 1–2, 5, 8, 47–48, 50, 57; death of, 79, 120; deification of, 145–146; and falconry, 103–105, 107, 110–112; and gift giving, 71–75; and the Imjin War, 75–78; and Ieyasu, 53–56; 61–64, 78–79; and ritual, 14, 81; and tea culture, 42–43, 45, 50, 56–61; and vengeance on Akechi Mitsuhide, 51–52
Tsuda Sōgyū, 27, 29–30, 45–46, 50–51, 57
Tsukumo Nasu, 2, **4,** 5, 25–26, 31, 57

Ueno Park, 161, 164
Uesugi Kagekatsu, 10, 62, 75, 83, 100, 108, 120–121, 192n15
Uesugi Kenshin, 72, 92
UNESCO World Heritage site, 143, 149, 172
unification, 13–15, 44–45, 50–52, 66, 69, 96, 108, 117, 145; *See also* national unification

wabi, 24, 42, 60, 138
war and ritual, 14–16, 32, 68, 118–119, 124, 126–130, 140–141
William Adams, 108

Xutang Zhiyu, 57, **58**

Yamashina Tokitsune, 75, 78, 86, 110
Yododono, 93, 132, 135
Yokota, **73,** 74
Yuan Dynasty, 22, **60,** 114
Yuanwu Kezin, 153
Yujian, 45, 47, 57, 153, **154**

Zen, 20, 23, 45, 57, 86, 142, 146, 153
Zhang Sigong, 20
Zhao Chang, 29
Zōjōji, 147–148